1996 E W9-DGO-718

GREENBERG'S®
POCKET PRICE GUIDE
LIONEL TRAINS
1901 – 1996

Founded by Bruce C. Greenberg, Ph.D.

Editor: Kent J. Johnson

Associate Editor:
Todd R. Wagner

Assistant Editor:
Julie LaFountain

Sixteenth Edition
Copyright © 1995
Kalmbach Publishing Co.
21027 Crossroads Circle
Waukesha, Wisconsin 53187
(414) 796-8776

Manufactured in the United States of America

ISBN: 0-89778-403-0

CONTENTS

This handy reference is divided into seven major sections: Prewar 1901–1942, Postwar 1945–1969, Modern Era (MPC) 1970–1986, Modern Era (LTI) 1987–1996, Special Production, Large Scale, and Catalogs. In the first four sections and in the Large Scale section, production is listed numerically, using the item's catalog number. In the prewar section, equipment is further described by gauge—Standard, O, OO, or 2⅞. The gauge type is within the parentheses.

Some steam locomotives in the prewar and modern era sections were not issued with a tender. These units are marked with a "T" after their wheel configuration. Otherwise, steam locomotives in all sections include value with tender, even if tenders are not listed in detail. Be advised that the value of steam locomotives, particularly those of the prewar period, may be significantly affected by the type of tender the item came with. For detailed information on tenders, consult the relevant comprehensive guides.

Cover photo: Partial view of a 2023 Union Pacific Alco A unit and 2483 observation car from the 1950 set 1464W. Models provided by Jack Sommerfeld.

INTRODUCTION

This **Pocket Price Guide** lists all major Lionel items numerically for the years 1901–1942 and 1945–1996 (there was no Lionel production during World War II). Announced product releases for 1996 were obtained from Lionel's 1995 Stocking Stuffers/1996 Spring Releases catalog, which was available in July 1995. This is a preliminary list of planned production, and these 1996 items are subject to change. Subsequent additions to the 1996 product line will be reported in the 1997 edition of this pocket guide.

The values quoted in this guide are for the most common variety of each item. Some rare variations are worth considerably more, and a few of the more important ones are cited. For more detailed information about variations, please consult these comprehensive guides: *Greenberg's Guide to Lionel Trains: 1901–1942, Volumes I, II,* and *III; Greenberg's Guide to Lionel Trains: 1945–1969, Volumes I, III, IV, V, VI,* and *VII; Greenberg's Guide to Lionel Trains: 1970–1991, Volumes I and II;* and *Greenberg's Guide to Lionel Paper and Collectibles.*

Dates cited in this guide are cataloged dates. If there is no catalog date, production dates are listed, if known. Lionel trains are frequently marked with "Built" or "New" dates. These dates often reflect the dates that Lionel's artists picked up from prototype photographs or the date when the artists prepared their drawings. These dates may or may not have any relation to catalog dates or actual production dates. In some cases, Lionel numbered cars with a number different from the catalog number. In these cases we also list this number and refer the reader to the catalog number, which we have enclosed in parentheses.

In recent years, reproductions of prewar and postwar Lionel trains and train parts have become a major concern for collectors. Today it is difficult to find a prewar or postwar Lionel item that has not had parts reproduced or remanufactured for it. Collectors need to be aware of this—while many reproductions are marked or exhibit distinct differences from the original to indicate that they are indeed reproductions, many others are virtually identical to the originals. In some reported cases reproduction markings have been removed. Very close and careful study of an item is advised before making a purchase.

Also, collectors should be aware that counterfeit reproductions of some popular Lionel prewar and postwar items do appear from time to time in the marketplace. These counterfeits often are extremely difficult to detect. If you have any doubts at all about an item's authenticity, you should seek the assistance of a knowledgeable and reputable collector.

We have provided several columns for items listed in Sections 1, 2, 3, 4, 6, and 7. The first two columns give the current market values for each piece. In the prewar and postwar sections, values are denoted by Good and Excellent. In both modern era sections, the Large Scale section, and the catalog section, values are given for Excellent and New. The "Color" column in the prewar and postwar sections is for noting colors, markings, or other distinguishing characteristics. The "Cond" column is for noting the condition of the piece. The "$" column is for recording your cost in acquiring the item.

We are constantly striving to improve **Greenberg's Pocket Price Guide**. If you find any missing items or detect any misinformation, please, by all means, write to us. If you have recommendations for improving a listing, we would also like to hear from you. Send your comments, new information, or corrections to:

Editor—Lionel Pocket Guide (10-8300)
Books Division
Kalmbach Publishing Co.
21027 Crossroads Circle
Waukesha, WI 53187-1612

HOW VALUES WERE DETERMINED

The values presented in this Pocket Price Guide are meant to serve only as a *guide* to collectors. They are an averaged reflection of prices for items bought and sold across the country, and are intended to assist the collector in making informed decisions concerning purchases and sales.

Values listed herein are based on values obtained at train meets held throughout the nation during the Spring and Summer of 1995, and from private transactions reported by members of our nationwide review panel. Values in your area may be consistent with values published in this guide, or higher or lower, depending upon the relative availability, scarcity, or desirability of a particular item. General economic conditions in your area may also affect values. Even regional preferences for specific road names may be a factor.

If you are selling a train to an individual who is planning to resell it—a retailer, for example—you will *not* obtain the values reported in this book. Rather, you may expect to receive about 50 percent of these prices. For your item to be of interest to such a buyer, it must be purchased for considerably less than the price listed here. But, if you are dealing one-to-one with another private collector, values may be expected to be more consistent with this guide.

Our studies of train values indicate that mail order and retail store prices are generally higher than prices found at train meets due to the cost and effort of running a retail establishment or producing and distributing a price list, as well as packing and shipping trains.

WE STRONGLY RECOMMEND THAT NOVICE COLLECTORS SEEK THE ADVICE AND ASSISTANCE OF FRIENDS OR ASSOCIATES WHO HAVE EXPERIENCE IN BUYING, SELLING, AND TRADING TRAINS.

NOTABLE FEATURES IN THIS EDITION

This edition lists Lionel production from 1970 to 1996 (which we define as modern era) in two subsections. The first modern era section covers 1970–1986, when Lionel Electric Trains were manufactured by various subsidiaries of General Mills—most notably Model Products Corporation (MPC) and the Fundimensions toy division. The second modern era section lists items manufactured by Richard Kughn's Lionel Trains, Inc. (LTI), from 1987 through pre-announced 1996 production. The enormous volume of production since 1970—and especially since 1987—made it both logical and necessary to better define the distinct entities that have manufactured Lionel trains in this period. Changes in Lionel's product numbering system from four digits to five digits contributed to the practicality of this restructuring. Our forthcoming comprehensive books detailing modern era Lionel production will follow this revised structure, and we are confident this will assist collectors in more easily identifying and accurately dating items of interest.

We are very grateful to Todd Wagner for his efforts in compiling, organizing, and confirming the extensive modern era lists. Special thanks, too, to Sherrie Weitzman, Steve Saxton, and Melissa Seifert, at Lionel Trains, Inc., for the valuable assistance they provided in verifying item numbers, production dates, and descriptions. This edition also involved the participation of many other people who generously gave of their time and knowledge. We appreciate their contributions to this publication and to our enjoyment of the hobby.

—Kent J. Johnson, Editor

DEFINITIONS

This Pocket Price Guide lists prices for prewar and postwar trains as Good and Excellent. Modern era (1970–1996) trains, Large Scale trains, and catalogs are priced Excellent and New. Prices for restored pieces fall between Good and Excellent, depending on the item. New pieces bring a substantial premium over Excellent pieces. Fair pieces bring substantially less than Good and Excellent pieces.

In the toy train field there is a great deal of concern with exterior appearance and less concern with operation. If operation is important to you, ask the seller if the train runs. If the seller indicates that he does not know whether the equipment operates, you should test it. Most train meets provide test tracks for this purpose.

Trains and related items are usually classified by condition relating to appearance. The following definitions apply for this guide:

- **FAIR**—well-scratched, chipped, dented, rusted, or warped condition.
- **GOOD**—scratched, small dents, and dirty.
- **VERY GOOD**—few scratches, no dents, rust or warpage; very clean.
- **EXCELLENT**—minute scratches or nicks; no dents or rust; exceptionally clean.
- **LIKE NEW**—free of blemishes, nicks or scratches; original condition throughout, with vibrant colors; only faint signs of handling or use; price includes original box.
- **NEW**—brand new, absolutely unmarred, all original and unused, in original packaging with all paperwork provided by the manufacturer.
- **RESTORED**—professionally refurbished and refinished with a color that approximates the original finish. Trim and ornamentation are present and in Like New condition. The finish appears in Like New condition.
- **REPRODUCTION**—a product intended to closely resemble the original item. It may or may not be marked as such, but should be so marked. Reproductions are currently available for many desirable prewar and postwar items.

- **CP (Current Production)** means that the item is now being advertised, manufactured, or is currently available from retail stores.
- **NRS (No Recorded Sales)** means that we do not know the current market value of the item. The item may be very scarce and bring a substantial premium over items in its general class, or it may be relatively common but unnoticed. Usually NRS listings occur when an older and previously unknown item is first reported, although we are still discovering relatively common variations that have not been previously reported. If you have confirmable information about the value of an NRS item, please write to us.
- **NM (Not Manufactured)** means that the item may have been cataloged or otherwise advertised, but it was not produced.
- **(#)** Numbers that have been put in parentheses by us do not appear on the actual items.
- **[#]** means decorations that make this item unique were not done by Lionel.
- **No Number** means the item may have lettering, but lacks an item number.
- **(no letters)** means no lettering or number appears on the item.
- ***** means excellent reproductions have been made.

NOTE: Values listed are for the most common variation. Many Prewar items have numerous known variations. Please consult the comprehensive Prewar Guides for complete descriptions.

		Good	Exc	Color	Cond	$
001	Steam 4-6-4 (OO), *38–42*	170	380	___	___	___
1	Bild-A-Motor, *28–31*	60	150	___	___	___
1	Trolley (Std.), *06–14*	1300	3500	___	___	___
1/111	Trolley Trailer (Std.), *06–14*	1000	3000	___	___	___
002	Steam 4-6-4 (OO), *39–42*	140	300	___	___	___
2	Bild-A-Motor, *28–31*	70	170	___	___	___
2	Countershafting, *04–11*		NRS	___	___	___
2	Trolley (Std.), *06–16**	1200	2500	___	___	___
2/200	Trolley Trailer (Std.), *06–16*	1000	2000	___	___	___
003	Steam 4-6-4 (OO), *39–42*	165	400	___	___	___
3	Trolley (Std.), *06–13*	1400	3500	___	___	___
3/300	Trolley Trailer (Std.), *06–13*	1300	3000	___	___	___
004	Steam 4-6-4 (OO), *39–42*	160	300	___	___	___
4	Electric 0-4-0 (O), *28–32**	500	900	___	___	___
4	Trolley (Std.), *06–12*	3000	5500	___	___	___
4U	#4 Kit form (O), *28–29*	1000	1500	___	___	___
5	Electric (2⅞") (see 100)					
5	Steam 0-4-0, no tender, Early (Std.), *06–07*	1000	1600	___	___	___
5	Steam 0-4-0, w/ tender, Early Special (Std.), *06–09*	1200	1800	___	___	___
5	Steam 0-4-0, no tender, Later (Std.), *10–11*	700	1300	___	___	___
5	Steam 0-4-0, w/ tender, Later Special (Std.), *10–11*	800	1500	___	___	___
5/51	Steam 0-4-0, w/ tender, Latest (Std.), *12–23*	750	1200	___	___	___
6	Steam 4-4-0 (Std.), *06–23*	800	1200	___	___	___
6	Steam 0-4-0 Special (Std.), *08–09*	2000	3250	___	___	___
7	Steam 4-4-0 (Std.), *10–23**	1800	2800	___	___	___
8	Electric 0-4-0 (Std.), *25–32*	140	200	___	___	___
8	Trolley (Std.), *08–14**	3000	6000	___	___	___

PREWAR (1901–1942)		Good	Exc	Color	Cond	$
8E	Electric 0-4-0 (Std.), *26–32*	150	225	___	___	___
9	Electric 0-4-0 (Std.), *29**	1200	2200	___	___	___
9	Trolley (Std.), *09*	3000	6000	___	___	___
9E	Electric 0-4-0 (Std.), *28–35**	600	1200	___	___	___
9U	Electric 0-4-0 Kit (Std.), *28–29*	1200	3000	___	___	___
9	Motor Car (Std.), *09–12*		NRS	___	___	___
10	Electric 0-4-0 (Std.), *25–29**	95	175	___	___	___
10	Interurban (Std.), *10–16*	1000	2000	___	___	___
10E	Electric 0-4-0 (Std.), *26–30*	125	225	___	___	___
011	Switches, pair (O), *33–37*	20	45	___	___	___
11	Flatcar, Early (Std.), *06–11*	150	350	___	___	___
11	Flatcar, Later (Std.), *11–16*	50	100	___	___	___
11	Flatcar, Latest (Std.), *16–18*	50	100	___	___	___
11	Flatcar, Lionel Corp. (Std.), *18–26*	40	80	___	___	___
012	Switches, pair (O), *27–33*	18	40	___	___	___
12	Gondola, Early (Std.), *06–11*	500	700	___	___	___
12	Gondola, Later (Std), *11–16*	50	100	___	___	___
12	Gondola, Latest (Std.), *16–18*	40	80	___	___	___
12	Gondola, Lionel Corp. (Std.), *18–26*	50	80	___	___	___
013	(2) 012 Switches and 439 Panel Board	70	170	___	___	___
13	Cattle Car, Early (Std.), *06–11*	200	450	___	___	___
13	Cattle Car, Later (Std.), *11–16*	150	300	___	___	___
13	Cattle Car, Latest (Std.), *16–18*	50	100	___	___	___
13	Cattle Car, Lionel Corp. (Std.), *18–26*	50	100	___	___	___
0014	Boxcar (OO), *38–42*	30	80	___	___	___
14	Boxcar, Early (Std.), *06–11*	175	400	___	___	___
14	Boxcar, Later (Std.), *11–16*	60	100	___	___	___
14	Boxcar, Latest (Std.), *16–18*	60	100	___	___	___
14	Boxcar, Lionel Corp. (Std.), *18–26*	50	75	___	___	___
0015	Tank Car (OO), *38–42*	30	70	___	___	___
15	Oil Car, Early (Std.), *06–11*	60	115	___	___	___
15	Oil Car, Later (Std.), *11–16*	60	115	___	___	___
15	Oil Car, Latest (Std.), *16–18*	60	115	___	___	___
15	Oil Car, Lionel Corp. (Std.), *18–26*	60	115	___	___	___
0016	Hopper Car (OO), *38–42*	48	100	___	___	___
16	Ballast (Dump) Car, Early (Std.), *06–26*	200	400	___	___	___
16	Ballast (Dump) Car,					

		Good	Exc	Color	Cond	$
	Later (Std.), *11–16*	90	175	___	___	___
16	Ballast (Dump) Car,					
	Latest (Std.), *16–18*	90	175	___	___	___
16	Ballast (Dump) Car,					
	Lionel Corp. (Std.), *18–26*	90	175	___	___	___
0017	Caboose (OO), *38–42*	30	65	___	___	___
17	Caboose, Early (Std.), *06–11*	175	400	___	___	___
17	Caboose, Later (Std.), *11–16*	60	150	___	___	___
17	Caboose, Latest (Std.), *16–18*	70	150	___	___	___
17	Caboose, Lionel Corp. (Std.), *18–26*	50	100	___	___	___
18	Pullman (Std.), *08*	800	1800	___	___	___
18	Pullman (Std.), *11–13*		NRS	___	___	___
18	Pullman (Std.), *13–15*	200	300	___	___	___
18	Pullman (Std.), *15–18*	200	300	___	___	___
18	Pullman (Std.), *18–22*	80	150	___	___	___
18	Pullman (Std.), *23–26*	275	600	___	___	___
19	Combine (Std.), *08*	800	1800	___	___	___
19	Combine (Std.), *11–13*		NRS	___	___	___
19	Combine (Std.), *13–15*	200	300	___	___	___
19	Combine (Std.), *15–18*	200	300	___	___	___
19	Combine (Std.), *18–22*	80	150	___	___	___
19	Combine (Std.), *23–26*	275	600	___	___	___
020	90° Crossover (O), *15–42*	2	6	___	___	___
020X	45° Crossover (O), *17–42*	3	9	___	___	___
20	90° Crossover (Std.),	4	10	___	___	___
20	Direct Current Reducer, *06*	—	300	___	___	___
20X	45° Crossover (Std.), *28–32*	5	10	___	___	___
021	Switches, pair (O), *15–37*	20	50	___	___	___
21	Switches, pair (Std.), *15–25*	40	110	___	___	___
21	90° Crossover (Std.), *06*	10	20	___	___	___
022	Switches, pair, Remote (O), *38–42*	35	70	___	___	___
22	Switches, pair (Std.), *06–25*	40	125	___	___	___
023	Bumper (O), *15–33*	10	40	___	___	___
23	Bumper (Std.), *06–23*	20	50	___	___	___
0024	PRR Boxcar (OO), *39–42*	35	70	___	___	___
24	Railway Station (Std.), *06*		NRS	___	___	___
025	Bumper (O), *28–42*	15	25	___	___	___
0025	Tank Car (OO), *39–42*	30	70	___	___	___
25	Open Station (Std.), *06*		NRS	___	___	___

|---|---|---|---|---|---|
25 Bumper (Std.), *27–42*	25	45	___	___	___
26 Passenger Bridge (Std.), *06*		NRS	___	___	___
0027 Caboose (OO), *39–42*	30	70	___	___	___
27 Lighting set, *11–23*	15	45	___	___	___
27 Station (Std.), *09–12*		NRS	___	___	___
28 Double Station w/ dome, *09–12*		NRS	___	___	___
29 Day Coach (Std.), *07–22*	1500	3000	___	___	___
29 (See #3 Trolley)					
31 Combine (Std.), *21–25*	60	85	___	___	___
32 Mail Car (Std.), *21–25*	60	85	___	___	___
32 Miniature Figures, *09–18*	75	140	___	___	___
33 Electric 0-6-0, Early (Std.), *13*	300	650	___	___	___
33 Electric 0-4-0, Later (Std.), *13–24*	60	125	___	___	___
34 Electric 0-6-0, Early (Std.), *12*	450	900	___	___	___
34 Electric 0-4-0 (Std.), *13*	175	400	___	___	___
35 Blvd. Lamp, 6⅛" high, *40–42*	25	55	___	___	___
35 Pullman (Std.), *12–13*	125	200	___	___	___
35 Pullman (Std.), *14–16*	40	60	___	___	___
35 Pullman (Std.), *15–18*	50	80	___	___	___
35 Pullman (Std.), *18–23*	25	40	___	___	___
35 Pullman (Std.), *24*	30	50			
35 Pullman (Std.), *25–26*	30	50			
36 Observation (Std.), *12–13*	125	200	___	___	___
36 Observation (Std.), *14–16*	40	60	___	___	___
36 Observation (Std.), *15–18*	50	80	___	___	___
36 Observation (Std.), *18–23*	25	40	___	___	___
36 Observation (Std.), *24*	30	50	___	___	___
36 Observation (Std.), *25–26*	30	50	___	___	___
38 Electric 0-4-0 (Std.), *13–24*	95	125	___	___	___
40 (See #4 Trolley)					
41 Accessory Contactor, *37–42*	1	3	___	___	___
042 Switches, pair (O), *38–42*	22	55	___	___	___
42 Electric 0-4-4-0, square hood, Early (Std.), *12**	900	1900	___	___	___
42 Electric 0-4-4-0, round hood, Later (Std.), *13–23*	225	500	___	___	___
043/43 Bild-A-Motor Gear set, *29*		NRS	___	___	___
43 Boat, Runabout, *33–36, 39–41*	370	600	___	___	___
0044 Boxcar (OO), *39–42*	25	60	___	___	___

		Good	Exc	Color	Cond	$
1044K	Boxcar Kit (OO), *39–42*	60	130	___	___	___
44	Boat, Speedster, *35–36*	370	650	___	___	___
1045	Tank Car (OO), *39–42*	30	75	___	___	___
1045K	Tank Car Kit (OO), *39–42*	60	135	___	___	___
45/045/45N	Automatic Gateman, *35–42*	40	80	___	___	___
1046	Hopper Car (OO), *39–42*	40	75	___	___	___
1046K	Hopper Car Kit (OO), *39–42*	50	100	___	___	___
46	Crossing Gate, *39–42*	45	95	___	___	___
1047	Caboose (OO), *39–42*	30	65	___	___	___
1047K	Caboose Kit (OO), *39–42*	60	130	___	___	___
47	Crossing Gate, *39–42*	60	125	___	___	___
48W	Whistle Station, *37–42*	25	70	___	___	___
49	Lionel Airport, *37–39*	100	325	___	___	___
50	Airplane, *36–39*	90	240	___	___	___
50	Electric 0-4-0 (Std.), *24*	100	200	___	___	___
50	Cardboard Train, Cars, Accessory (O), *43**	200	400	___	___	___
51	Steam 0-4-0, 5 Late eight-wheel (Std.), *12–23*	750	1200	___	___	___
51	Lionel Airport, *36, 38*	100	350	___	___	___
52	Lamp Post, *33–41*	45	95	___	___	___
53	Electric 0-4-4-0, Early (Std.), *12–14*	1000	2500	___	___	___
53	Electric 0-4-0, Later (Std.), *15–19*	450	900	___	___	___
53	Electric 0-4-0, Latest (Std.), *20–21*	150	400	___	___	___
53	Lamp Post, *31–42*	35	75	___	___	___
53	Electric 0-6-6-0, Early (Std.), *11*		NRS	___	___	___
54	Electric 0-4-4-0, Early (Std.), *12**	2500	4000	___	___	___
54	Electric 0-4-4-0, Late (Std.), *13–23*	1800	3000	___	___	___
54	Lamp Post, *29–35*	40	85	___	___	___
55	Airplane w/ stand, *37–39*	160	485	___	___	___
56	Lamp Post, removable lens and cap, *24–42*	30	85	___	___	___
57	Lamp Post w/ street names, *22–42*	45	100	___	___	___
58	Lamp Post, 7⅜" high, *22–42*	25	55	___	___	___
59	Lamp Post, 8¾" high, *20–36*	40	95	___	___	___
60/060	Telegraph Post (Std./O), *29–42*	7	18	___	___	___
60	Electric 0-4-0, F.A.O.S. (Std.), *15 u*	-	NRS	___	___	___
61	Electric 0-4-4-0, F.A.O.S. (Std.), *15 u*		NRS	___	___	___

		Good	Exc	Color	Cond
61	Lamp Post, one globe, *14–36*	45	85	___	___ ___
62	Electric 0-4-0, F.A.O.S. (Std.), *24–32 u*		NRS	___	___ ___
62	Semaphore, *20–32*	25	55	___	___ ___
63	Lamp Post, two globes, *33–42*	120	220	___	___ ___
63	Semaphore, *15–21*	25	55	___	___ ___
64	Lamp Post, *40–42*	20	60	___	___ ___
64	Semaphore, 6¾" high, *15–21*	30	65	___	___ ___
65	Semaphore, one-arm, *15–26*	30	65	___	___ ___
65	Whistle Contoller, *35*	3	6	___	___ ___
66	Semaphore, two-arm, *15–26*	35	75	___	___ ___
66	Whistle Controller, *36–39*	4	8	___	___ ___
67	Lamp Post, *15–32*	70	120	___	___ ___
67	Whistle Controller, *36–39*	4	8	___	___ ___
68/068	Crossing Sign, *25–42*	10	12	___	___ ___
69/069/69N	Electric Warning Signal, *21–42*	25	60	___	___ ___
70	Outfit: (2) 62s (1) 59 (1) 68	50	120	___	___ ___
071	(6) 060 Telegraph Poles (Std.), *24–42*	70	145	___	___ ___
71	(6) 60 Telegraph Poles (Std.)	70	145	___	___ ___
0072	Switches, pair (OO), *38–42*	130	225	___	___ ___
0074	Boxcar (OO), *39–42*	30	75	___	___ ___
0075	Tank Car (OO), *39–42*	40	100	___	___ ___
076/76	Block Signal, *23–28*	25	70	___	___ ___
76	Warning Bell and Shack, *39–42*	80	180	___	___ ___
0077	Caboose (OO), *39–42*	30	60	___	___ ___
77/077/77N	Automatic Crossing Gate, *23–39*	25	50	___	___ ___
78/078	Train Signal (Std.), *24–32*	35	85	___	___ ___
79	Flashing Signal, *28–40*	65	160	___	___ ___
80	Automobile, *12–16*	720	1600	___	___ ___
80/080/80N	Semaphore (Std), *26–42*	50	130	___	___ ___
81	Automobile, *12–16*	720	1600	___	___ ___
81	Controlling Rheostat, *27–33*	2	5	___	___ ___
82/082/82N	Semaphore, *27–42*	55	120	___	___ ___
83	Flashing Traffic Signal, *27–42*	45	120	___	___ ___
084	Semaphore, *28–32*	55	95	___	___ ___
84	Semaphore, *27–32*	55	95	___	___ ___
84	(2) Automobiles	1400	3200	___	___ ___

		Good	Exc	Color	Cond	$
5	Telegraph Pole (Std.), 29–42	12	25	___	___	___
5	(2) Automobiles	1400	3200	___	___	___
6	(6) Telegraph Poles, 29–42	65	155	___	___	___
7	Flashing Crossing Signal, 27–42	55	125	___	___	___
8	Battery Rheostat, 15–27	2	5	___	___	___
8	Rheostat Controller, 33–42	3	5	___	___	___
9	Flag Pole, 23–34	35	75	___	___	___
0	Flag Pole, 27–42	35	85	___	___	___
1	Circuit Breaker, 30–42	20	45	___	___	___
92	Signal Tower, 23–27	75	155	___	___	___
2	Floodlight Tower, 31–42*	105	220	___	___	___
3	Water Tower, 31–42	25	65	___	___	___
4	High Tension Tower, 32–42*	95	220	___	___	___
5	Controlling Rheostat, 34–42	2	5	___	___	___
6	Coal Elevator, manual, 38–40	150	290	___	___	___
97	Telegraph set (O)	50	85	___	___	___
7	Coal Elevator, 38–42	125	265	___	___	___
8	Coal Bunker, 38–40	195	470	___	___	___
9/099/99N	Train Control, 32–42	45	110	___	___	___
00	Electric Loco (2⅞"), 03–05*	3000	6000	___	___	___
00	Trolley (Std.), 10–16	1300	3000	___	___	___
00	(2) Bridge Apprch. (Std.), 20–31	15	35	___	___	___
00	Wooden Gondola (2⅞"), 01		NRS	___	___	___
01	Bridge Span (2) Approaches (Std.), 20–31	25	70	___	___	___
01	Summer Trolley (Std.), 10–13	1300	3000	___	___	___
02	(2) Bridge Spans (2) Approaches (Std.), 20–31	35	110	___	___	___
03	Bridge (Std.), 13–16	25	60	___	___	___
03	(3) Bridge Spans (2) Approaches (Std.), 20–31	60	160	___	___	___
04	Bridge Span (Std.), 20–31	20	45	___	___	___
04	Tunnel (Std.), 09–14	50	130	___	___	___
05	Bridge (Std.), 11–14	20	65	___	___	___
05	(2) Bridge Apprchs. (O), 20–31	20	50	___	___	___
06	Bridge Span, (2) Approaches (O), 20–31	30	70	___	___	___
07	DC Reducer, 110V, 23–32		NRS	___	___	___
08	(2) Bridge Spans,					

PREWAR (1901–1942)	Good	Exc	Color	Cond	$
(2) Approaches (O), *20–31*	40	80	____	____	____
109 (3) Bridge Spans,					
(2) Approaches (O), *20–32*	35	125	____	____	____
109 Tunnel (Std.), *13–14*	30	65	____	____	____
110 Bridge Span (O), *20–31*	12	25	____	____	____
111 Box of 50 Bulbs, *20–31*	—	125	____	____	____
112 Gondola, Early (Std.), *10–12*	150	300	____	____	____
112 Gondola, Later (Std.), *12–16*	40	70	____	____	____
112 Gondola, Latest (Std.), *16–18*	40	70	____	____	____
112 Gondola, Lionel Corp. (Std.), *18–26*	35	60	____	____	____
112 Station, *31–35*	120	255	____	____	____
113 Cattle Car, Later (Std.), *12–16*	50	80	____	____	____
113 Cattle Car, Latest (Std.), *16–18*	50	80	____	____	____
113 Cattle Car, Lionel Corp. (Std.), *18–26*	40	60	____	____	____
113 Station, *31–34*	135	300	____	____	____
114 Boxcar, Later (Std.), *12–16*	35	60	____	____	____
114 Boxcar, Latest (Std.), *16–18*	35	60	____	____	____
114 Boxcar, Lionel Corp. (Std.), *18–26*	35	60	____	____	____
114 Station, *31–34*	510	1300	____	____	____
115 Station, *35–42**	165	320	____	____	____
116 Station, *35–42**	600	1400			
116 Ballast Car, Early and Later (Std.), *10–16*	50	80	____	____	____
116 Ballast Car, Latest (Std.), *16–18*	50	80	____	____	____
116 Ballast Car, Lionel Corp. (Std.), *18–26*	50	80	____	____	____
117 Caboose, Early (Std.), *12*	40	70	____	____	____
117 Caboose, Later (Std.), *12–16*	40	70	____	____	____
117 Caboose, Latest (Std.), *16–18*	40	70	____	____	____
117 Caboose, Lionel Corp. (Std.), *18–26*	40	70	____	____	____
117 Station, *36–42*	90	280	____	____	____
118 Tunnel, 8" long (O), *22–32*	15	45	____	____	____
118L Tunnel, 8" long, *27*	15	45	____	____	____
119 Tunnel, 12" long, *20–42*	12	45	____	____	____
119L Tunnel, 12" long, *27–33*	15	45	____	____	____
120 Tunnel, 17" long, *22–27*	20	75	____	____	____
120L Tunnel, *27–42*	40	100	____	____	____
121 Station (Std.), *09–16*	140	335	____	____	____

		Good	Exc	Color	Cond	$
21	Station (Std.), *20–26*	75	165	___	___	___
21X	Station (Std.), *17–19*	110	285	___	___	___
22	Station (Std.), *20–30*	65	160	___	___	___
23	Station (Std.), *20–23*	70	225	___	___	___
23	Tunnel, 18½" long (O), *33–42*	65	190	___	___	___
24	Station, "Lionel City", *20–36**	75	175	___	___	___
25	Station, "Lionelville", *23–25*	75	180	___	___	___
25	Track Template, *38*	1	4	___	___	___
26	Station, "Lionelville", *23–36*	70	170	___	___	___
27	Station, "Lionel Town", *23–36*	70	145	___	___	___
28	124 Station & Terrace, *31–34**	800	1995	___	___	___
28	115 Station & Terrace, *35–42**	800	1795	___	___	___
29	Terrace, *28–42**	600	1200	___	___	___
30	Tunnel, 26" long, *20–36*	130	400	___	___	___
30L	Tunnel, 26" long, *27–33*	120	400	___	___	___
31	Corner Display, *24–28*	125	325	___	___	___
32	Corner Grass Plot, *24–28*	125	325	___	___	___
33	Heart Shaped Plot, *24–28*	125	325			
34	Oval Shaped Plot, *24–28*	125	325	___	___	___
34	Station, "Lionel City", w/ stop, *37–42*	175	350	___	___	___
35	Circular Plot, *24–28*	125	325	___	___	___
36	Large Elevation, *24–28*		NRS	___	___	___
36	Station, "Lionelville", w/ stop, *37–42*	70	155	___	___	___
37	Station, w/ stop, *37–42*	60	140	___	___	___
40L	Tunnel, 37" long, *27–32*	300	850	___	___	___
50	Electric 0-4-0, Early (O), *17*	80	165	___	___	___
50	Electric 0-4-0, Late (O), *18–25*	70	115	___	___	___
52	Electric 0-4-0 (O), *17–27*	80	130	___	___	___
52	Crossing Gate, *40–42*	18	45	___	___	___
53	Block Signal, *40–42*	20	55	___	___	___
53	Electric 0-4-0 (O), *24–25*	90	170	___	___	___
54	Electric 0-4-0 (O), *17–23*	90	170	___	___	___
54	Highway Signal, *40–42*	18	45	___	___	___
55	Freight Shed, *30–42**	150	350	___	___	___
56	Electric 4-4-4 (O), *17–23*	475	900	___	___	___
56	Electric 0-4-0 (O), *17–23*	380	750	___	___	___
56	Station Platform, *39–42*	75	150	___	___	___
56X	Electric 0-4-0 (O), *23–24*	380	550	___	___	___

		Good	Exc	Color	Cond	$
157	Hand Truck, *30–32*	20	45	___	___	___
158	Electric 0-4-0 (O), *19–23*	70	185	___	___	___
158	(2) 156s and (1) 136, *40–42*	100	235	___	___	___
159	Block Actuator, *40*	10	30	___	___	___
161	Baggage Truck, *30–32**	30	75	___	___	___
162	Dump Truck, *30–32**	30	75	___	___	___
163	(2) 157 (1) 162 (1) 161, boxed, *30–42**	120	385	___	___	___
164	Log Loader, *40–42*	125	275	___	___	___
165	Magnetic Crane, *40–42*	150	300	___	___	___
166	Whistle Controller, *40–42*	3	6	___	___	___
167	Whistle Controller, *40–42*	4	10	___	___	___
167X	Whistle Controller (OO), *40–42*	5	12	___	___	___
169	Controller, *40–42*	2	6	___	___	___
170	DC Reducer, 220V, *14–38*	2	5	___	___	___
171	DC to AC Inverter, 110V, *36–42*	2	5	___	___	___
172	DC to AC Inverter, 229V, *39–42*	2	5	___	___	___
180	Pullman (Std.), *11–13*	100	175	___	___	___
180	Pullman (Std.), *13–15*	80	175	___	___	___
180	Pullman (Std.), *15–18*	80	175	___	___	___
180	Pullman (Std.), *18–22*	80	100	___	___	___
181	Combine (Std.), *11–13*	100	175	___	___	___
181	Combine (Std.), *13–15*	80	175	___	___	___
181	Combine (Std.), *15–18*	80	175	___	___	___
181	Combine (Std.), *18–22*	80	100	___	___	___
182	Observation (Std.), *11–13*	100	175	___	___	___
182	Observation (Std.), *13–15*	80	175	___	___	___
182	Observation (Std.), *15–18*	80	175	___	___	___
182	Observation (Std.), *18–22*	80	100	___	___	___
183	Pullman (Std.)		NM			
184	Bungalow, Illuminated, *23–32**	55	95	___	___	___
184	Combine (Std.), *11*		NM			
185	Bungalow, *23–24*	45	95	___	___	___
185	Observation (Std.), *11*		NM			
186	(5) 184 Bungalows, *23–32*	140	500	___	___	___
186	Log Loader Outfit, *40–41*	130	350	___	___	___
187	(5) 185 Bungalows, *23–24*	145	525	___	___	___
188	Elevator and Car set, *38–41*	110	350	___	___	___
189	Villa, Illuminated, *23–32**	115	225	___	___	___

PREWAR (1901–1942)	Good	Exc	Color	Cond	$
190 Observation (Std.), *08*	800	1800	___	___	___
190 Observation (Std.), *11–13*		NRS	___	___	___
190 Observation (Std.), *13–15*	200	300	___	___	___
190 Observation (Std.), *15–18*	200	300	___	___	___
190 Observation (Std.), *18–22*	80	150	___	___	___
190 Observation (Std.), *23–26*	250	575	___	___	___
191 Villa, Illuminated, *23–32**	135	250	___	___	___
192 Villa set, Illuminated :					
(1) 189; (1) 191; (2) 184, *27–32*		NRS	___	___	___
193 Accessory set, boxed, *27–29*	145	360	___	___	___
194 Accessory set, boxed, *27–29*	145	360	___	___	___
195 Terrace, *27–30*	320	820	___	___	___
196 Accessory set, *27*	160	370	___	___	___
200 Electric Express (2⅞"), *03*	4000	6000	___	___	___
200 Turntable, *28–33**	80	195	___	___	___
200 Wooden Gondola (2⅞"), *01–02*		NRS	___	___	___
200 Trailer, matches #2 Trolley					
(Std.), *11–16*	—	3600	___	___	___
200 Electric Express (2⅞"), *03–05**	4000	7000	___	___	___
201 Steam 0-6-0 (O), *40–42*	350	785	___	___	___
202 Summer Trolley (Std.), *10–13*	1300	3000	___	___	___
203 Armored 0-4-0 (O), *17–21*	1000	1850	___	___	___
203 Steam 0-6-0 (O), *40–42*	280	500	___	___	___
204 Steam 2-4-2 (O), *40–42 u*	55	115	___	___	___
205 (3) Merch. Containers, *30–38**	125	300	___	___	___
206 Sack of Coal, *38–42*	5	18	___	___	___
208 Tool set, boxed, *34–42**	40	120	___	___	___
0209 Barrels, *34–42*	5	15	___	___	___
209 Wooden Barrels, *34–42*	8	20	___	___	___
210 Switches, pair (Std.), *26, 34–42*	30	75	___	___	___
211 Flatcar (Std.), *26–40**	70	130	___	___	___
212 Gondola (Std.), *26–40**	75	150	___	___	___
213 Cattle Car (Std.), *26–40**	125	250	___	___	___
214 Boxcar (Std.), *26–40**	150	250	___	___	___
214R Refrigerator Car (Std.), *29–40**	325	550	___	___	___
215 Tank Car (Std.), *26–40**	120	200	___	___	___
216 Hopper Car (Std.), *26–38**	200	300	___	___	___
217 Caboose (Std.), *26–40**	125	250	___	___	___
217 Lighting set, *14–23*		NRS	___	___	___

PREWAR (1901–1942)	Good	Exc	Color	Cond	$
218 Dump Car (Std.), *26–38**	175	325	___	___	___
219 Crane (Std.), *26–40**	125	225	___	___	___
220 Floodlight Car (Std.), *31–40**	200	375	___	___	___
220 Switches, pair (Std.), *26**	20	55	___	___	___
222 Switches, pair (Std.), *26–32*	40	85	___	___	___
223 Switches, pair (Std.), *32–42*	35	95	___	___	___
224/224E Steam 2-6-2 (O), *38–42*	100	200	___	___	___
225 222 Switches, 439 Panel, *29–32*	75	185	___	___	___
225/225E Steam 2-6-2 (O), *38–42*	200	350	___	___	___
226/226E Steam 2-6-4 (O), *38–41*	350	750	___	___	___
227 Steam 0-6-0 (O), *39–42*	550	1300	___	___	___
228 Steam 0-6-0 (O), *39–42*	550	1300	___	___	___
229 Steam 2-4-2 (O), *39–42*	75	125	___	___	___
230 Steam 0-6-0 (O), *39–42*	920	1880	___	___	___
231 Steam 0-6-0 (O), *39*	900	1800	___	___	___
232 Steam 0-6-0 (O), *40–42*	950	1900	___	___	___
233 Steam 0-6-0 (O), *40–42*	1000	2000	___	___	___
238 Steam 4-4-2 (O), *39–40, u*	250	475	___	___	___
238E Steam 4-4-2 (O), *36–38*	150	295	___	___	___
248 Electric 0-4-0 (O), *27–32*	80	160	___	___	___
249/249E Steam 2-4-2 (O), *36–39*	100	220	___	___	___
250 Electric 0-4-0, Early (O), *26*	100	220	___	___	___
250 Electric 0-4-0, Late (O), *34*	120	240	___	___	___
250E Steam 4-4-2 Hiawatha (O), *35–42**	700	1500	___	___	___
251 Electric 0-4-0 (O), *25–32*	175	310	___	___	___
251E Electric 0-4-0 (O), *27–32*	180	320	___	___	___
252 Electric 0-4-0 (O), *26–32*	85	160	___	___	___
252E Electric 0-4-0 (O), *33–35*	125	175	___	___	___
253 Electric 0-4-0 (O), *24–32*	100	190	___	___	___
253E Electric 0-4-0 (O), *31–36*	150	210	___	___	___
254 Electric 0-4-0 (O), *24–32*	120	240	___	___	___
254E Electric 0-4-0 (O), *27–34*	160	265	___	___	___
255E Steam 2-4-2 (O), *35–36*	400	800	___	___	___
256 Electric 0-4-4-0 (O), *24–30**	440	900	___	___	___
257 Steam 2-4-0 (O), *30–35 u*	140	320	___	___	___
258 Steam 2-4-0, Early (O), *30–35 u*	75	185	___	___	___
258 Steam 2-4-2, Late (O), *41 u*	45	100	___	___	___
259 Steam 2-4-2 (O), *32*	60	120	___	___	___
259E Steam 2-4-2 (O), *33–42*	60	120	___	___	___

		Good	Exc	Color	Cond	$
260E	Steam 2-4-2 (O), *30–35**	350	580	___	___	___
261	Steam 2-4-2 (O), *31*	155	245	___	___	___
261E	Steam 2-4-2 (O), *35*	170	275	___	___	___
262	Steam 2-4-2 (O), *31–32*	120	215	___	___	___
262E	Steam 2-4-2 (O), *33–36*	135	235	___	___	___
263E	Steam 2-4-2 (O), *36–39**	300	620	___	___	___
264E	Steam 2-4-2 (O), *35–36*	150	325	___	___	___
265E	Steam 2-4-2 (O), *35–40*	150	350	___	___	___
267E/267W	Sets: 616,					
	(2) 617s, 618, *35–41*	300	450	___	___	___
270	Bridge, 10" long (O), *31–42*	15	50	___	___	___
270	Lighting set, *15–23*		NRS	___	___	___
271	(2) 270 Spans (O), *31–33, 35–40*	35	100	___	___	___
271	Lighting set, *15–23*		NRS	___	___	___
272	(3) 270 Spans (O), *31–33, 35–40*	38	110	___	___	___
280	Bridge, 14" long (Std.), *31–42*	35	100	___	___	___
281	(2) Bridge Spans (Std.),					
	31–33, 35–40	65	140	___	___	___
282	(3) Bridge Spans (Std.),					
	31–33, 35–40	85	175	___	___	___
289E	Steam 2-4-2 (O), *37u*	125	350	___	___	___
300	Electric Trolley Car					
	(2⅞"), *01–05*	2000	4000	___	___	___
300	Hell Gate Bridge (Std.), *28–42**	580	1500	___	___	___
300	(See #3 Trolley)					
301	Batteries, set of 4 (2⅞"), *03–05*		NRS	___	___	___
302	Plunge Battery (2⅞"), *01–02*		NRS	___	___	___
303	Summer Trolley, *10–13*	1500	3500	___	___	___
303	Carbon Cylinders (2⅞"), *02*		NRS	___	___	___
304	Composite Zincs (2⅞"), *02*		NRS	___	___	___
306	Glass Jars (2⅞"), *02*		NRS	___	___	___
308	(5) Signs (O), *40–42*	15	35	___	___	___
309	Electric Trolley Trailer					
	(2⅞"), *01–05*	2500	4500	___	___	___
309	Pullman (Std.), *26–39*	100	175	___	___	___
310	Baggage (Std.), *26–39*	100	175	___	___	___
310	Rails and Ties, complete					
	section (2⅞"), *01–02*	5	15	___	___	___
312	Observation (Std.), *24–39*	100	175	___	___	___

PREWAR (1901–1942)		Good	Exc	Color	Cond	$
313	Bascule Bridge (O), *40–42*	220	495	___	___	___
314	Girder Bridge (O), *40–42*	10	30	___	___	___
315	Trestle Bridge (O), *40–42*	25	75	___	___	___
316	Trestle Bridge (O), *40–42*	20	48	___	___	___
318	Electric 0-4-0 (Std.), *24–32*	150	260	___	___	___
318E	Electric 0-4-0, *26–35*	150	275	___	___	___
319	Pullman (Std.), *24–27*	110	175	___	___	___
320	Baggage (Std.), *25–27*	100	175	___	___	___
320	Switch and Signal (2⅞"), *02–05*		NRS	___	___	___
322	Observation (Std.), *24–27, 29–30 u*	100	175	___	___	___
330	Crossing, 90° (2⅞"), *02–05*		NRS	___	___	___
332	Baggage (Std.), *26–33*	75	100	___	___	___
337	Pullman (Std.), *25–32*	100	200	___	___	___
338	Observation (Std.), *25–32*	100	200	___	___	___
339	Pullman (Std.), *25–33*	50	80	___	___	___
340	Suspension Bridge (2⅞"), *02–05*＊		NRS	___	___	___
341	Observation (Std.), *25–33*	50	80	___	___	___
350	Track Bumper (2⅞"), *02–05*		NRS	___	___	___
370	Jars and Plates (2⅞"), *02–03*		NRS	___	___	___
380	Electric 0-4-0 (Std.), *23–27*	200	350	___	___	___
380	Elevated Pillars (2⅞"), *04–05*＊	30	75	___	___	___
380E	Electric 0-4-0 (Std.), *26–29*	300	400	___	___	___
381	Electric 4-4-4 (Std.), *28–29*＊	1800	3000	___	___	___
381E	Electric 4-4-4 (Std.), *28–36*＊	1500	3000	___	___	___
381U	Electric 4-4-4 Kit (Std.), *28–29*	1600	4300	___	___	___
384	Steam 2-4-0 (Std.), *30–32*＊	400	500	___	___	___
384E	Steam 2-4-0 (Std.), *30–32*＊	400	500	___	___	___
385E	Steam 2-4-2 (Std.), *33–39*＊	400	675	___	___	___
390	Steam 2-4-2 (Std.), *29*＊	400	725	___	___	___
390E	Steam 2-4-2 (Std.), *29–31*＊	450	700	___	___	___
392E	Steam 4-4-2 (Std.), *32–39*＊	650	1200	___	___	___
400	Express Trail Car (2⅞"), *03–05*＊	3500	6500	___	___	___
400E	Steam 4-4-4 (Std.), *31–39*＊	1200	2000	___	___	___
402	Electric 0-4-4-0 (Std.), *23–27*	300	500	___	___	___
402E	Electric 0-4-4-0 (Std.), *26–29*	300	500	___	___	___
404	Summer Trolley (Std.), *10*		NRS	___	___	___
408E	Electric 0-4-4-0 (Std.), *27–36*＊	700	1300	___	___	___
412	Pullman, "California" (Std.), *29–35*＊	600	2000	___	___	___

		Good	Exc	Color	Cond	$
413	Pullman, "Colorado" (Std.), *29–35**	600	2000			
414	Pullman, "Illinois" (Std.), *29–35**	600	2000	___	___	___
416	Observation, "New York" (Std.), *29–35**	600	2000	___	___	___
418	Pullman (Std.), *23–32**	190	280	___	___	___
419	Combination (Std.), *23–32**	190	280	___	___	___
420	Pullman, "Faye" (Std.), *30–40**	525	1000	___	___	___
421	Pullman, "Westphal" (Std.), *30–40**	550	1000	___	___	___
422	Observation, "Tempel" (Std.), *30–40**	525	1000	___	___	___
424	Pullman, "Liberty Belle" (Std.), *31–40**	325	530	___	___	___
425	Pullman, "Stephen Girard" (Std.), *31–40**	325	550	___	___	___
426	Observation, "Coral Isle" (Std.), *31–40**	325	550	___	___	___
427	Diner (Std.), *30*		NM			
428	Pullman (Std.), *26–30**	250	325	___	___	___
429	Combine (Std.), *26–30**	250	325	___	___	___
430	Observation (Std.), *26–30**	250	325	___	___	___
431	Diner (Std.), *27–32**	350	600	___	___	___
435	Power Station, *26–38**	130	275	___	___	___
436	Power Station, *26–37**	120	255	___	___	___
437	Switch/Signal Tower, *26–37**	210	480	___	___	___
438	Signal Tower, *27–39**	215	465	___	___	___
439	Panel Board, *28–42**	75	135	___	___	___
440/0440/440N	Signal Bridge, *32–42**	190	460	___	___	___
440C	Panel Board, *32–42*	75	135	___	___	___
441	Weighing Station (Std.), *32–36*	450	1500	___	___	___
442	Landscape Diner, *38–42*	135	200	___	___	___
444	Roundhouse (Std.), *32–35**	1100	3000	___	___	___
444-18	Roundhouse Clip, *33*		NRS	___	___	___
450	Electric 0-4-0, Macy's (O), *30 u*	300	695	___	___	___
450	Set: 450; matching 605; (2) 606s, *30 u*	750	1400	___	___	___
455	Electric Range, *30, 32–33*	320	980	___	___	___
490	Observation (Std.), *23–32**	190	280	___	___	___
500	Dealer Display, *27–28*		NRS	___	___	___
500	Electric Derrick Car					

PREWAR (1901–1942)		Good	Exc	Color	Cond	$
	(2⅞"), 03–04*	5000	7000	___	___	___
501	Dealer Display, 27–28		NRS	___	___	___
502	Dealer Display, 27–28		NRS	___	___	___
503	Dealer Display, 27–28		NRS	___	___	___
504	Dealer Display, 24–28		NRS	___	___	___
505	Dealer Display, 24–28		NRS	___	___	___
506	Dealer Display, 24–28		NRS	___	___	___
507	Dealer Display, 24–28		NRS	___	___	___
508	Dealer Display, 24–28		NRS	___	___	___
509	Dealer Display, 24–28		NRS	___	___	___
510	Dealer Display, 27–28		NRS	___	___	___
511	Flatcar (Std.), 27–40	50	90	___	___	___
512	Gondola (Std.), 27–39	40	85	___	___	___
513	Cattle Car (Std.), 27–38	70	135	___	___	___
514	Boxcar (Std.), 29–40	85	150	___	___	___
514	Refrigerator Car (Std.), 27–28	225	400	___	___	___
514R	Refrigerator Car (Std.), 29–40	140	200	___	___	___
515	Tank Car (Std.), 27–40	90	150	___	___	___
516	Hopper Car (Std.), 28–40	170	250	___	___	___
517	Caboose (Std.), 27–40	45	90	___	___	___
520	Floodlight Car (Std.), 31–40	95	200	___	___	___
529	Pullman (O), 26–32	15	35			
530	Observation (O), 26–32	15	35	___	___	___
550	Miniature Figures, boxed (Std.), 32–36*	130	230	___	___	___
551	Engineer (Std.), 32	20	40	___	___	___
552	Conductor (Std.), 32	20	40	___	___	___
553	Porter (Std.), 32	20	40	___	___	___
554	Male Passenger (Std.), 32	20	40	___	___	___
555	Female Passenger (Std.), 32	20	40	___	___	___
556	Red Cap Figure (Std.), 32	20	40	___	___	___
600	Derrick Trailer (2⅞"), 03–04*	4500	9500	___	___	___
600	Pullman, Early (O), 15–23	40	80	___	___	___
600	Pullman, Late (O), 33–42	50	100	___	___	___
601	Observation, Late (O), 33–42	50	100	___	___	___
601	Pullman, Early (O), 15–23	30	60	___	___	___
602	Baggage, Lionel Lines, Late (O), 33–42	60	120	___	___	___
602	Baggage, NYC (O), 15–23	20	45	___	___	___

PREWAR (1901–1942)	Good	Exc	Color	Cond	$
602 Observation (O), *22 u*	20	35	____	____	____
603 Pullman, Early (O), *22 u*	25	70	____	____	____
603 Pullman, Later (O), *20–25*	18	50	____	____	____
603 Pullman, Latest (O), *31–36*	35	65	____	____	____
604 Observation, Later (O), *20–25*	35	65	____	____	____
604 Observation, Latest (O), *31–36*	35	65	____	____	____
605 Pullman (O), *25–32*	85	190	____	____	____
606 Observation (O), *25–32*	85	190	____	____	____
607 Pullman (O), *26–27*	35	75	____	____	____
608 Observation (O), *26–37*	35	75	____	____	____
609 Pullman (O), *37*	35	75	____	____	____
610 Pullman, Early (O), *15–25*	30	70	____	____	____
610 Pullman, Late (O), *26–30*	50	85	____	____	____
611 Observation (O), *37*	35	95	____	____	____
612 Observation, Early (O), *15–25*	25	65	____	____	____
612 Observation, Late (O), *26–30*	50	85	____	____	____
613 Pullman (O), *31–40**	60	125	____	____	____
614 Observation (O), *31–40**	60	125	____	____	____
615 Baggage (O), *33–40**	85	195	____	____	____
616E/616W Diesel only (O), *35–41*	80	190	____	____	____
616E/616W Set: 616, (2) 617s, 618	260	425	____	____	____
617 Coach (O), *35–41*	40	85	____	____	____
618 Observation (O), *35–41*	40	85	____	____	____
619 Combine (O)	100	235	____	____	____
620 Floodlight Car (O), *37–42*	35	65	____	____	____
629 Pullman (O), *24–32*	15	35	____	____	____
630 Observation, *24–32*	15	35	____	____	____
636W Diesel only (O), *36–39*	90	165	____	____	____
636W Set: 636W (2) 637s, 638, *36–39*	250	525	____	____	____
637 Coach (O), *36–39*	70	115	____	____	____
638 Observation (O), *36–39*	70	115	____	____	____
651 Flatcar (O), *35–40*	20	45	____	____	____
652 Gondola (O), *35–40*	20	45	____	____	____
653 Hopper Car (O), *34–40*	30	65	____	____	____
654 Tank Car (O), *34–42*	25	45	____	____	____
655 Boxcar (O), *34–42*	25	45	____	____	____
656 Cattle Car (O), *35–40*	30	70	____	____	____
657 Caboose (O), *34–42*	17	40	____	____	____
659 Dump Car (O), *35–42*	40	70	____	____	____

PREWAR (1901–1942)		Good	Exc	Color	Cond	$
700	Electric 0-4-0 (O), *15–16*	360	700	___	___	___
700	Window Display (2⅞"), *03–05*		NRS	___	___	___
700E	Steam 4-6-4, Scale Hudson,					
	5344 (O), *37–42**	1900	4000	___	___	___
700K	Steam 4-6-4, unbuilt (O), *38–42*	3550	5400	___	___	___
701	Electric 0-4-0 (O), *15–16*	400	720	___	___	___
701	Steam 0-6-0 (see 708)					
702	Baggage (O), *17–21*	120	350	___	___	___
703	Electric 4-4-4 (O), *15–16*	1400	2600	___	___	___
706	Electric 0-4-0 (O), *15–16*	350	700	___	___	___
708	Steam 0-6-0, "8976"					
	on boiler front (O), *39–42**	1500	3000	___	___	___
710	Pullman (O), *24–34*	150	240	___	___	___
711	R.C. Switches, pair (O72), *35–42*	75	170	___	___	___
712	Observation (O), *24–34*	140	280	___	___	___
714	Boxcar (O), *40–42**	300	600	___	___	___
714K	Boxcar, unbuilt (O), *40–42*	—	925	___	___	___
715	Tank Car (O), *40–42**	340	675	___	___	___
715K	Tank Car, unbuilt (O), *40–42*	—	745	___	___	___
716	Hopper Car (O), *40–42**	400	830	___	___	___
716K	Hopper, unbuilt (O), *40–42*	—	975	___	___	___
717	Caboose (O), *40–42**	390	625	___	___	___
717K	Caboose, unbuilt (O), *40–42*	—	745	___	___	___
720	90° Crossing (O72), *35–42*	20	42	___	___	___
721	Manual Switches, pair (O72), *35–42*	45	100			
730	90° Crossing (O72), *35–42*	20	40	___	___	___
731	R.C. Switches, pair, T-rail					
	(O72), *35–42*	90	175	___	___	___
751E/751W Set: 752; (2) 753s; 754						
	(O), *34–41**	500	950	___	___	___
752E	Diesel only (O), *34–41*	160	325	___	___	___
753	Coach (O), *36–41*	95	200	___	___	___
754	Observation (O), *36–41*	95	200	___	___	___
760	16-piece Curved Track (O72), *35–42*	35	80	___	___	___
761	Curved Track (O72), *34–42*	1	3	___	___	___
762	Straight Track (O72), *34–42*	1	3	___	___	___
762	Inside Straight Track (O72), *34–42*	2	5	___	___	___
763E	Steam 4-6-4 (O), *37–42*	1200	3000	___	___	___
771	Curved Track, T-rail (O72), *35–42*	3	8	___	___	___

		Good	Exc	Color	Cond	$
772	Straight Track, T-rail (O72), *35–42*	4	12	___	___	___
773	Fishplate Outfit (O72), *36–42*	25	35	___	___	___
782	Hiawatha Combine (O), *35–41**	185	450	___	___	___
783	Hiawatha Coach (O), *35–41**	185	450	___	___	___
784	Hiawatha Observation (O), *35–41**	185	450	___	___	___
792	Rail Chief Combine (O), *37–41**	300	925	___	___	___
793	Rail Chief Coach (O), *37–41**	300	925	___	___	___
794	Rail Chief Observation (O), *37–41**	300	925	___	___	___
800	Boxcar (O), *15–26*	30	55	___	___	___
800	Boxcar (2⅞"), *04–05**	2500	4500	___	___	___
801	Caboose (O), *15–26*	30	50	___	___	___
802	Stock Car (O), *15–26*	40	60	___	___	___
803	Hopper Car, Early (O), *23–28*	20	40	___	___	___
803	Hopper Car, Late (O), *29–34*	25	45	___	___	___
804	Tank Car (O), *23–28*	25	50	___	___	___
805	Boxcar (O), *27–34*	25	45	___	___	___
806	Stock Car (O), *27–34*	25	45	___	___	___
807	Caboose (O), *27–40*	15	25	___	___	___
809	Dump Car (O), *31–41*	35	70	___	___	___
810	Crane (O), *30–42*	125	195	___	___	___
811	Flatcar (O), *26–40*	40	80	___	___	___
812	Gondola (O), *26–42*	30	65	___	___	___
813	Stock Car (O), *26–42*	55	125	___	___	___
814	Boxcar (O), *26–42*	50	100	___	___	___
814R	Refrigerator Car (O), *29–42*	100	185	___	___	___
815	Tank Car (O), *26–42*	50	115	___	___	___
816	Hopper Car (O), *27–42*	65	130	___	___	___
817	Caboose (O), *26–42*	45	90	___	___	___
820	Boxcar (O), *15–26*	45	75	___	___	___
820	Floodlight Car (O), *31–42*	105	200	___	___	___
821	Stock Car (O), *15–16, 25–26*	45	95	___	___	___
822	Caboose (O), *15–26*	35	75	___	___	___
831	Flatcar (O), *27–34*	20	40	___	___	___
840	Industrial Power Station, *28–40**	1200	3400	___	___	___
900	Ammunition Car (O), *17–21*	125	390	___	___	___
900	Box Trail Car (2⅞"), *04–05**	2000	4000	___	___	___
901	Gondola (O), *19–27*	20	40	___	___	___
902	Gondola (O), *27–34*	25	35	___	___	___
910	Grove of Trees, *32–42*	70	170	___	___	___

		Good	Exc	Color	Cond	$
911	Country Estate	175	400	___	___	___
912	Suburban Home	175	400	___	___	___
913	Landscaped Bungalow, *40–42*	140	315	___	___	___
914	Park Landscape, *32–35*	90	230	___	___	___
915	Tunnel, *32, 34–35*	160	485	___	___	___
916	Tunnel, 29¼" long, *35*	95	200	___	___	___
917	Scenic Hillside, *32–36*	90	230	___	___	___
918	Scenic Hillside, *32–36*	90	230	___	___	___
919	Park Grass, bag, *32–42*	7	17	___	___	___
920	Village, *32–33*	600	1750	___	___	___
921	Scenic Park, 3 pieces, *32–33*	980	2875	___	___	___
921C	Park Center, *32–33*	400	1160	___	___	___
922	Terrace, *32–36*	80	170	___	___	___
923	Tunnel, 40¼" long, *33–42*	90	250	___	___	___
924	Tunnel, 30" long (O72), *35–42*	50	150	___	___	___
925	Lubricant, *35–42*	1	3	___	___	___
927	Flag Plot, *37–42*	70	150	___	___	___
1000	Passenger Car (2⅞"), *05* *	4500	7500	___	___	___
1000	Trolley Trailer (Std.), *10–16*	1400	2500	___	___	___
1010	Electric 0-4-0, Winner (O), *31–32*	55	130	___	___	___
1010	Interurban Trailer (Std.), *10–16*	1000	2000	___	___	___
1011	Pullman, Winner (O), *31–32*	30	40	___	___	___
1011	Interurban (Std.), *10*		NM			
1012	Station, *32*	35	65	___	___	___
1012	(See #1011 Interurban)					
1015	Steam 0-4-0 (O), *31–32*	75	200	___	___	___
1017	Winner Station, *33*	25	75	___	___	___
1019	Observation (O), *31–32*	30	60	___	___	___
1020	Baggage (O), *31–32*	65	115	___	___	___
1021	90° Crossover (O27), *32–42*	1	4	___	___	___
1022	Tunnel, 18¾" long (O), *35–42*	15	32	___	___	___
1023	Tunnel, 19" long, *34–42*	20	45	___	___	___
1024	Switches, pair (O27), *37–42*	4	16	___	___	___
1025	Bumper (O27), *40–42*	11	25	___	___	___
1027	Transformer, Tin Station, *34*	35	95	___	___	___
1028	Transformer, 40 watts, *39*	3	12	___	___	___
1030	Electric 0-4-0 (O), *32*	70	150	___	___	___
1035	Steam 0-4-0 (O), *32*	75	125			
1045	Watchman, *38–42*	15	55	___	___	___

		Good	Exc	Color	Cond	$
1050	Passenger Car Trailer (2⅞"), 05*	5000	8000	___	___	___
1100	Handcar, Mickey Mouse, 35–37*	400	685	___	___	___
1100	Summer Trolley Trailer (Std.), 10–13		NRS	___	___	___
1103	Handcar, Peter Rabbit (O), 35–37*	400	1050	___	___	___
1105	Handcar, Santa Claus (O), 35–35*	575	1200	___	___	___
1107	Transformer, Tin Station, 33	25	75	___	___	___
1107	Handcar, Donald Duck (O), 36–37*	450	1200	___	___	___
1121	Switches, pair (O27), 37–42	15	35	___	___	___
1506L	Steam 0-4-0 (O), 33–34	95	140	___	___	___
1506M	Steam 0-4-0 (O), 35	250	475	___	___	___
1508	Steam 0-4-0, Commodore Vanderbilt w/ Mickey in 1509 Stoker Tender, 35	320	525	___	___	___
1511	Steam 0-4-0 (O), 36–37	110	180	___	___	___
1512	Gondola (O), 31–33, 36–37	20	45	___	___	___
1514	Boxcar (O), 31–37	20	45	___	___	___
1515	Tank Car (O), 33–37	20	45	___	___	___
1517	Caboose (O), 31–37	20	45	___	___	___
1518	Mickey Mouse Diner (O), 35	75	225	___	___	___
1519	Mickey Mouse Band (O), 35	75	225	___	___	___
1520	Mickey Mouse Animal (O), 35	75	225	___	___	___
1536	Circus: 1508, 1509, 1518, 1519, 1520	700	1450	___	___	___
1550	Switches, pair, windup, 33–37	2	6	___	___	___
1555	90° Crossover, windup, 33–37	1	3	___	___	___
1560	Station, 33–37	15	38	___	___	___
1569	Accessory set, 8 pieces, 33–37	20	55	___	___	___
1588	Steam 0-4-0 (O), 36–37	150	275	___	___	___
1630	Pullman (O), 38–42	25	55	___	___	___
1631	Observation (O), 38–42	30	65	___	___	___
1651E	Electric 0-4-0 (O), 33	120	250	___	___	___
1661E	Steam 2-4-0 (O), 33	75	160	___	___	___
1662	Steam 0-4-0 (O27), 40–42	155	260	___	___	___
1663	Steam 0-4-0 (O27), 40–42	190	320	___	___	___
1664/1664E	Steam 2-4-2 (O27), 38–42	55	85	___	___	___
1666/1666E	Steam 2-6-2 (O27), 38–42	100	150	___	___	___
1668/1668E	Steam 2-6-2 (O27), 37–41	75	140	___	___	___

PREWAR (1901–1942)	Good	Exc	Color	Cond	$
1673 Coach (O), *36–37*	30	75	___	___	___
1674 Pullman (O), *36–37*	30	75	___	___	___
1675 Observation (O), *36–37*	30	75	___	___	___
1677 Gondola (O), *33–35, 39–42*	15	40	___	___	___
1679 Boxcar (O), *33–42*	20	40	___	___	___
1680 Tank Car (O), *33–42*	15	35	___	___	___
1681 Steam 2-4-0 (O), *34–35*	55	110	___	___	___
1681E Steam 2-4-0 (O), *34–35*	65	140	___	___	___
1682 Caboose (O), *33–42*	10	30	___	___	___
1684 Steam 2-4-2 (O27), *41–42*	45	80	___	___	___
1685 Coach (O), *u*	150	310	___	___	___
1686 Baggage (O), *u*	150	310	___	___	___
1687 Observation (O), *u*	150	310	___	___	___
1688/1688E Steam 2-4-2 (O27), *36–46*	50	90	___	___	___
1689E Steam 2-4-2 (O27), *36–37*	60	100	___	___	___
1690 Pullman (O), *33–40*	25	55	___	___	___
1691 Observation (O), *33–40*	22	55	___	___	___
1692 Pullman (O27), *39 u*	40	70	___	___	___
1693 Observation (O27), *39 u*	40	70	___	___	___
1700E Diesel, power unit only (O27), *35–37*	45	75	___	___	___
1700E Set: 1700 (2) 1701s, 1702 (O27), *35–37 u*	125	210	___	___	___
1701 Coach (O27), *35–37*	20	50	___	___	___
1702 Observation (O27), *35–37*	20	50	___	___	___
1703 Observation w/hooked coupler, *u*	35	85	___	___	___
1717 Gondola (O), *33–40 u*	20	40	___	___	___
1717X Gondola (O), *40 u*	20	45	___	___	___
1719 Boxcar (O), *33–40 u*	25	50	___	___	___
1719X Boxcar (O), *41–42 u*	25	50	___	___	___
1722 Caboose (O), *33–42 u*	20	45	___	___	___
1722X Caboose (O), *39–40 u*	15	35	___	___	___
1766 Pullman (Std.), *34–40**	300	600	___	___	___
1767 Baggage Car (Std.), *34–40**	300	800	___	___	___
1768 Observation (Std.), *34–40**	300	600	___	___	___
1811 Pullman (O), *33–37*	30	65	___	___	___
1812 Observation (O), *33–37*	30	65	___	___	___
1813 Baggage Car (O), *33–37*	60	120	___	___	___
1816/1816W Diesel (O), *35–37*	95	250	___	___	___

		Good	Exc	Color	Cond	$
817	Coach (O), *35–37*	20	50	___	___	___
818	Observation (O), *35–37*	20	50	___	___	___
835E	Steam 2-4-2 (Std.), *34–39*	450	850	___	___	___
910	Electric 0-6-0, Early (Std.), *10–11*	800	1800	___	___	___
910	Electric 0-6-0, Late (Std.), *12*	550	1100	___	___	___
910	Pullman (Std.), *u*	1000	2000	___	___	___
911	Electric 0-4-0, Early (Std.), *10–12*	1000	2000	___	___	___
911	Electric 0-4-0, Late (Std.), *13*	700	1200	___	___	___
911	Electric 0-4-4-0, Special (Std.), *11–12*	1000	2500	___	___	___
912	Electric 0-4-4-0 (Std.), *10–12**	1500	2700	___	___	___
912	Electric 0-4-4-0 Special (Std.), *11**	2500	5000	___	___	___
2200	Summer Trolley Trailer (Std.), *10–13*	1100	2500	___	___	___
2600	Pullman (O), *38–42*	55	140	___	___	___
2601	Observation (O), *38–42*	55	140	___	___	___
2602	Baggage Car (O), *38–42*	70	160	___	___	___
2613	Pullman (O), *38–42**	90	270	___	___	___
2614	Observation (O), *38–42**	90	270	___	___	___
2615	Baggage Car (O), *38–42**	115	285	___	___	___
2620	Floodlight Car (O), *38–42*	38	85	___	___	___
2623	Pullman (O), *41–42*	155	325	___	___	___
2624	Pullman (O), *41–42*	750	1890	___	___	___
2630	Pullman (O), *38–42*	25	60	___	___	___
2631	Observation (O), *38–42*	25	60	___	___	___
2640	Pullman Illuminated (O), *38–42*	25	65	___	___	___
2641	Observation Illuminated (O), *38–42*	25	65	___	___	___
2642	Pullman (O), *41–42*	25	60	___	___	___
2643	Observation (O), *41–42*	25	60	___	___	___
2651	Flatcar (O), *38–42*	25	45	___	___	___
2652	Gondola (O), *38–41*	25	45	___	___	___
2653	Hopper Car (O), *38–42*	35	60	___	___	___
2654	Tank Car (O), *38–42*	30	60	___	___	___
2655	Boxcar (O), *38–42*	25	70	___	___	___
2656	Stock Car (O), *38–41*	35	85	___	___	___
2657	Caboose (O), *40–41*	15	35	___	___	___
2657X	Caboose (O), *40–41*	25	40	___	___	___
2659	Dump Car (O), *38–41*	40	65	___	___	___

PREWAR (1901–1942)	Good	Exc	Color	Cond	$
2660 Crane (O), *38–42*	50	85	___	___	___
2672 Caboose (O27), *41–42*	15	35	___	___	___
2677 Gondola (O27), *39–41*	15	35	___	___	___
2679 Boxcar (O27), *38–42*	12	30	___	___	___
2680 Tank Car (O27), *38–42*	12	30	___	___	___
2682 Caboose (O27), *38–42*	15	30	___	___	___
2682X Caboose (O27), *38–42*	20	35	___	___	___
2717 Gondola (O), *38–42u*	20	35	___	___	___
2719 Boxcar (O), *38–42u*	20	45	___	___	___
2722 Caboose (O), *38–42u*	20	45	___	___	___
2755 Tank Car (O), *41–42*	35	80	___	___	___
2757 Caboose (O), *41–42*	20	35	___	___	___
2757X Caboose (O), *41–42*	25	40	___	___	___
2758 Automobile Boxcar (O), *41–42*	35	50	___	___	___
2810 Crane (O), *38–42*	150	225	___	___	___
2811 Flatcar (O), *38–42*	65	130	___	___	___
2812 Gondola (O), *38–42*	38	95	___	___	___
2813 Stock Car (O), *38–42*	110	220	___	___	___
2814 Boxcar (O), *38–42*	90	205	___	___	___
2814R Refrigerator Car (O), *38–42*	130	255	___	___	___
2815 Tank Car (O), *38–42*	65	165	___	___	___
2816 Hopper Car (O), *35–42*	110	230	___	___	___
2817 Caboose (O), *36–42*	85	155	___	___	___
2820 Floodlight Car (O), *38–42*	95	210	___	___	___
2954 Boxcar (O), *40–42**	225	620	___	___	___
2955 Sunoco Tank Car (O), *40–42**	225	620	___	___	___
2956 Hopper Car (O), *40–42**	200	590	___	___	___
2957 Caboose (O), *40–42**	200	550	___	___	___
3300 Summer Trolley Trailer (Std.), *10–13*	1400	2500	___	___	___
3651 Operating Lumber Car (O), *39–42*	15	40	___	___	___
3652 Operating Gondola (O), *39–42*	20	60	___	___	___
3659 Operating Dump Car (O), *39–42*	15	35	___	___	___
3811 Operating Lumber Car (O), *39–42*	35	70	___	___	___
3814 Operating Merchandise Car (O), *39–42*	110	240	___	___	___
3859 Operating Dump Car (O), *38–42*	40	85	___	___	___
4351 (See 14, 17, 117)					
4400 (See #404 Summer Trolley)					

		Good	Exc	Color	Cond	$
344	(See 700E)					
906	(See 14, 17)					
118	(See 14)					
976	(See 227, 228, 229, 230, 706, 708)					
9050	(See 14)					
1906	(See 17)					
4078	(See 14, 114)					
2976	(See 114)					
5784	(See 12, 16, 112)					
6399	(See 16, 112)					
8237	(See 14, 114)					
42715	(See 17)					
A	Miniature Motor, *04*	50	105	___	___	___
A	Transformer, 40, 60 watts, *27–37*	8	26	___	___	___
B	New Departure Motor, *06–16*	50	112	___	___	___
B	Transformer, 50, 75 watts, *16–38*	6	25	___	___	___
C	New Departure Motor, *06–16*	50	125	___	___	___
D	New Departure Motor, *06–14*	50	125	___	___	___
E	New Departure Motor, *06–14*	50	125	___	___	___
F	New Departure Motor, *06–14*	50	125	___	___	___
G	Battery Fan Motor, *06–14*	50	125	___	___	___
K	Power Motor, *05*	50	125	___	___	___
K	Transformer, 150, 200 watts	30	125	___	___	___
L	Power Motor, *05*	50	110	___	___	___
L	Transformer, 50, 75 watts	7	24	___	___	___
M	Battery Motor, *15–20*	30	90	___	___	___
N	Transformer, 50 watts	7	25	___	___	___
Q	Transformer, 50, 75 watts	15	45	___	___	___
R	Battery Motor, *15–20*	30	85	___	___	___
R	Transformer, 100 watts, *38–42*	17	55	___	___	___
S	Transformer, 50, 80 watts	11	35	___	___	___
T	Transformer, 75, 100,150 watts	10	30	___	___	___
U	Transformer, Aladdin	6	18	___	___	___
V	Transformer, 150 watts, *39–42*	65	150	___	___	___
W	Transformer, 75 watts	7	25	___	___	___
Y	Battery Motor, *15–20*	40	90	___	___	___
Z	Transformer, 250 watts, *39–42*	120	225	___	___	___

Other Transformers and Rheostats made by Lionel

		Good	Exc	Color	Cond
106	Rheostat, *11–14*	3	10	___ ___ ___
1029	25 watts, *36*	6	20	___ ___ ___
1030	40 watts, *35–38*	6	25	___ ___ ___
1031	Rheosat, circa 1938	2	4	___ ___ ___
1036	Rheostat, circa 1941	2	5	___ ___ ___
1037	Tranformer, 40 watts, *40–42*	7	25	___ ___ ___
1038	Rheostat, circa 1940	2	4	___ ___ ___
1039	Transformer, 35 watts, *37–40*	7	20	___ ___ ___
1040	Transformer, 60 watts, *37–39*	12	30	___ ___ ___
1041	Transformer, 60 watts, *39–42*	12	30	___ ___ ___

Track, Lockons, and Contactors

	Good	Exc	Color	Cond
O Straight	.25	.75	___ ___ ___
O Curve	.25	.75	___ ___ ___
O72 Straight	1	2	___ ___ ___
O72 Curve	1	2	___ ___ ___
O27 Straight	.10	.50	___ ___ ___
O27 Curve	.10	.50	___ ___ ___
Standard Straight	.60	2	___ ___ ___
Standard Curve	.60	2	___ ___ ___
O Gauge Lockon	.10	.50	___ ___ ___
Standard Gauge Lockon	.25	1	___ ___ ___
UTC Lockon	.25	.75	___ ___ ___
145C Contactor	.50	2	___ ___ ___
153C Contactor	.50	3	___ ___ ___

		Good	Exc	Color	Cond	$
011-11	Fiber Pins (O), *46–50*	.10	.15	___	___	___
011-43	Insulating Pins, dz. (O), *61*	1	1.50	___	___	___
020	90° Crossover (O), *45–61*	5	8	___	___	___
020X	45° Crossover (O), *46–59*	6	8	___	___	___
022	R.C. Switches, pair (O), *45–69*	30	55	___	___	___
022-500	Adapter set (O), *57–61*	1	2	___	___	___
022A	R.C. Switches, pair (O), *47*	70	115	___	___	___
025	Bumper (O), *46–47*	7	20	___	___	___
026	Bumper, *48–50*	9	20	___	___	___
027C-1	Track Clips, dz. (027), *47, 49*	.50	1	___	___	___
30	Water Tower, *47–50*	75	150	___	___	___
31	Curved Track (Super O), *57–66*	1	1.50	___	___	___
31-7	Power Blade Con. (Super O), *57–61*	—	.50	___	___	___
31-15	Ground Rail Pin (Super O), *57–66*	—	.90	___	___	___
31-45	Power Blade Connection (Super O), *61–66*	—	.90	___	___	___
32	Straight Track (Super O), *57–66*	.65	1.40	___	___	___
32-10	Insulating Pin (Super O)	—	.50	___	___	___
32-20	Power Blade Ins. (Super O)	—	.25	___	___	___
32-25	Insulating Pin (Super O)	—	.25	___	___	___
32-30	Ground Pin (Super O)	—	.25	___	___	___
32-31	Power Pin (Super O)	—	.25	___	___	___
32-32	Insulating Pin (Super O)	—	.25	___	___	___
32-33	Ground Pin (Super O)	—	.25	___	___	___
32-34	Power Pin (Super O)	—	.25	___	___	___
32-45	Power Blade Insulators, dz. (Super O)	1	2	___	___	___
32-55	Insulating Pins, dz. (Super O)	1	2	___	___	___
33	Half Curved Track (Super O), *57–66*	1	2	___	___	___
34	Half Straight Track (Super O), *57–66*	1	1.50	___	___	___
35	Boulevard Lamp, *45–49*	15	35	___	___	___
36	Remote Control set (Super O), *57–66*	6	12	___	___	___
37	Uncoupling Track set (Super O),					

		Good	Exc	Color	Cond	$
	57–66	6	12	___	___	___
38	Water Tower, *46–47*	100	250	___	___	___
38	Accessory Adapter Track (Super O)	5	12	___	___	___
39	Operating set (Super O), *57*	4	9	___	___	___
39-5	Operating set (Super O), *57–58*	4	9	___	___	___
39-10	Operating set (Super O), *58*	4	9	___	___	___
39-15	Operating set, w/ blade (Super O), *57–58*	4	9	___	___	___
39-20	Operating set (Super O), *57–58*	4	9	___	___	___
39-25	Operating set (Super O), *61–66*	4	9	___	___	___
39-35	Operating set (Super O), *59*	4	9	___	___	___
40	Hookup Wire, *50–51, 53–63*	2	4	___	___	___
40-25	Conductor Wire, *56–59*	3	5	___	___	___
40-50	Cable Reel, *60–61*	4	6	___	___	___
41	Contactor (Super O)	.50	1	___	___	___
41	U.S. Army Switcher, *55–57*	100	150	___	___	___
42	Picatinny Arsenal Switcher, *57*	150	300	___	___	___
042/42	Manual Switches, pr. (O), *46–59*	20	40	___	___	___
43	Power Track (Super O), *59–66*	3	6	___	___	___
44	U.S. Army Mobile Launcher, *59–62*	110	205	___	___	___
45	U.S. Marines Mobile Launcher, *60–62*	125	255	___	___	___
45	Automatic Gateman, *46–49*	25	50	___	___	___
45N	Automatic Gateman, *45*	30	60	___	___	___
48	Insl. Straight Track (Super O), *57–66*	4	9	___	___	___
49	Insl. Curved Track (Super O), *57–66*	4	9	___	___	___
50	Lionel Gang Car, *54–64*	30	55	___	___	___
51	Navy Yard Switcher, *56–57*	100	190	___	___	___
52	Fire Car, *58–61*	105	225	___	___	___
53	Rio Grande Snowplow, *57–60*					
	(A) Backwards "a" in Rio Grande	180	330	___	___	___
	(B) Correctly printed "a"	370	680	___	___	___
54	Ballast Tamper, *58–61, 66, 68–69*	100	225	___	___	___
54-6446	(See 6446 or 6446-25)					
55	Tie-jector, *57–61*	120	235	___	___	___
55-150	Ties, *57–60*	2	5	___	___	___
56	Lamp Post, *46–49*	20	50	___	___	___
56	M&St L Mine Transport, *58*	250	560	___	___	___

		Good	Exc	Color	Cond	$
57	AEC Switcher, *59–60*	325	750	___	___	___
58	Lamp Post, *46–50*	20	50	___	___	___
58	GN Snowplow, *59–61*	325	650	___	___	___
59	Minuteman Switcher, *62–63*	300	600	___	___	___
60	Lionelville Rapid Transit Trolley, *55–58*	100	195	___	___	___
61	Ground Lockon (Super O), *57–66*	.25	.50	___	___	___
62	Power Lockon (Super O), *57–66*	.25	.50	___	___	___
62-78	Wooden Barrels, *52–57*	5	10	___	___	___
64	Street Lamp, *45–49*	23	50	___	___	___
65	Lionel Lines Handcar, *62–66*	150	375	___	___	___
68	Executive Inspection Car, *58–61*	200	350	___	___	___
69	Lionel Maintenance Car, *60–62*	175	310	___	___	___
70	Yard Light, *49–50*	22	50	___	___	___
71	Lamp Post, *49–59*	8	20	___	___	___
75	Goose Neck Lamp, set of 2, *61–63*	11	22	___	___	___
76	Blvd. Street Lamp, *59–66, 68–69*	9	22	___	___	___
80	Controller	10	18	___	___	___
88	Controller, *46–60*	4	8	___	___	___
89	Flagpole, *56–58*	16	50	___	___	___
90	Controller	3	6	___	___	___
91	Circuit Breaker, *57–60*	8	20	___	___	___
92	Circuit Breaker, *59–66, 68–69*	6	12	___	___	___
93	Water Tower, *46–49*	15	35	___	___	___
96C	Controller	2	5	___	___	___
97	Coal Elevator, *46–50*	118	225	___	___	___
100	Multivolt-DC/AC, Trans., *58–66*		NRS	___	___	___
108	Trestle set		NRS	___	___	___
109	Partial Trestle set		NRS	___	___	___
110	Graduated Trestle set, *55–69*	11	22	___	___	___
111	Elevated Trestle set, *56–69*	8	18	___	___	___
111-100	Two Elevated Trestle Piers, *60–63*	10	20	___	___	___
112	R.C. Switches, pr. (Super O), *57–66*	50	100	___	___	___
114	Newsstand w/ horn, *57–59*	50	120	___	___	___
115	Passenger Station, *46–49*	175	350	___	___	___
118	Newsstand w/ whistle, *57–58*	45	100	___	___	___
119	Landscaped Tunnel, *57–58*		NRS	___	___	___
120	90° Crossing (Super O), *57–66*	6	12	___	___	___

		Good	Exc	Color	Cond	$
121	Landscaped Tunnel, *59–66*		NRS			
122	Lamp Assortment		NRS			
123	Lamp Assortment, *55–59*		NRS			
123-60	Lamp Assortment, *60–63*		NRS			
125	Whistle Shack, *50–55*	17	40			
128	Animated Newsstand, *57–60*	80	220			
130	60° Crossing (Super O)	9	15			
131	Curved Tunnel, *59–66*		NRS			
132	Passenger Station, *49–55*	45	100			
133	Passenger Station, *57, 61–62, 66*	30	90			
137	Passenger Station (See Prewar section), *46*		NM			
138	Water Tower, *53–57*	75	145			
140	Automatic Banjo Signal, *54–66*	25	45			
142	Man. Switches, pr. (Super O), *57–66*	30	60			
145C	Contactor, *50–60*	1	3			
145	Automatic Gateman, *50–66*	25	45			
147	Whistle Controller, *61–66*	1	4			
148	Dwarf Trackside Signal, *57–60*	18	45			
150	Telegraph Pole set, *47–50*	20	55			
151	Auto. Semaphore, *47–69*	15	40			
152	Auto. Crossing Gate, *45–49*	12	35			
153	Auto. Block Control, Signal, *45–59*	15	38			
153C	Contactor	1	5			
154	Auto. Highway Signal, *45–69*	12	35			
155	Blinking Light Signal w/bell, *55–57*	30	65			
156	Station Platform, *46–49*	25	80			
157	Station Platform, *52–59*	15	40			
160	Unloading Bin, *52–57*	1	3			
161	Mail Pickup set, *61–63*	32	90			
163	Single Target Block Signal, *61–69*	15	30			
164	Log Loader, *46–50*	110	270			
167	Whistle Controller, *45–46*	4	10			
175	Rocket Launcher, *58–60*	110	300			
175-50	Extra Rocket, *59–60*	5	20			
182	Magnetic Crane, *46–49*	110	225			
192	Oper. Control Tower, *59–60*	100	215			
193	Industrial Water Tower, *53–55*	50	100			

		Good	Exc	Color	Cond	$
195	Floodlight Tower, *57–69*	28	55	___	___	___
195-75	Eight-Bulb Extension, *58–60*	7	18	___	___	___
196	Smoke Pellets, *46–47*	—	45	___	___	___
197	Rotating Radar Antenna, *57–59*	50	110	___	___	___
199	Microwave Relay Tower, *58–59*	32	85	___	___	___
202	UP Alco A unit, *57*	60	100	___	___	___
204	Santa Fe Alco AA units, *57*	75	150	___	___	___
205	Missouri Pacific Alco AA units, *57–58*	75	160	___	___	___
206	Artificial Coal, large bag, *46–68*	—	10	___	___	___
207	Artificial Coal, small bag	—	7	___	___	___
208	Santa Fe Alco AA units, *58–59*	78	165	___	___	___
209	New Haven Alco AA units, *58*	350	775	___	___	___
209	Wooden Barrels, set of 4, *46–50*	5	15	___	___	___
210	Texas Special Alco AA units, *58*	110	210	___	___	___
211	Texas Special Alco AA units, *62–66*	80	180	___	___	___
212	USMC Alco A unit, *58–59*	75	150	___	___	___
212	Santa Fe Alco AA units, *64–66*	78	150	___	___	___
212T	USMC dummy A unit, *58–59 u*	285	575	___	___	___
213	Railroad Lift Bridge, *50*		NM			
213	M&St L Alco AA units, *64*	75	175	___	___	___
214	Plate Girder Bridge, *53–69*	8	20	___	___	___
215	Santa Fe Alco units, *65 u*					
	(A) AB units	80	180	___	___	___
	(B) Double A units (usually w/ 212T)	78	165	___	___	___
216	Burlington Alco A unit, *58*	100	310	___	___	___
216	M&St L Alco AA units, (usually w/ 213T), *64 u*	90	200	___	___	___
217	B&M Alco AB units, *59*	75	185	___	___	___
218	Santa Fe Alco units, *59–63*					
	(A) Double A units	70	170	___	___	___
	(B) AB units	70	165	___	___	___
219	Missouri Pacific Alco AA units, *59 u*	68	150	___	___	___
220	Santa Fe Alco units, *60–61*					
	(A) A unit only	75	135	___	___	___
	(B) AA units	100	230	___	___	___
221	2-6-4, 221T/221W Tender, *46–47*	60	125	___	___	___

		Good	Exc	Color	Cond	$
221	Rio Grande Alco A unit, *63–64*	35	75	___	___	___
221	USMC Alco A unit, *63–64 u*	100	255	___	___	___
221	Santa Fe Alco A unit, *63–64 u*	175	420	___	___	___
222	Rio Grande Alco A unit, *62 adv. cat.*	35	75	___	___	___
223	218C Santa Fe Alco AB units, *63*	85	185	___	___	___
224	Steam 2-6-2, 2466T/2466W Tender, *45–46*	80	110	___	___	___
224	U.S. Navy Alco AB units, *60*	100	200	___	___	___
225	C&O Alco A unit, *60*	65	120	___	___	___
226	B&M Alco AB units, *60 u*	85	190	___	___	___
227	CN Alco A unit, *60 u*	78	160	___	___	___
228	CN Alco A unit, *61 u*	70	140	___	___	___
229	M&St L Alco units, *61–62*					
	(A) A unit only, 61	60	120	___	___	___
	(B) AB units, *62*	95	225	___	___	___
230	C&O Alco A unit, *61*	55	105	___	___	___
231	Rock Island Alco A unit, *61–63*	50	115	___	___	___
232	New Haven Alco A unit, *62*	62	130	___	___	___
233	Steam 2-4-2, 233W Tender, *61–62*	50	105			
235	Steam 2-4-2, 1130T/1060T Tender, *61 u*	18	45	___	___	___
236	Steam 2-4-2, 1130T/1050T Tender, *61–62*	18	45	___	___	___
237	Steam 2-4-2, *63–66*					
	(A) w/ 1060T Tender	25	60	___	___	___
	(B) w/ 234W Tender	48	105	___	___	___
238	Steam 2-4-2, 234W Tender, *63–64*	55	125	___	___	___
239	Steam 2-4-2, 234W Tender, *65–66*	55	100	___	___	___
240	Steam 2-4-2, 242T, *64 u*	130	260	___	___	___
241	Steam 2-4-2 w/ 234W Tender, *65 u*	75	165	___	___	___
242	Steam 2-4-2 w/ 1060T Tender or 1062T Tender, *62–66*	20	60	___	___	___
243	Steam 2-4-2, 243W Tender, *60*	70	150	___	___	___
244	Steam 2-4-2, 244T/1130T Tender, *60–61*	25	40	___	___	___
245	Steam 2-4-2, w/ 1060T Tender, *59–60 u*	35	70	___	___	___
246	Steam 2-4-2, 244T/1130T Tender, *59–61*	25	45	___	___	___

		Good	Exc	Color	Cond	$
247	Steam 2-4-2, 247T Tender, *59*	28	65	___	___	___
248	Steam 2-4-2, 1130T Tender, *58*	28	65	___	___	___
249	Steam 2-4-2, 250T Tender, *58*	18	49	___	___	___
250	Steam 2-4-2, 250T Tender, *57*	20	52	___	___	___
251	Steam 2-4-2, 1062T Tender, *66 u*	140	280	___	___	___
252	Crossing Gate, *50–62*	13	25	___	___	___
253	Block Control Signal, *56–59*	15	35	___	___	___
256	Illuminated Freight Station, *50–53*	22	30	___	___	___
257	Freight Station w/ diesel horn, *56–57*	32	90	___	___	___
260	Bumper, *51–69*					
	(A) Die-cast	9	18	___	___	___
	(B) Black plastic	25	50	___	___	___
262	Highway Crossing Gate, *62–69*	18	55	___	___	___
264	Operating Fork Lift Platform, includes 6264, *57–60*	120	225	___	___	___
270	Metal Bridge (O)	18	40	___	___	___
282	Gantry Crane, *54–57*	100	195	___	___	___
282R	Gantry Crane, *56–57*	120	225	___	___	___
299	Code Transmitter Beacon set, *61–63*	65	145	___	___	___
308	Railroad Sign set, *45–49*	15	30	___	___	___
309	Yard Sign set, die-cast, *50–59*	10	20	___	___	___
310	Billboard set, *50–68*	7	15	___	___	___
313	Bascule Bridge, *46–49*	255	550	___	___	___
313-82	Fiber Pins, *46–60*	—	.05	___	___	___
313-121	Fiber Pins, *61*	—	1.50	___	___	___
314	Scale Model Girder Bridge, *45–50*	9	24	___	___	___
315	Trestle Bridge, *46–48*	50	100	___	___	___
316	Trestle Bridge, *49*	15	40	___	___	___
317	Trestle Bridge, *50–56*	10	30	___	___	___
321	Trestle Bridge, *58–64*	11	35	___	___	___
332	Arch-Under Bridge, *59–66*	20	50	___	___	___
334	Operating Dispatching Board, *57–60*	100	245	___	___	___
342	Culvert Loader, *56–58*	125	285	___	___	___
344-80	Missiles, *59–60*	5	15	___	___	___
345	Culvert Unloader, *57–59*	175	365	___	___	___
346	Manual Culvert Unloader, *65*	65	170	___	___	___
347	Cannon Firing Range set, *64 u*	120	460	___	___	___

		Good	Exc	Color	Cond	$
348	Manual Culvert Unloader, *66–69*	70	185			
350	Engine Transfer Table, *57–60*	155	350			
350-50	Transfer Table Extension, *57–60*	75	165			
352	Ice Depot, includes 6352, *55–57*	120	225			
353	Trackside Control Signal, *60–61*	14	40			
356	Operating Freight Station, *52–57*	38	95			
362	Barrel Loader, *52–57*	50	125			
364	Conveyor Lumber Loader, *48–57*	80	120			
364C	On/Off Switch, *48–64*	3	7			
365	Dispatching Station, *58–59*	65	130			
375	Turntable, *62–64*	150	275			
390C	Switch, d.p.d.t., *60–64*	3	9			
394	Rotary Beacon, *49–53*	25	42			
395	Floodlight Tower, *49–56*	22	45			
397	Diesel Operating Coal Loader, *48–57*	90	165			
400	B&O RDC Passenger, *56–58*	150	250			
404	B&O RDC Baggage-Mail, *57–58*	165	300			
410	Billboard Blinker, *56–58*	25	45			
413	Countdown Control Panel, *62*	38	72			
415	Diesel Fueling Station, *55–57*	95	160			
419	Heliport Control Tower, *62*	150	375			
443	Missile Launch Platform, w/ 943 Ammo Dump, *60–62*	15	40			
445	Switch Tower, lighted, *52–57*	35	60			
448	Missile Firing Range set, w/6448, *61–63*	75	150			
450	Signal Bridge, two-track, *52–58*	30	60			
450L	Signal Light Head	15	30			
452	Signal Bridge, single-track, *61–63*	65	125			
455	Operating Oil Derrick, *50–54*	120	190			
456	Coal Ramp w/ 3456 Hopper, *50–55*	75	165			
460	Piggyback Transportation, includes 3460, *55–57*	65	145			
460P	Piggyback Platform, *55–57*	30	80			
461	Platform w/ Truck and Trailer, *66*	70	150			
462	Derrick Platform set, *61–62*	150	300			
464	Lumber Mill, *56–60*	80	165			
465	Sound Dispatching Station, *56–57*	60	135			
470	Missile Launching Platform					

POSTWAR (1945–1969)	Good	Exc	Color	Cond	$
w/ 6470, *59–62*	105	150	___	___	___
480-25 Conversion Coupler, *50–60*	1	3	___	___	___
480-32 Conv. Magnetic Coupler, *61–69*	1	3	___	___	___
494 Rotary Beacon, *54–66*	25	50	___	___	___
497 Coaling Station, *53–58*	80	150	___	___	___
520 Lionel Lines Box Cab Electric, *56–57*	70	140	___	___	___
600 MKT NW-2 Switcher, *55*					
(A) Black frame and end rails	90	170	___	___	___
(B) Gray frame and yellow end rails	220	400	___	___	___
601 Seaboard NW-2 Switcher, *56*	80	170	___	___	___
602 Seaboard NW-2 Switcher, *57–58*	85	195	___	___	___
610 Erie NW-2 Switcher, *55*					
(A) Black frame	85	160	___	___	___
(B) Yellow frame	280	590	___	___	___
611 Jersey Central NW-2 Switcher, *57–58*	120	205	___	___	___
613 UP NW-2 Switcher, *58*	125	415	___	___	___
614 Alaska NW-2 Switcher, *59–60*	120	200	___	___	___
616 Santa Fe NW-2 Switcher, *61–62*	85	175	___	___	___
617 Santa Fe NW-2 Switcher, *63*	120	250	___	___	___
621 Jersey Central NW-2 Switcher, *56–57*	60	145	___	___	___
622 Santa Fe NW-2 Switcher, *49–50*	150	325	___	___	___
623 Santa Fe NW-2 Switcher, *52–54*	95	200	___	___	___
624 C&O NW-2 Switcher, *52–54*	110	270	___	___	___
625 LV GE 44-ton Switcher, *57–58*	75	150	___	___	___
626 B&O GE 44-ton Switcher, *59*	120	375	___	___	___
627 LV GE 44-ton Switcher, *56–57*	80	145	___	___	___
628 NP GE 44-ton Switcher, *56–57*	80	145	___	___	___
629 Burlington GE 44-ton Switcher, *56*	110	350	___	___	___
633 Santa Fe NW-2 Switcher, *62*	100	215	___	___	___
634 Santa Fe NW-2 Switcher, *63, 65–66*					
(A) w/ safety stripes	80	185	___	___	___
(B) w/o safety stripes	55	120	___	___	___
635 UP NW-2 Switcher, *65 u*	60	120	___	___	___
637 Steam 2-6-4, 2046W/736W Tender, *59–63*	60	160	___	___	___

		Good	Exc	Color	Cond	$
638-2361	Van Camp's Pork & Beans Boxcar, *62 u*	25	50	___	___	___
645	Union Pacific NW-2 Switcher, *69*	60	130	___	___	___
646	Steam 4-6-4, 2046W Tdr., *54–58*	125	250	___	___	___
665	Steam 4-6-4, 2046W/6026W/ 736W Tender, *54–59, 66*	100	245	___	___	___
670	Pennsylvania Turbine, 6-8-6, *52*		NM			
671	Steam 6-8-6, *46–49*					
	(A) 671W Tender	120	250	___	___	___
	(B) 2671W Tender	115	225	___	___	___
671R	Steam 6-8-6, 4424W/4671 Tender, *46–49*	130	315	___	___	___
671RR	Steam 6-8-6, 2046W-50 Tender, *52*	130	260	___	___	___
671S	Smoke Conversion Kit	—	45	___	___	___
674	Steam 2-6-4, *52*		NM			
675	Steam 2-6-2, 2466W/2466WX/ 6466WX Tender, *47–49;* 2-6-4, *52*	80	165	___	___	___
681	Steam Turbine, 6-8-6, 2046W-50/ 2671W Tender, *50–51, 53*	120	265	___	___	___
682	Steam 6-8-6, 2046W-50 Tender, *54–55*	210	415	___	___	___
685	Steam 4-6-4, 6026W Tender, *53*	115	265	___	___	___
703	Steam 4-6-4, Hudson, *46*		NM			
703-10	Special Smoke Bulb, *46*	—	35	___	___	___
711	Remote Control Switches (O72)	90	180	___	___	___
721	Manual Switches (O72)	65	110	___	___	___
725	Steam 2-8-4, Berkshire, *52*		NM			
726	Steam 2-8-4 Berkshire					
	(A) 2426W Tender, *46*	275	450	___	___	___
	(B) 2426W Tender, *47–49*	265	425	___	___	___
726RR	Steam 2-8-4 Berkshire, 2046W Tender, *52*	210	385	___	___	___
726S	Smoke Conversion Kit		NRS	___	___	___
736	Steam 2-8-4, 2671WX/2046W/ 736W Tender, *50–66*	250	400	___	___	___
746	N&W Steam 4-8-4, *57–60*					
	(A) Long stripe Tender	580	1275	___	___	___
	(B) Short stripe Tender	500	1195	___	___	___

		Good	Exc	Color	Cond	$
760	Curved Track, 16 sec. (O72), *54–57*	18	40	___	___	___
773	Steam 4-6-4 Hudson, 2426W Tender, *50*	700	1400	___	___	___
773	Steam 4-6-4 Hudson, *64–66*					
	(A) w/ 773W Tender	500	1000	___	___	___
	(B) w/ 736W Tender	455	800	___	___	___
902	Elevated Trestle set, *60*		NRS	___	___	___
909	Smoke Fluid, *57–68*	—	10	___	___	___
919	Artificial Grass, *46–64*	—	12	___	___	___
920	Scenic Display set, *57–58*	50	100	___	___	___
920-2	Tunnel Portals, pair, *58–59*	20	35	___	___	___
920-3	Green Grass, *57*	—	15	___	___	___
920-4	Yellow Grass, *57*	—	15	___	___	___
920-5	Artificial Rock, *58*	2	6	___	___	___
920-8	Lichen, *58*	1	2	___	___	___
925	Lionel Lubricant, lg. tube, *46–69*	1	5	___	___	___
926	Lionel Lubricant, sm. tube, *55*	1	2	___	___	___
926-5	Instruction Booklet, *46–48*	1	5	___	___	___
927	Lubricating Kit, *50–59*	10	25	___	___	___
928	Maint. & Lubricating Kit, *60–63*	20	45	___	___	___
943	Ammo Dump, *59–61*	25	45	___	___	___
950	U.S. Railroad Map, *58–66*	20	50	___	___	___
951	Farm set, *58*	15	45	___	___	___
952	Miniature Figure set, *58*	18	45	___	___	___
953	Miniature Figure set, *60–62*	20	50	___	___	___
954	Swimming Pool/Playground set, *59*	15	35	___	___	___
955	Highway set, *58*	15	40	___	___	___
956	Stockyard set, *59*	15	35	___	___	___
957	Farm Building and Animal set, *58*	20	45	___	___	___
958	Vehicle set, *58*	12	35	___	___	___
959	Barn set, *58*	15	40	___	___	___
960	Barnyard set, *59–61*	12	38	___	___	___
961	School set, *59*	12	38	___	___	___
962	Turnpike set, *58*	20	55	___	___	___
963	Frontier set, *59–60*	20	60	___	___	___
963-100	Frontier set w/ box for Halloween General set	95	200	___	___	___

		Good	Exc	Color	Cond	$
964	Factory set, *59*	15	40	___	___	___
965	Farm set, *59*	15	38	___	___	___
966	Firehouse set, *58*	15	40	___	___	___
967	Post Office set, *58*	15	40	___	___	___
968	TV Transmitter set, *58*	12	35	___	___	___
969	Construction set, *60*	12	35	___	___	___
970	Ticket Booth, *58–60*	40	120	___	___	___
971	Lichen Package, *60–64*	5	10	___	___	___
972	Landscape Tree Assortment, *61–64*	5	10	___	___	___
973	Complete Landscaping set, *60–64*	10	25	___	___	___
974	Scenery set, *62–63*	5	15	___	___	___
980	Ranch set, *60*	15	45	___	___	___
981	Freight Yard set, *60*	12	40	___	___	___
982	Suburban Split Level set, *60*	12	40	___	___	___
983	Farm set, *60–61*	12	40	___	___	___
984	Railroad set, *61–62*	12	40	___	___	___
985	Freight Area set, *61*	13	38	___	___	___
986	Farm set, *62*	18	36	___	___	___
987	Town set, *62*	18	36	___	___	___
988	Railroad Structure set, *62*	18	36	___	___	___
1001	Steam 2-4-2, 1001T Tender, *48*	22	45	___	___	___
1002	Lionel Gondola, *48–52*					
	(A) Black w/ white lettering	5	10	___	___	___
	(B) Blue w/ white lettering	6	12	___	___	___
	(C) Silver w/ black lettering	100	325	___	___	___
	(D) Yellow w/ black lettering	100	340	___	___	___
	(E) Red w/ white lettering	110	350	___	___	___
	(F) Light blue w/ black lettering		NRS	___	___	___
X1004	PRR Baby Ruth Boxcar, *48–52*	5	12	___	___	___
1005	Sunoco 1-D Tank Car, *48–50*	3	10	___	___	___
1007	LL SP-Type Caboose, *48–52*	3	8	___	___	___
1008	Camtrol Uncoupling Unit (027), *57–62*	.50	1	___	___	___
1008-50	Camtrol w/ track (027), *48*	.25	1	___	___	___
1010	Transformer, 35 watts, *61–66*	8	16	___	___	___
1011	Transformer, 25 watts, *48–49*	8	16	___	___	___
1012	Transformer, 35 watts, *50–54*	7	14	___	___	___
1013	Curved Track (027), *45–69*	.10	.20	___	___	___
1013-17	Steel Pins (027), *46–60*	—	.05	___	___	___

		Good	Exc	Color	Cond	$
1013-42	Steel Pins (O27), *61–68*	—	.60	___	___	___
1014	Transformer, 40 watts, *55*	11	25	___	___	___
1015	Transformer, 45 watts, *56–60*	8	25	___	___	___
1016	Transformer, 35 watts, *59–60*	6	25	___	___	___
1018	Straight Track (O27), *45–69*	.15	.40	___	___	___
1018	½ Straight Track (O27), *55–69*	.15	.40	___	___	___
1019	R.C. Track set (O27), *46–48*	2	8	___	___	___
1020	90° Crossing (O27), *55–69*	2	6	___	___	___
1021	90° Crossing (O27), *45–54*	2	6	___	___	___
1022	Man. Switches, pr. (O27), *53–69*	10	20	___	___	___
1122-34	R.C. Switches, pair, *52–53*	14	38	___	___	___
1023	45° Crossing (O27), *56–69*	2	5	___	___	___
1024	Man. Switches, pr. (O27), *46–52*	7	15	___	___	___
1025	Illuminated Bumper (O27), *46–47*	6	15	___	___	___
1025	Transformer, 45 watts, *61–69*	12	25	___	___	___
1026	Transformer, 25 watts, *61–64*	5	12	___	___	___
1032	Transformer, 75 watts, *48*	30	60	___	___	___
1033	Transformer, 90 watts, *48–56*	25	50	___	___	___
1034	Transformer, 75 watts, *48–54*	15	30	___	___	___
1035	Transformer, 60 watts, *47*	22	45	___	___	___
1037	Transformer, 40 watts, *46–47*	10	28	___	___	___
1041	Transformer, 60 watts, *45–46*	12	25	___	___	___
1042	Transformer, 75 watts, *47–48*	18	48	___	___	___
1043	Transformer					
	(A) 50 watts, black, *53–57*	12	25	___	___	___
	(B) 60 watts, ivory, *57–58*	55	115	___	___	___
1044	Transformer, 90 watts, *57–69*	40	75	___	___	___
1045	Operating Watchman, *46–50*	15	40	___	___	___
1047	Operating Switchman, *59–61*	50	165	___	___	___
1050	Steam 0-4-0, 1050 Tender, *59 u*	50	150	___	___	___
1053	Transformer, 60 watts, *56–60*	18	40	___	___	___
1055	Texas Special Alco A unit, *59–60 adv. cat.*	30	50	___	___	___
1060	Steam 2-4-2, 1050T/1060T Tender, *60–62 adv. cat.*	12	30	___	___	___
1061	Steam 0-4-0, 1061T Tender, *64; 2–4–2, 69*	12	30	___	___	___
1062	Steam 2-4-2, 1062T Tender, *63–64*	12	30	___	___	___
1063	Transformer, 75 watts, *60–64*	18	55	___	___	___

		Good	Exc	Color	Cond	$
1065	Union Pacific Alco A unit, *61 adv. cat.*	35	90	___	___	
1066	Union Pacific Alco A unit, *64 u*	50	105	___	___	
1073	Transformer, 60 watts, *61–66*	20	55	___	___	
1101	Steam 2-4-2, 1001T Tender, *48*	20	42	___	___	
1101	Transformer, 25 watts, *48*	8	15	___	___	
1110	Steam 2-4-2, 1001T Tender, *49, 51–52*	10	38	___	___	
1120	Steam 2-4-2, 1001T Tender, *50*	15	30	___	___	
1121	R.C. Switches, pr. (O27), *46–51*	12	35	___	___	
1122	R.C. Switches, pr. (O27), *52–53*	12	35	___	___	
1122E	R.C. Switches, pr. (O27), *53–69*	15	40	___	___	
1122-500	Gauge Adapter (O27), *57–66*	.25	1	___	___	
1130	Steam 2-4-2, 6066T/1130T Tender, *53–54*	16	35	___	___	
1615	Steam 0-4-0, 1615T Tender, *55–57*	85	200	___	___	
1625	Steam 0-4-0, 1625T Tender, *58*	90	225	___	___	
1640-100	Presidential Kit, *60*	60	175	___	___	
1654	Steam 2-4-2, 1654W Tender, *46–47*	35	80	___	___	
1655	Steam 2-4-2, 6654W Tender, *48–49*	35	70	___	___	
1656	Steam 0-4-0, 6403B Tender, *48–49*	125	295	___	___	
1665	Steam 0-4-0, 2403B Tender, *46*	150	350			
1666	Steam 2-6-2, 2466W/2466WX Tender, *46–47*	50	135	___	___	
1862	General 4-4-0, 1862T Tender, *59–62*	100	225	___	___	
1865	Western & Atlantic Coach, *59–62*	18	40	___	___	
1866	Western & Atlantic Baggage, *59–62*	18	40	___	___	
1872	General 4-4-0, 1872T Tender, *59–62*	100	300	___	___	
1875	Western & Atlantic Coach, *59–62*	125	250	___	___	
1875W	W&A Coach w/ whistle, *59–62*	85	175	___	___	
1876	Western & Atlantic Baggage, *59–62*	30	85	___	___	
1877	Flatcar w/ fence and horses, *59–62*	30	80	___	___	
1882	General 4-4-0, 1882T Tender, *60 u*	200	420	___	___	
1885	Western & Atlantic Coach, *60 u*	95	275	___	___	

		Good	Exc	Color	Cond	$
1887	Flatcar w/ fences and horses, *60 u*	80	180	___	___	___
2001	Track Make-up Kit (O27), *63*		NRS	___	___	___
2002	Track Make-up Kit (O27), *63*		NRS	___	___	___
2003	Track Make-up Kit (O27), *63*		NRS	___	___	___
2016	Steam 2-6-4, 6026W Tender, *55–56*	50	125	___	___	___
2018	Steam 2-6-4, *56–59, 61*					
	(A) 6026T Tender	40	80	___	___	___
	(B) 6026W Tender	60	120	___	___	___
	(C) 1130T Tender	40	80	___	___	___
2020	Steam 6-8-6, 2020W/6020W					
	Tender, *46–49*	100	200	___	___	___
2023	Union Pacific Alco AA units, *50–51*					
	(A) Yellow body	150	295	___	___	___
	(B) Silver body	150	295	___	___	___
2024	C&O Alco A, *69*	30	80	___	___	___
2025	Steam 2-6-2, 2-6-4, with 2466W/					
	6466W Tender, *47–49, 52*	70	140	___	___	___
2026	Steam 2-6-2, 2-6-4, *48–49, 51–53*					
	(A) 6466W or 6466WX	60	115	___	___	___
	(B) 6466T or 6066T	40	85	___	___	___
2028	Pennsylvania GP-7, *55*					
	(A) Gold lettering	165	410	___	___	___
	(B) Yellow lettering	140	375	___	___	___
	(C) Tan frame	250	565	___	___	___
2029	Steam 2-6-4, 234W Tdr., *64–69*	70	125	___	___	___
2031	Rock Island Alco AA units, *52–54*	150	380	___	___	___
2032	Erie Alco AA Units, *52–54*	125	250	___	___	___
2033	Union Pacific Alco AA units,					
	52–54	155	350	___	___	___
2034	Steam 2-4-2, 6066T Tender, *52*	25	50	___	___	___
2035	Steam 2-6-4, 6466W Tender,					
	50–51	65	175	___	___	___
2036	Steam 2-6-4, 6466W Tender, *50*	65	150	___	___	___
2037	Steam 2-6-4, black engine,					
	54–55, 57–63					
	(A) w/ 6026T, 1130T	45	90	___	___	___
	(B) w/ 6026W, 233W, 234W	60	125	___	___	___
2037-500	Steam 2-6-4, pink engine, w/					
	1130T-500 Tender, *57–58*	360	800	___	___	___

POSTWAR (1945–1969)		Good	Exc	Color	Cond	$
2041	Rock Island Alco AA units, *69*	60	120	___	___	___
2046	Steam 4-6-4, 2046W Tender, *50–51, 53*	135	235	___	___	___
2055	Steam 4-6-4, 2046W/6026W Tender, *53–55*	75	195	___	___	___
2056	Steam 4-6-4, 2046W Tender, *52*	105	250	___	___	___
2065	Steam 4-6-4, 2046W/6026W Tender, *54–56*	100	225	___	___	___
2240	Wabash F-3 AB units, *56*	400	800	___	___	___
2242	New Haven F-3 AB units, *58–59*	500	1200	___	___	___
2243	Santa Fe F-3 AB units, *55–57*	300	495	___	___	___
2243C	Santa Fe F-3 B units, *55–57*	100	220	___	___	___
2245	Texas Special F-3 AB units, *54–55*					
	(A) B unit w/ portholes, *54*	300	550	___	___	___
	(B) B unit w/o portholes, *55*	430	835	___	___	___
2257	Lionel SP-Type caboose, *47*					
	(A) Red, no stack	5	10	___	___	___
	(B) Tuscan, w/ stack	50	200	___	___	___
2257	Caboose, red w/ plastic stack		NRS	___	___	___
2321	Lackawanna Train Master, *54–56*					
	(A) Gray roof	300	500	___	___	___
	(B) Maroon roof	400	800	___	___	___
2322	Virginian Train Master, *65–66*					
	(A) Unpainted blue stripe	300	625	___	___	___
	(B) Painted blue stripe	400	825	___	___	___
2328	Burlington GP-7, *55–56*	200	425	___	___	___
2329	Virginian Rectifier, *58–59*	315	750	___	___	___
2330	Pennsylvania GG-1, green, *50*	625	1350	___	___	___
2331	Virginian Train Master, *55–58*					
	(A) Black stripe/gold lettering, *55*	720	1400	___	___	___
	(B) Blue stripe/yellow lettering, *56–58*	400	900	___	___	___
	(C) Blue and yellow, gray mold	600	1200	___	___	___
2332	Pennsylvania GG-1, *47–49*					
	(A) Black	900	2000	___	___	___
	(B) Green	320	600	___	___	___
2333	Santa Fe F-3 AA units, *48–49*	275	515	___	___	___
2333	NYC F-3 AA units, *48–49*					
	(A) Rubber-stamped lettering	425	900	___	___	___

		Good	Exc	Color	Cond	$
	(B) Heat-stamped lettering	295	700	___	___	___
2337	Wabash GP-7, *58*	110	315	___	___	___
2338	Milwaukee Road GP-7, *55–56*					
	(A) Orange band around shell	800	1800	___	___	___
	(B) Interrupted orange band	150	250	___	___	___
2339	Wabash GP-7, *57*	165	325	___	___	___
2340	Pennsylvania GG-1, *55*					
	(A) Tuscan	700	1450	___	___	___
	(B) Dark green	650	1325	___	___	___
2341	Jersey Central Train Master, *56*					
	(A) High gloss orange	1100	2300	___	___	___
	(B) Dull orange	950	2000			
2343	Santa Fe F-3 AA units, *50–52*	250	575	___	___	___
2343C	Santa Fe F-3 B unit, *50–55*	100	215	___	___	___
2344	NYC F-3 AA units, *50–52*	290	600	___	___	___
2344C	NYC F-3 B unit, *50–55*	120	250	___	___	___
2345	Western Pacific F-3 AA units, *52*	1100	2075	___	___	___
2346	B&M GP-9, *65–66*	145	290	___	___	___
2347	C&O GP-7, *65 u*	1200	2600	___	___	___
2348	M&St L GP-9, *58–59*	175	425	___	___	___
2349	Northern Pacific GP-9, *59–60*	175	415	___	___	___
2350	New Haven EP-5, *56–58*					
	(A) White "N" painted nose	370	750	___	___	___
	(B) White "N" decal nose	220	500	___	___	___
	(C) Orange "N" painted nose	900	1600	___	___	___
	(D) Orange "N" decal nose	500	1100	___	___	___
	(E) White "N" orange paint through doors	380	800	___	___	___
2351	Milwaukee Road EP-5, *57–58*	200	575	___	___	___
2352	Pennsylvania EP-5, *58–59*					
	(A) Tuscan body	225	500	___	___	___
	(B) Chocolate brown body	230	550	___	___	___
2353	Santa Fe F-3 AA units, *53–55*	270	575	___	___	___
2354	NYC F-3 AA units, *53–55*	225	600	___	___	___
2355	Western Pacific F-3 AA units, *53*	800	1600	___	___	___
2356	Southern F-3 AA units, *54–56*	500	1000	___	___	___
2356C	Southern F-3 B unit, *54–56*	160	300	___	___	___
2357	Lionel SP-Type Caboose, *47–48*					
	(A) Red w/ red stack	115	275	___	___	___

		Good	Exc	Color	Cond	$
	(B) Tuscan w/ Tuscan stack	15	30			
2358	Great Northern EP-5, *59–60*	350	1000			
2359	Boston & Maine GP-9, *61–62*	185	300			
2360	Penn GG-1, *56–58, 61–63*					
	(A) Tuscan, 5 gold stripes	600	1500			
	(B) Dark green, 5 gold stripes	575	1300			
	(C) Tuscan, single gold stripe, heat-stamped lettering	500	1000			
	(D) Tuscan, single gold stripe, decal lettering	500	885			
2363	Illinois Central F-3 AB units, *55–56*	450	1100			
2365	C&O GP-7, *62–63*	135	300			
2367	Wabash F-3 AB units, *55*	400	1000			
2368	B&O F-3 AB units, *56*	650	1700			
2373	CP F-3 AA units, *57*	950	2100			
2378	Milwaukee Road F-3 AB units, *56*					
	(A) w/ roof line stripes	1050	1800			
	(B) w/o roof line stripes	1000	1700			
2379	Rio Grande F-3 AB units, *57–58*	580	1100			
2383	Santa Fe F-3 AA units, *58–66*	225	475			
2400	Maplewood Pullman, green, *48–49*	60	150			
2401	Hillside Obs., green, *48–49*	60	150			
2402	Chatham Pullman, green, *48–49*	60	150			
2404	Santa Fe Vista Dome, *64–65*	30	70			
2405	Santa Fe Pullman, *64–65*	30	70			
2406	Santa Fe Observation, *64–65*	30	70			
2408	Santa Fe Vista Dome, *66*	35	78			
2409	Santa Fe Pullman, *66*	35	78			
2410	Santa Fe Observation, *66*	35	75			
2411	Lionel Lines Flatcar, *46–48*					
	(A) w/ pipes, *46*	50	90			
	(B) w/ logs, *47–48*	15	30			
2412	Santa Fe Vista Dome, *59–63*	25	85			
2414	Santa Fe Pullman, *59–63*	25	85			
2416	Santa Fe Observation, *59–63*	22	65			
2419	DL&W Work Caboose, *46–47*	22	45			
2420	DL&W Work Caboose, w/ light, *46–48*	40	100			

		Good	Exc	Color	Cond	$
2421	Maplewood Pullman, *50–53*					
	(A) Gray roof	40	85	___	___	___
	(B) Silver roof	40	70	___	___	___
2422	Chatham Pullman, *50–53*					
	(A) Gray roof	40	85	___	___	___
	(B) Silver roof	35	70	___	___	___
2423	Hillside Observation, *50–53*					
	(A) Gray roof	40	80	___	___	___
	(B) Silver roof	35	65	___	___	___
2429	Livingston Pullman, *52–53*	50	120	___	___	___
2430	Blue Pullman, *46–47*	20	65	___	___	___
2431	Blue Observation, *46–47*	20	65	___	___	___
2432	Clifton Vista Dome, *54–58*	20	48	___	___	___
2434	Newark Pullman, *54–58*	20	48	___	___	___
2435	Elizabeth Pullman, *54–58*	30	75	___	___	___
2436	Mooseheart Observation, *57–58*	20	60	___	___	___
2436	Summit Observation, *54–56*	25	60	___	___	___
2440	Green Pullman, *46–47*	20	55	___	___	___
2441	Green Observation, *46–47*	20	50	___	___	___
2442	Clifton Vista Dome, *56*	45	100	___	___	___
2442	Brown Pullman, *46–48*	20	70	___	___	___
2443	Brown Observation, *46–48*	20	70	___	___	___
2444	Newark Pullman, *56*	25	80	___	___	___
2445	Elizabeth Pullman, *56*	45	190	___	___	___
2446	Summit Observation, *56*	40	100	___	___	___
2452	Pennsylvania Gondola, *45–47*	8	18	___	___	___
2452X	Pennsylvania Gondola, *46–47*	5	10	___	___	___
X2454	Pennsylvania Boxcar, *46*	70	180	___	___	___
X2454	Baby Ruth Boxcar, "PRR" logo, *46–47*	7	22	___	___	___
2456	Lehigh Valley Hopper, *48*	7	20	___	___	___
2457	PRR Caboose, metal, N5, *45–47*	15	30	___	___	___
X2458	Pennsylvania Boxcar, *46–47*	15	50	___	___	___
2460	Bucyrus Erie Crane, 12-wheel, *46–50*					
	(A) Gray Cab	75	200	___	___	___
	(B) Black Cab	35	75	___	___	___
2461	Transformer Car, die-cast, *47–48*					
	(A) Red transformer	40	110	___	___	___
	(B) Black transformer	30	85	___	___	___

		Good	Exc	Color	Cond	$
2465	Sunoco 2-D Tank Car, *46–48*	5	17			
2472	PRR Caboose, metal, N5, *46–47*	10	25			
2481	Plainfield Pullman, yellow, *50*	105	275			
2482	Westfield Pullman, yellow, *50*	105	275			
2483	Livingston Observation, yellow, *50*	85	230			
2521	President McKinley Obs., *62–66*	60	180			
2522	President Harrison V. D., *62–66*	80	180			
2523	President Garfield Pullman, *62–66*	80	180			
2530	REA Baggage, *54–60*					
	(A) Large doors	250	500			
	(B) Small doors	100	180			
2531	Silver Dawn Observation, *52–60*	65	110			
2532	Silver Range Vista Dome, *52–60*	65	110			
2533	Silver Cloud Pullman, *52–59*	65	110			
2534	Silver Bluff Pullman, *52–59*	65	110			
2541	Alexander Hamilton Obs., *55–56**	75	200			
2542	Betsy Ross Vista Dome, *55–56**	75	200			
2543	William Penn Pullman, *55–56**	75	200			
2544	Molly Pitcher Pullman, *55–56**	75	200			
2550	B&O RDC Baggage/Mail, *57–58*	200	550			
2551	Banff Park Observation, *57**	100	250			
2552	Skyline 500 Vista Dome, *57**	100	250			
2553	Blair Manor Pullman, *57**	175	375			
2554	Craig Manor Pullman, *57**	150	350			
2555	Sunoco 1-D Tank Car, *46–48*	15	40			
2559	B&O RDC Passenger, *57–58*	150	305			
2560	Lionel Lines Crane, 8-wheel, *46–47*	20	55			
2561	Vista Valley Observation, *59–61**	100	245			
2562	Regal Pass Vista Dome, *59–61**	125	310			
2563	Indian Falls Pullman, *59–61**	125	310			
2625	Madison Pullman, *46–47**	95	235			
2625	Manhattan Pullman, *46–47**	100	240			
2625	Irvington Pullman, *46–50**					
	(A) No silhouettes	95	220			
	(B) w/ silhouettes	105	275			
2627	Madison Pullman, *48–50**					
	(A) No silhouettes	95	225			
	(B) w/ silhouettes	95	255			
2628	Manhattan Pullman, *48–50**					

| --- | --- | --- | --- | --- | --- |
(A) No silhouettes	95	220	___	___	___
(B) w/ silhouettes	105	260	___	___	___
2671 TCA Tender, *68*	—	75	___	___	___
2755 SUNX 1-D Tank Car, *45*	35	125	___	___	___
2855 SUNX 1-D Tank Car, *46–47*					
(A) Black	65	200	___	___	___
(B) Gray	50	175	___	___	___
2856 B&O Scale Hopper Car, *46–47*	NM				
2857 NYC Scale Caboose, *46*	NM				
X2954 Pennsylvania Scale Boxcar, *41–42*	125	250	___	___	___
2955 SUNX 1-D Scale Tank Car, *40–42, 46*	100	250	___	___	___
2956 B&O Scale Hopper Car, *40–42*	150	310	___	___	___
2957 NYC Scale Caboose, *46*	60	225	___	___	___
(3309) Turbo Missile Launch Car, *63–64*					
(A) Red body	25	60	___	___	___
(B) Olive body	100	325	___	___	___
3330 Flatcar w/ Submarine Kit, *60–62*	60	150	___	___	___
3330-100 Oper. Submarine Kit, *60–61*	50	100	___	___	___
(3349) Turbo Missile Launch Car, *62–65*	25	60	___	___	___
3356 Operating Horse Car only, *56–60, 64–66*	40	85	___	___	___
3356 Operating Horse Car and Corral set, *56–60, 64–66*	70	175	___	___	___
3356-100 (9) Black Horses, *56–59*	6	20	___	___	___
3356-150 Horse Car Corral	30	85	___	___	___
3357 Hydraulic Maintenance Car, *62–64*	20	65	___	___	___
3359 Lionel Lines Two-bin Dump, *55–58*	18	52	___	___	___
3360 Operating Burro Crane, *56–57*	130	265	___	___	___
3361 Operating Log Dump Car, *55–58*	20	45	___	___	___
3362 Flatcar w/ helium tanks or logs, *61–63*	12	42	___	___	___
3362/3364 Log Dump Car, *65–69*	12	35	___	___	___
3366 Circus Car Corral set, *59–62*	125	250	___	___	___
3366 Circus Car only, *59–62*	50	100	___	___	___
3366-100 (9) White Horses, *59–60*	20	45	___	___	___
3370 W&A Outlaw Car, *61–64*	18	58	___	___	___
3376 Bronx Zoo Car, *60–66, 69*					
(A) Blue w/ white lettering	20	55	___	___	___

		Good	Exc	Color	Cond	$
	(B) Green w/ yellow lettering	35	110			
	(C) Blue w/ yellow lettering	110	310			
3386	Bronx Zoo Car, *60 adv. cat.*	25	65			
3409	Helicopter Car, *61 adv. cat.*	45	120			
3410	Helicopter Car, *61–63*	40	95			
(3413)	Mercury Capsule Car, *62–64*	65	145			
3419	Helicopter Car, *59–65*	40	110			
3424	Wabash Operating Boxcar, *56–58*	30	80			
3424-100	Low Bridge Signal set	10	40			
3428	U.S. Mail Oper. Boxcar, *59–60*	30	105			
3429	USMC Helicopter Car, *60*	200	465			
3434	Poultry Dispatch car, *59–60, 64–66*	50	100			
3435	Traveling Aquarium Car, *59–62*					
	(A) Gold circle	400	1000			
	(B) Tank 1, Tank 2	280	800			
	(C) Gold lettering	150	300			
	(D) Yellow rubber stamp	100	250			
3444	Erie Operating Gondola, *57–59*	30	60			
3451	Operating Log Dump Car, *46–48*	12	32			
3454	PRR Operating Merchandise Car, *46–47*					
	(A) Red lettering		NRS			
	(B) Blue lettering	65	130			
3456	N&W Operating Hopper Car, *50–55*	15	50			
3459	LL Operating Dump Car, *46–48*					
	(A) Aluminum bin	100	275			
	(B) Black bin	15	50			
	(C) Green bin	20	65			
3460	Flatcar w/ trailers, *55–57*	22	65			
3461	Lionel Operating Log Car, *49–55*	10	35			
3462	Automatic Milk Car, *47–48*	20	55			
3462P	Milk Car Platform	5	15			
X3464	ATSF Operating Boxcar, *49–52*	10	25			
X3464	NYC Operating Boxcar, *49–52*	10	25			
3469	LL Operating Dump Car, *49–55*	12	45			
3470	Target Launcher, *62–64*	30	75			
3472	Automatic Milk Car, *49–53*	15	45			
3474	Western Pacific Boxcar, *52–53*	15	55			
3482	Automatic Milk Car, *54–55*	20	55			
3484	Pennsylvania Operating Boxcar, *53*	15	50			

	Good	Exc	Color	Cond	$
3484-25 ATSF Operating Boxcar, *54*	30	90	___	___	___
3494-1 NYC Pacemaker Boxcar, *55*	40	105	___	___	___
3494-150 MP Operating Boxcar, *56*	55	110	___	___	___
3494-275 State of Maine Operating Boxcar, *56–58*	55	130	___	___	___
3494-550 Monon Operating Boxcar, *57–58*	100	400	___	___	___
3494-625 Soo Operating Boxcar, *57–58*	115	400	___	___	___
3509 Satellite Car, *61*	22	60	___	___	___
(3510) Satellite Car, *62 adv. cat.*	40	155	___	___	___
3512 Fireman and Ladder Car, *59–61*					
(A) Black rooftop ladder	30	95	___	___	___
(B) Silver rooftop ladder	40	125	___	___	___
3519 Satellite Car, *61–64*	20	55	___	___	___
3520 Searchlight Car, *52–53*	30	58	___	___	___
3530 GM Generator Car, *56–58*	60	135	___	___	___
3530-50 Searchlight w/ pole and base	24	75	___	___	___
3535 A E C Security Car, *60–61*	35	125	___	___	___
3540 Operating Radar Car, *59–60*	35	135	___	___	___
3545 Lionel TV Car, *61–62*	50	170	___	___	___
3559 Operating Coal Dump Car, *46–48*	15	40	___	___	___
3562-1 ATSF Operating Barrel Car, black, *54*	75	200	___	___	___
3562-25 ATSF Operating Barrel Car, gray, *54*					
(A) Red lettering	125	325	___	___	___
(B) Blue lettering	20	55	___	___	___
3562-50 ATSF Oper. Barrel Car, yellow, *55–56*					
(A) Painted	35	85	___	___	___
(B) Unpainted	20	55	___	___	___
3562-75 ATSF Operating Barrel Car, orange, *57–58*	35	65	___	___	___
3619 Helicopter Boxcar, *62–64*					
(A) Light yellow	30	90	___	___	___
(B) Dark yellow	40	150	___	___	___
3620 Searchlight Car, *54–56*	25	45	___	___	___
3650 Extension Searchlight Car, *56–59*					
(A) Light gray	40	68	___	___	___
(B) Dark gray	65	140	___	___	___
3656 Armour Operating Cattle Car, *49–55*					

		Good	Exc	Color	Cond	$
	(A) Black letters, Armour sticker	70	200	___	___	___
	(B) White letters, Armour sticker	35	65	___	___	___
	(C) White lettering	25	75	___	___	___
3656	Stockyard w/ cattle	20	55	___	___	___
3662	Automatic Milk Car, *55–60, 64–66*	30	70	___	___	___
3665	Minuteman Operating Car, *61–64*					
	(A) Medium blue roof	75	170	___	___	___
	(B) Dark blue roof	50	110	___	___	___
3666	Minuteman Boxcar w/ missile, *64 u*	170	500	___	___	___
3672	Bosco Operating Boxcar, *59–60*					
	(A) Unpainted	80	225	___	___	___
	(B) Painted	95	265	___	___	___
3820	Flatcar w/ submarine, *60–62*	60	190	___	___	___
3830	Flatcar w/ submarine, *60–63*	50	120	___	___	___
3854	Operating Merchandise Car, *46–47*	180	425	___	___	___
3927	Lionel Lines Track Cleaner, *56–60*	50	120	___	___	___
3927-50	Track Cleaning Fluid, *57–69*	3	7	___	___	___
3927-75	Track Cleaning Pads, *57–69*	5	15	___	___	___
4357	PRR SP-Type Caboose, elec., *48–49*	55	165	___	___	___
4452	PRR Gondola, electronic, *46–49*	40	100	___	___	___
4454	Baby Ruth PRR Boxcar, elec., *46–49*	60	175	___	___	___
4457	PRR N5 Caboose, electronic, *46–47*	45	165	___	___	___
4681	Steam 6-8-6, electronic, *50*		NM			
4776-18	(See 2457, 2472)					
5159	Maintenance Kit, *63–65*	2	5	___	___	___
5159-50	Maintenance and Lube Kit, *66–69*	2	5	___	___	___
5160	Viewing Stand	50	145	___	___	___
5459	LL Dump Car, electronic, *46–49*	55	175	___	___	___
6002	NYC Gondola, *50*	4	14	___	___	___
X6004	Baby Ruth PRR Boxcar, *50*	4	8	___	___	___
6007	Lionel Lines SP-Type Caboose, *50*	3	7	___	___	___
6009	R.C. Uncoupling Track, *53–54*	1	4	___	___	___
6012	Lionel Gondola, *51–56*	2	8	___	___	___
6014	Airex Boxcar, *60, u*	25	65	___	___	___
6014	Bosco PRR Boxcar, *58*					
	(A) White body	35	70	___	___	___
	(B) Red body	5	10	___	___	___
	(C) Orange body	5	10	___	___	___

		Good	Exc	Color	Cond	$
6014	Chun King Boxcar, *57 u*	60	130	___	___	___
6014	Frisco Boxcar, *57, 63–69*					
	(A) White body	4	8	___	___	___
	(B) Red body	4	8	___	___	___
	(C) White w/ coin slot	25	50	___	___	___
	(D) Orange body	20	40	___	___	___
X6014	Baby Ruth PRR Boxcar	5	9	___	___	___
6014-150	Wix Boxcar, *59 u*	85	170	___	___	___
6015	Sunoco 1-D Tank Car, *54–55*					
	(A) Painted tank	35	90	___	___	___
	(B) Unpainted tank	4	8	___	___	___
6017	Lionel Lines SP-Type Caboose, *51–62*	2	6	___	___	___
6017	Lionel SP-Type Caboose, *56 only*	15	40	___	___	___
6017-50	USMC SP-Type Caboose, *58*	20	55	___	___	___
6017-85	LL SP-Type Caboose, gray, *58*	20	50	___	___	___
6017-100	B&M SP-Type Caboose, *59, 62, 65–66*					
	(A) Purplish blue	250	520	___	___	___
	(B) Medium or light blue	10	40	___	___	___
6017-185	ATSF SP-Type Caboose, *59–60*	10	35	___	___	___
6017-200	U.S. Navy SP-Type Caboose, *60*	35	85	___	___	___
6017-225	ATSF SP-Type Caboose, *c. 63 u*	15	45	___	___	___
6017-235	ATSF SP-Type Caboose, *62*	25	50	___	___	___
6019	RCS Track set (O27), *48–66*	2	6	___	___	___
6024	Nabisco Shredded Wheat Boxcar, *57*	12	24	___	___	___
6024	RCA Whirlpool Boxcar, *57 u*	30	70	___	___	___
6025	Gulf 1-D Tank Car, *56–58*	5	15	___	___	___
6029	Remote Control Uncoupling Track, *55–63*	1	4	___	___	___
6032	Lionel Gondola, black (O27), *52–54*	2	5	___	___	___
X6034	Baby Ruth PRR Boxcar, *53–54*	5	12	___	___	___
6035	Sunoco 1-D Tank Car, *52–53*	3	6	___	___	___
6037	Lionel Lines SP-Type Caboose, *52–54*	2	5	___	___	___
6042	Lionel Gondola, *59–61, 62–64 u*	2	6	___	___	___
6044	Airex Boxcar, orange lettering, *59–60 u*					
	(A) Medium blue	6	18	___	___	___

POSTWAR (1945–1969)	Good	Exc	Color	Cond	$
(B) Teal blue	40	85	___	___	___
(C) Dark blue/purple	80	270	___	___	___
6044-1X Nestles/McCall's Boxcar					
(no lettering), *62–63 u*	450	900	___	___	___
6045 LL 2-D Tank Car, *59–64 adv. cat.*					
(A) Gray	15	25	___	___	___
(B) Orange	15	42	___	___	___
6045 Cities Service 2-D Tank, *60 u*	12	35	___	___	___
6047 Lionel Lines SP-Type Caboose, *62*	2	4	___	___	___
6050 Lionel Savings Bank Boxcar, *61*	12	35	___	___	___
6050 Swift Refrigerator Car, *62–63*	10	20	___	___	___
6050 Libby's Boxcar, *63 u*	18	45	___	___	___
6057 LL SP-Type Caboose, *59–62*	3	9	___	___	___
6057-50 LL SP-Type Caboose, orange, *62*	12	25	___	___	___
6058 C&O SP-Type Caboose, *61*	15	45	___	___	___
6059 M&St L SP-Type Caboose, *61–69*					
(A) Painted, red	8	16	___	___	___
(B) Unpainted, red	4	8	___	___	___
(C) Unpainted, maroon	6	12	___	___	___
6062 NYC Gondola, w/ cable reels, *59–62*	7	18	___	___	___
6062-50 NYC Gondola, w/ 2 canisters, *69*	5	20	___	___	___
(6067) Caboose (no lett.), SP-Type, *62*	3	6	___	___	___
6076 ATSF Hopper, *63 u*	10	22	___	___	___
6076 LV Hopper, red, black or gray body	7	14	___	___	___
(6076) Hopper, no lettering, gray or yellow body	10	20	___	___	___
6110 Steam 2-4-2, 6001T Tender, *50–51*	15	35	___	___	___
(6111) Flatcar w/ logs, *55–57*	6	14	___	___	___
6112 Lionel Gondola, *56–58*					
(A) Black body	3	7	___	___	___
(B) Blue body	4	9	___	___	___
(C) White body	10	25	___	___	___
6119 DL&W Work Caboose, red, *55–56*	10	25	___	___	___
6119-25 DL&W Work Caboose, orange, *56–59*	10	30	___	___	___
6119-50 DL&W Caboose, brown, *56*	15	55	___	___	___
6119-75 DL&W Caboose, gray, *57*	12	35	___	___	___
6119-100 DL&W Work Caboose,					

	Good	Exc	Color	Cond	$
red/gray, *57–66, 69*	12	40			
(6119-125) Rescue Unit Work Caboose					
(no number), olive drab, *63–64 u.*	60	140			
(6120) Work Caboose (no lettering),					
yellow, *61–62 adv. cat.*	7	25			
(6121) Flatcar (various colors)					
w/ pipes, *56–57*	5	15			
6130 ATSF Work Caboose, *61, 65–69*	10	30			
6139 R.C. Uncoupling Track (O27), *63*	1	4			
6142 Lionel Gondola; green, blue					
or black, *63–66, 69*	2	6			
6149 Remote Control Uncoupling					
Track (O27), *64–69*	1	5			
(6151) Flatcar (various colors)					
w/ patrol truck, *58*	40	120			
6162 NYC Gondola, *59–68*					
(A) Blue body	5	12			
(B) Red body	40	105			
6162-60 Alaska Gondola, *59*	25	65			
6167 LL SP-Type Caboose, red, *63*	3	8			
(6167) Unstamped SP-Type Caboose					
w/o end rails					
(A) Red body	3	10			
(B) Yellow body	10	25			
(C) Brown body	15	40			
6167-85 UP SP-Type Caboose, *69*	10	30			
6175 Flatcar w/ rocket, red or					
black body, *58–61*	25	70			
6176 LV Hopper, yellow, gray					
or black body, *64–66, 69*	3	9			
(6176) Hopper (no lettering)					
(A) Yellow	6	18			
(B) Gray	5	15			
(C) Olive	30	80			
6219 C&O Work Caboose, *60*	25	75			
6220 Santa Fe NW-2 Switcher, *49–50*	125	295			
6250 Seaboard NW-2 Switcher, *54–55*					
(A) Decals	125	300			
(B) Rubber-stamped	110	285			

		Good	Exc	Color	Cond	$
6257	Lionel SP-Type Caboose, *48–56, 63–64*	3	8	___	___	___
6257-100	Lionel Lines SP-Type Caboose	6	18	___	___	___
6257-25	Lionel SP-Type Caboose	3	7	___	___	___
6257-50	Lionel SP-Type Caboose	3	6	___	___	___
6257X	Lionel SP-Type Caboose	12	30	___	___	___
6262	Flatcar w/ wheels, *56–57*					
	(A) Black, *56–57*	30	65	___	___	___
	(B) Red, *56*	160	450	___	___	___
6264	Flatcar w/ lumber for Fork Lift set, *57–60*	20	55	___	___	___
6311	Flatcar w/ three pipes, *55*	15	40	___	___	___
6315	Gulf 1-D Chemical Tank Car, *56–59, 68–69*					
	(A) Early, painted	20	50	___	___	___
	(B) Late, unpainted	30	60	___	___	___
	(C) Late, unpainted w/ built date	40	75	___	___	___
6315	Lionel Lines 1-D Tank Car, *63–66*	13	35	___	___	___
6342	NYC Gondola, *56–58, 64–66*	9	25	___	___	___
6343	Barrel Ramp Car, *61–62*	15	40	___	___	___
6346	Alcoa Quad Hopper, *56*	20	45	___	___	___
6352	PFE Reefer from 352 Ice Depot, *55–57*	45	110	___	___	___
6356	NYC Stock Car, 2 level, *54–55*	12	35	___	___	___
6357	Lionel SP-Type Caboose, *48–61*	6	18	___	___	___
6357-50	ATSF SP-Type Caboose	320	900	___	___	___
6361	Flatcar w/ timber, *60–61, 64–69*	25	70	___	___	___
6362	Truck Car w/ three trucks, *55–56*					
	(A) Shiny orange	20	60	___	___	___
	(B) Dull orange	85	150	___	___	___
6376	LL Circus Stock Car, *56–57*	30	70	___	___	___
(6401)	Flatcar, no load, gray	2	8	___	___	___
(6402)	Flatcar w/ reels or boat, *62, 64–66, 69*					
	(A) w/ reels	6	15	___	___	___
	(B) w/ boat	25	65	___	___	___
6404	Black Flatcar w/ brown auto, *60*	—	270	___	___	___
6405	Maroon Flatcar w/ trailer, *61*	12	40	___	___	___
(6406)	Flatcar w/ yellow auto, *61*	35	85	___	___	___

		Good	Exc	Color	Cond	$
(6407)	Flatcar w/ rocket, *63*	125	450	___	___	___
(6408)	Flatcar w/ pipes, *63*	10	20	___	___	___
(6409)	Flatcar w/ pipes, *63*	10	20	___	___	___
6411	Flatcar w/ logs, *48–50*	11	25	___	___	___
6413	Mercury Project Car, *62–63*	70	140	___	___	___
6414	Evans Auto Loader w/ four cars, *55–66*					
	(A) Early premium cars w/ windows, chrome bumpers and rubber tires; red, yellow, blue and white	40	100	___	___	___
	(B) Four cheap cars, w/o trim, two red, two yellow	300	600	___	___	___
	(C) Four red cars w/ gray bumpers	50	175	___	___	___
	(D) Four yellow cars w/ gray bumpers	150	400	___	___	___
	(E) Four brown cars w/ gray bumpers	300	750	___	___	___
	(F) Four green cars w/ gray bumpers	400	950	___	___	___
6415	Sunoco 3-D Tank Car, *53–55, 64–66, 69*	10	30	___	___	___
6416	Boat Loader Car, *61–63*	80	200	___	___	___
6417	PRR Porthole Caboose, *53–57*					
	(A) w/ "NEW YORK ZONE"	10	35	___	___	___
	(B) w/o "NEW YORK ZONE"	100	230	___	___	___
6417-3	(See 6417-25)					
6417-25	Lionel Lines N5C Caboose, *54*	15	40	___	___	___
6417-50	LV N5C Caboose, *54*					
	(A) Tuscan	350	1000	___	___	___
	(B) Gray	50	140	___	___	___
6417-51	(See 6417-50)					
6417-53	(See 6417-25)					
6418	(See 214)					
6418	Flatcar w/ steel girders, *55–57*	45	100	___	___	___
6419	DL&W Work Caboose, early frame, *48–50, 52–57*	15	40	___	___	___
6419-25	DL&W Work Caboose, *54–55*	13	30	___	___	___
6419-50	DL&W Work Caboose, late frame, *56–57*	15	50	___	___	___
6419-57	(See 6419-100)					

		Good	Exc	Color	Cond	$
6419-75	DL&W Work Caboose, late frame, _56–57_	15	50	___	___	___
6419-100	N&W Work Caboose, _57–58_	45	135	___	___	___
6420	DL&W Work Caboose, w/ light, _48–50_	35	105	___	___	___
6424	Flatcar w/ two autos, _56–59_	16	42	___	___	___
6425	Gulf 3-D Tank Car, _56–58_	15	40	___	___	___
6427	Lionel Lines N5C Caboose, _54–60_	12	30	___	___	___
6427-60	Virginian N5C Caboose, _58_	115	315	___	___	___
6427-500	PRR N5C Girls' Caboose, _57–58*_	125	350	___	___	___
6428	U.S. Mail Boxcar, _60–61, 65–66_	15	30	___	___	___
6429	DL&W Work Caboose, AAR trucks, _63_	125	310	___	___	___
6430	Flat. w/ Cooper-Jarrett vans, _56–58_	20	60	___	___	___
6431	Flatcar w/ vans, _66_	80	250	___	___	___
6434	Poultry Dispatch, _58–59_	40	80	___	___	___
6436-1	LV Quad Hopper, black, _55_	15	35	___	___	___
6436-25	LV Quad Hopper, maroon, _55–57_	15	30	___	___	___
6436-57	(See 6436-500)					
6436-110	LV Quad Hopper, red, _63–68_					
	(A) w/o cover	17	30	___	___	___
	(B) w/ cover and "NEW 3-55"	80	155	___	___	___
6436-500	LV Girls' Hopper, lilac, "643657," _57–58*_	75	225	___	___	___
6436-1969	TCA Quad Hopper, _69_	50	110	___	___	___
6437	Pennsylvania N5C Caboose, _61–68_	15	30	___	___	___
6440	Flatcar with vans, _61–63_	25	95	___	___	___
6440	Green Pullman, _48–49_	20	45	___	___	___
6441	Green Observation, _48–49_	20	45	___	___	___
6442	Brown Pullman, _49_	30	70	___	___	___
6443	Brown Observation, _49_	30	70	___	___	___
6445	Fort Knox Gold Reserve, _61–63_	60	140	___	___	___
(6446)	N&W Quad Hopper "546446", black or gray, _54–55_	18	45	___	___	___
6446-25	N&W Quad Hopper "644625", black or gray, _55–57_	18	75	___	___	___
6446-60	See 6436-110(B)					

		Good	Exc	Color	Cond	$
6447	Pennsylvania N5C Caboose, *63*	125	350	___	___	___
6448	Target Car, *61–64*	10	30	___	___	___
6452	Pennsylvania Gondola, black, *48–49*	6	18	___	___	___
X6454	(A) Baby Ruth PRR Boxcar, *48*	60	200	___	___	___
X6454	(B) NYC Boxcar, orange, *48*	45	155	___	___	___
X6454	(C) NYC Boxcar, brown, *48*	15	50	___	___	___
X6454	(D) NYC Boxcar, tan, *48*	15	28	___	___	___
X6454	(E) ATSF Boxcar, *48*	15	38	___	___	___
X6454	(F) SP Boxcar, *49–52*	15	40	___	___	___
X645	(G) Erie Boxcar, *49–52*	20	45	___	___	___
X645	(H) PRR Boxcar, *49–52*	20	50	___	___	___
6456	Lehigh Valley Short Hopper, *48–55*					
	(A) Black	6	12	___	___	___
	(B) Maroon	5	11	___	___	___
	(C) Gray	15	35	___	___	___
	(D) Enamel red, yellow lettering	50	115	___	___	___
	(E) Enamel red, white lettering	200	500	___	___	___
6457	Lionel SP-Type Caboose, *49–52*	12	25	___	___	___
6460	Bucyrus Erie black cab Crane, 8-wheel, *52–54*	20	60	___	___	___
6460-25	Bucyrus Erie red cab Crane, 8-wheel, w/ box, *54*	40	95	___	___	___
6461	Transformer Car, *49–50*	25	75	___	___	___
6462	NYC Gondola, *49–57*					
	(A) Black,	5	10	___	___	___
	(B) Green,	7	18	___	___	___
	(C) Red,	5	12	___	___	___
6462-500	NYC Girls' Gondola, pink, *57–58**	65	170	___	___	___
6463	Rocket Fuel 2-D Tank, *62–63*	10	40	___	___	___
6464-1	WP Boxcar, *53–54*					
	(A) Blue lettering	35	85	___	___	___
	(B) Red lettering	450	1250	___	___	___
6464-25	GN Boxcar, *53–54*	35	90	___	___	___
6464-50	M&St L Boxcar, *53–56*	38	75	___	___	___
6464-75	RI Boxcar, *53–54, 69*	40	85	___	___	___
6464-100	WP Boxcar, *54–55*					
	(A) Silver body, yellow feather	60	125	___	___	___
	(B) Orange body, blue feather	350	830	___	___	___
6464-125	NYC Boxcar, *54–56*	40	120	___	___	___

POSTWAR (1945–1969)	Good	Exc	Color	Cond	$
6464-150 MP Boxcar, *54–55, 57*	32	125	___	___	___
6464-175 Rock Island Boxcar, *54–55*					
(A) Blue lettering	50	125	___	___	___
(B) Black lettering	450	1050	___	___	___
6464-200 Pennsylvania Boxcar, *54–55, 69*	70	140	___	___	___
6464-225 SP Boxcar, *54–56*	50	100	___	___	___
6464-250 WP Boxcar, *66*	90	200	___	___	___
6464-275 State of Maine Boxcar, *55, 57–59*					
(A) Striped doors	50	100	___	___	___
(B) Solid doors	55	130	___	___	___
6464-300 Rutland Boxcar, *55–56*					
(A) Rubber-stamped	40	95	___	___	___
(B) Split door	310	725	___	___	___
(C) Solid shield	850	2500	___	___	___
(D) Heat-stamped	50	150	___	___	___
6464-325 B&O Sentinel Boxcar, *56*	280	605	___	___	___
6464-350 MKT Katy Boxcar, *56*	115	290	___	___	___
6464-375 Central of Georgia Boxcar, *56–57, 66*					
(A) Unpainted, maroon body	45	120	___	___	___
(B) Painted, red body	800	1700	___	___	___
6464-400 B&O Time-saver Boxcar, *56–57, 69*	40	110	___	___	___
6464-425 New Haven Boxcar, *56–58*	30	75	___	___	___
6464-450 Great Northern Boxcar, *56–57, 66*	60	135	___	___	___
6464-475 B&M Boxcar, *57–60, 65–66, 68*	30	60	___	___	___
6464-500 Timken Boxcar, yellow and white, charcoal lettering (Also see 6464-500 in MPC) *57–58, 69*	60	130	___	___	___
6464-510 NYC Pacemaker Boxcar, *57–58*	300	620	___	___	___
6464-515 MKT Boxcar, *57–58*	260	590	___	___	___
6464-525 M&St L Boxcar, *57–58, 64–66*	30	65	___	___	___
6464-650 D&RGW Boxcar, *57–58, 66*					
(A) Unpainted yellow body	50	130	___	___	___
(B) Painted yellow body & roof	500	1000	___	___	___
6464-700 Santa Fe Boxcar, *61, 66*	50	130	___	___	___
6464-725 New Haven Boxcar, *62–66, 68*					
(A) Orange body	30	60	___	___	___

	Good	Exc	Color	Cond	$
(B) Black body	65	215	___	___	___
6464-825 Alaska Boxcar, *59–60*	105	255	___	___	___
6464-900 NYC Boxcar, *60–66*	50	120	___	___	___
6464-1965 TCA Pittsburgh Boxcar, *65*	—	270	___	___	___
6464-1970 (See MPC)					
6464-1971 (See MPC)					
6465 Sunoco 2-D Tank Car, *48–56*	4	12	___	___	___
6465 Cities Service 2-D Tank, *60–62*	12	30	___	___	___
6465 Gulf 2-D Tank Car, *58*					
(A) Black tank	25	75	___	___	___
(B) Gray tank	10	25	___	___	___
6465 LL 2-D Tank Car, *59, 63–64*					
(A) Black tank	10	30	___	___	___
(B) Orange tank	5	15	___	___	___
6467 Bulkhead Flatcar, *56*	18	50	___	___	___
6468 B&O Auto Boxcar, *53–55*					
(A) Tuscan	140	320	___	___	___
(B) Blue	20	60	___	___	___
6468-25 NH Auto Boxcar, *56–58*	25	60	___	___	___
(6469) Lionel Liquefied Gases Car, *63*	55	150	___	___	___
6470 Explosives Boxcar, *59–60*	12	40	___	___	___
6472 Refrigerator Car, *50–53*	18	38	___	___	___
6473 Horse Transport Car, *62–69*	10	28	___	___	___
6475 Heinz 57 Vat Car, post-factory alteration	50	100	___	___	___
6475 Libby's Crushed Pineapple Vat Car, *63, u*	18	65	___	___	___
6475 Pickles Vat Car, *60–62*	15	45	___	___	___
6476 LV Hopper, red, black, and gray body, *57–69*	4	10	___	___	___
6476-1 LV Hopper, gray, TTOS, *69*	25	75	___	___	___
6476-135 LV Hopper, yellow, *64–66, 68*	6	12	___	___	___
6476-160 LV Hopper, black, *69*	6	15	___	___	___
6476-185 LV Hopper, yellow, *69*	6	14	___	___	___
6477 Bulkhead Car w/ pipes, *57–58*	15	65	___	___	___
6480 Explosives Boxcar, red, *61, adv. cat.*	18	50	___	___	___
6482 Refrigerator Car, *57*	30	60	___	___	___
(6500) Flatcar w/ Bonanza plane, *62, 65*	280	540	___	___	___
(6501) Flatcar w/ jet boat, *62–63*	55	120	___	___	___

		Good	Exc	Color	Cond	$
(6502)	Flatcar w/ bridge girder, *62*	20	50	___	___	___
6511	Flatcar w/ pipes, *53–56*	11	35	___	___	___
(6512)	Cherry Picker Car, *62–63*	35	105	___	___	___
6517	LL Bay Window Caboose, *55–59*					
	(A) Underscored	30	80	___	___	___
	(B) Not underscored	20	60	___	___	___
6517-75	Erie B/W Caboose, *66*	180	465	___	___	___
6517-1966	TCA B/W Caboose, *66*	90	200	___	___	___
6518	Transformer Car, *56–58*	45	115	___	___	___
6519	Allis-Chalmers Flatcar, *58–61*					
	(A) Dark/medium orange base	35	75	___	___	___
	(B) Dull light orange base	40	110	___	___	___
6520	Searchlight Car, *49–51*					
	(A) Tan diesel generator	200	500	___	___	___
	(B) Green diesel generator	150	300	___	___	___
	(C) Maroon or orange diesel gen.	25	60	___	___	___
6530	Fire Fighting Car, red, *60–61*	40	75	___	___	___
6536	M&St L Quad Hopper, *58–59, 63*	20	50	___	___	___
6544	Missile Firing Car, *60–64*					
	(A) White-lettered console	45	110	___	___	___
	(B) Black-lettered console	175	415	___	___	___
6555	Sunoco 1-D Tank Car, *49–50*	15	40	___	___	___
6556	MKT Stock Car, *58*	70	240	___	___	___
6557	Lionel SP-Type Caboose, smoke, *58–59*	85	250	___	___	___
6560	Bucyrus Erie Crane w/ stack, 8-wheel, *55–58, 68–69*					
	(A) Reddish-orange or black cab, early construction	65	185	___	___	___
	(B) Gray cab	40	85	___	___	___
	(C) Red cab	20	45	___	___	___
	(D) Dark blue (Hagerstown)	40	95	___	___	___
6560-25	Bucyrus Erie Crane, 8-whl., *56*	45	110	___	___	___
6561	Reel Car, *53–56*					
	(A) Orange reels	20	65	___	___	___
	(B) Gray reels	25	75	___	___	___
6562	NYC Gondola w/ canisters, black, red, or gray, *56–58*	12	35	___	___	___
6572	REA Refrig. Car, *58–59, 63*	45	100	___	___	___

POSTWAR (1945–1969)	Good	Exc	Color	Cond	$
6630 IRBM Rocket Launcher, *61, adv. cat.*	30	105			
6636 Alaska Quad Hopper, *59–60*	15	45			
6640 USMC Rocket Launcher, *60*	85	225			
6646 Lionel Lines Stock Car, *57*	12	35			
6650 IRBM Rocket Launcher, *59–63*	25	60			
6650-80 Missile, *60*	3	10			
6651 USMC Cannon Car, *64 u*	60	160			
6656 Lionel Lines Stock Car, *49–55*	8	20			
6657 Rio Grande SP-Type Caboose, *57–58*	50	175			
6660 Flatcar w/ crane, *58*	30	80			
6670 Flatcar w/ crane, *59–60*	20	70			
6672 Santa Fe Refrigerator Car, *54–56*					
(A) Blue lettering, two lines	25	70			
(B) Black lettering, two lines	22	75			
(C) Blue lettering, three lines	70	225			
6736 Detroit & Mack. Quad Hopper, *60–62*	15	45			
6800 Flatcar w/ airplane, *57–60*	75	175			
6801 Flatcar w/ boat, *57–60*	45	110			
6802 Flatcar w/ bridge, *58–59*	12	30			
6803 Flatcar w/ tank and truck, *58–59*	70	205			
6804 Flatcar w/ USMC trucks, *58–59*	70	205			
6805 Atomic Disposal Flatcar, *58–59*	35	125			
6806 Flatcar w/ USMC trucks, *58–59*	70	175			
6807 Lionel Flatcar w/ boat, *58–59*	60	150			
6808 Flatcar w/ USMC trucks, *58–59*	100	250			
6809 Flatcar w/ USMC trucks, *58–59*	85	210			
6810 Flatcar w/ trailer, *58*	18	45			
6812 Track Maintenance Car, *59*	18	90			
6814 Lionel Rescue Caboose, *59–61*	30	115			
6816 Flatcar w/ bulldozer, *59–60*					
(A) Red car	200	420			
(B) Black car	260	650			
6816-100 Allis-Chalmers Tractor, *59–60*	50	170			
6817 Flatcar w/ scraper, *59–60*					
(A) Black car	340	700			
(B) Red car	200	425			
6817-100 Allis-Chalmers Scraper, *59–60*	75	200			

POSTWAR (1945–1969)		Good	Exc	Color	Cond	$
6818	Transformer Car, *58*	25	60			
6819	Flatcar w/ helicopter, *59–60*	25	70			
6820	Flatcar w/ missile transport helicopter, *60–61*					
	(A) Light blue-painted flatcar	80	225			
	(B) Darker blue flatcar	50	150			
6821	Flatcar w/ crates, *59–60*	20	35			
6822	Searchlight Car, *61–69*	20	45			
6823	Flatcar w/ IRBM missiles, *59–60*	25	60			
6824	USMC Work Caboose, *60*	60	175			
6825	Flatcar w/ bridge, *59–62*	15	42			
6826	Flatcar w/ trees, *59–60*	50	145			
6827	Flatcar w/ steam shovel, *60–63*	65	140			
6827-100	Harnischfeger Shovel, *60*	50	100			
6828	Flatcar w/ crane, *60–63, 66*	80	180			
6828-100	Harnischfeger Crane, *60*	40	95			
6830	Flatcar w/ submarine, *60–61*	50	120			
6844	Flatcar w/ missiles, *59–60*					
	(A) Black plastic flatcar	20	60			
	(B) Red plastic flatcar	300	650			
63132	(See 3464)					
64173	(See 6427 LL)					
65400	(See 2454 or 6454)					
81000	(See 6417 PRR)					
96743	(See 6454)					
159000	(See 3464)					
336155	(See 3361)					
477618	(See 2457 or 2472)					
536417	(See 6417 PRR)					
546446	(See 6446)					
576419	(See 6419-100)					
576427	(See 6427-500)					
641751	(See 6417-50)					
A	Transformer, 90 watts, *47–48*	25	75			
CTC	Lockon (O and O27), *47–69*	—	1			
ECU-1	Electronic Control Unit, *46*	18	60			
KW	Transformer, 190 watts, *50–65*	100	180			
LTC	Lockon (O and O27), *50–69*	—	5			
LW	Transformer, 125 watts, *55–56*	85	135			

POSTWAR (1945–1969)

		Good	Exc	Color	Cond	$
OC	Curved Track (O), *45–61*	—	1.50	___	___	___
OC½	Half Sec. Curve Track (O), *45–66*	—	1.50	___	___	___
OCS	Curved Insulated Track (O), *46–50*		NRS	___	___	___
OS	Straight Track (O), *45–61*	—	1.50	___	___	___
OSS	Straight Insulated Track, *46–50*		NRS	___	___	___
OTC	Lockon Track (O and O27)	—	5	___	___	___
Q	Transformer, 75 watts, *46*	20	65	___	___	___
R	Transformer, 110 watts, *46–47*	30	80	___	___	___
RW	Transformer, 110 watts, *48–54*	40	85	___	___	___
RCS	Remote Control Track (O), *45–48*	5	9	___	___	___
SP	Smoke Pellets, bottle, *48–69*	5	15	___	___	___
SW	Transformer, 130 watts, *61–66*	60	125	___	___	___
TW	Transformer, 175 watts, *53–60*	85	165	___	___	___
TOC	Curved Track (O), *62–66, 68–69*	—	2	___	___	___
TOC½	Half Sec. Str. Trk. (O), *62–66*	—	2	___	___	___
TOS	Straight Track (O), *62–69*	—	2	___	___	___
UCS	Remote Control Track (O), *45–69*	—	15	___	___	___
UTC	Lockon (O, O27, Standard), *45*	—	1.50	___	___	___
V	Transformer, 150 watts, *46–47*	75	145	___	___	___
VW	Transformer, 150 watts, *48–49*	70	155	___	___	___
Z	Transformer, 250 watts, *45–47*	100	225	___	___	___
ZW	Transformer, 250 watts, *48–49*	120	300	___	___	___
ZW	Transformer, 275 watts, *50–66*	150	320	___	___	___

No Number SP-Type Caboose, (see 6067, 6167)

No Number Work Caboose,
    (see 6119-125, 6120)

No Number Flatcar (see 6401, 6402, 6406)

No Number Gondola (see 6142)

No Number Hopper (see 6176)

No Number Turbo Missile Car (see 3309, 3349)

No Number Rolling Stock
    (see 3413, 3510, 6111, 6121, 6151, 6407,
    6408, 6409, 6469, 6500, 6501, 6502, 6512)

		Exc	New	Cond/$
3	(See 8104, 8630, 8701)			
[4]	Midwest TCA C&NW F-3 A Unit, shell only, *77 u*		NRS	____
[00005]	Midwest TCA Covered Quad Hopper, *78 u*		NRS	____
[10]	METCA Jersey Central F-3 A Unit, shell only, *71 u*		NRS	____
[303]	LOTS Stauffer Chemical 1-D Tank Car, *85 u*	60	75	____
484	(See 8587)			
491	(See 7203)			
(0511)	TCA St. Louis Baggage Car "1981", *81 u*	60	75	____
0512	Toy Fair Reefer, *81 u*	100	125	____
550	(See 8378)			
(550C)	Curved Track 31" (O), *70*	.75	1.25	____
(550S)	Straight Track (O), *70*	.75	1.25	____
577	(See 9562)			
578	(See 9563)			
579	(See 9564)			
580	(See 9565)			
581	(See 9566)			
582	(See 9567)			
611	(See 8100)			
634	Santa Fe NW-2, *70 u*	55	100	____
659	(See 8101)			
665E	Johnny Cash "Blue Train" 4-6-4, *71 u*		NRS	____
672	(See 8610)			
779	(See 8215)			
0780	LRRC Boxcar, *82 u*	75	95	____
0781	LRRC Flatcar w/ trailers, *83 u*	100	125	____
0782	LRRC 1-D Tank Car, *85 u*	60	75	____
783	(See 8406)			
0784	LRRC Covered Quad Hopper, *84 u*	75	95	____
784	(See 8606)			
[1018-1979]	TCA Mortgage Burning Hi-cube Boxcar, *79 u*	40	50	____

| --- | --- | --- | --- | --- |
(1050)	New Englander set, *80–81*	160	195	_____
(1051)	T&P Diesel set, *80*		NM	
(1052)	Chesapeake Flyer set, *80*	140	160	_____
(1053)	The James Gang set, *80–82*	225	245	_____
(1070)	The Royal Limited set, *80*	400	450	_____
(1071)	Mid Atlantic Limited set, *80*	375	415	_____
(1072)	Cross Country Express set, *80–81*	325	425	_____
(1076)	Lionel Clock, *76–77 u*	200	250	_____
(1081)	Wabash Cannonball set, *70–72*	110	125	_____
(1082)	Yard Boss set, *70*	125	160	_____
(1083)	Pacemaker set, *70*	110	125	_____
(1084)	Grand Trunk & Western set, *70*	125	150	_____
(1085)	Santa Fe Express Diesel Freight set, *70*	175	200	_____
(1085)	Santa Fe Twin Diesel set, *71*	175	200	_____
(1086)	The Mountaineer set, *70*		NM	
(1087)	Midnight Express set, *70*		NM	
(1091)	Sears Special set, *70 u*		NRS	_____
(1092)	79N97081C Sears set, *70 u*		NRS	_____
(1092)	79C97105C Sears 6-unit set, *71 u*		NRS	_____
(1100)	Happy Huff n' Puff, *74–75 u*	50	60	_____
(1150)	L.A.S.E.R. Train set, *81–82*	175	200	_____
(1151)	Union Pacific Thunder Freight set, *81–82*	160	185	_____
(1153)	JCPenney Thunderball Freight set, *81 u*	170	190	_____
(1154)	Reading Yard King set, *81–82*	225	250	_____
(1155)	Cannonball Freight set, *82*	75	90	_____
(1157)	Lionel Leisure Wabash Cannonball set, *81 u*		NRS	_____
(1158)	Maple Leaf Limited set, *81*	500	550	_____
(1159)	Toys "R" Us Midnight Flyer set, *81 u*	135	150	_____
(1160)	Great Lakes Limited set, *81*	400	475	_____
(T-1171)	Canadian National Steam Loco set, *71 u*	195	225	_____
(T-1172)	Yardmaster set, *71 u*		NRS	_____
(T-1173)	Grand Trunk & Western set, *71–73 u*	185	210	_____
(T-1174)	Canadian National set, *71–73 u*	300	350	_____
(1182)	The Yardmaster set, *71–72*	85	110	_____
(1183)	The Silver Star set, *71–72*	75	100	_____
(1184)	The Allegheny set, *71*	125	160	_____
(1186)	Cross Country Express set, *71–72*	200	250	_____
(1187)	Illinois Central set, *71 (SSS)*	450	550	_____
(1190)	Sears Special #1 set, *71 u*		NRS	_____

		Exc	New	Cond/$
(1195)	JCPenney Special set, *71 u*		NRS	___
(1198)	Unnamed set, *71 u*		NRS	___
(1199)	Ford-Autolite Allegheny set, *71 u*	185	210	___
(1200)	Gravel Gus, *75 u*		NRS	___
[1203]	NETCA B&M NW-2, shell only, *72 u*	—	70	___
[1223]	LOTS Seattle & North Coast Hi-cube Boxcar, *86 u*	125	150	___
(1250)	New York Central set, *72 (SSS)*	400	475	___
(1252)	Heavy Iron set, *82–83*	100	145	___
(1253)	Quicksilver Express set, *82–83*	275	325	___
(1254)	Black Cave Flyer set, *82*	80	110	___
(1260)	Continental Limited set, *82*	450	550	___
(1261)	49N95211 Sears Black Cave Flyer set, *82 u*		NRS	___
(1262)	Toys "R" Us Heavy Iron set, *82 u*		NRS	___
(1263)	XU671-0701A JCPenney Overland Freight set, *82 u*		NRS	___
(1264)	Nibco Express set, *82 u*	175	225	___
(1265)	Tappan Special set, *82 u*	135	165	___
(T-1272)	Yardmaster set, *72–73 u*		NRS	___
(T-1273)	Silver Star set, *72–73 u*		NRS	___
(1280)	Kickapoo Valley & Northern set, *72*	60	75	___
(1284)	Allegheny set, *72*	150	175	___
(1285)	Santa Fe Twin Diesel set, *72*	100	150	___
(1287)	Pioneer Dockside Switcher set, *72*	—	100	___
[1287]	Midwest TCA C&NW Reefer, *84 u*		NRS	___
(1290)	Sears set, *72 u*		NRS	___
(1291)	Sears set, *72 u*		NRS	___
(1300)	Gravel Gus Junior, *75 u*		NRS	___
(1350)	Canadian Pacific set, *73 (SSS)*	800	1000	___
(1351)	Baltimore & Ohio set, *83–84*	200	245	___
(1352)	Rocky Mountain Freight set, *83–84*	75	100	___
(1353)	Southern Streak set, *83–85*	75	100	___
(1354)	Northern Freight Flyer set, *83–85*	275	325	___
(1355)	Commando Assault Train set, *83–84*	150	200	___
(1359)	Train Display Case for set 1355, *83 u*	75	100	___
(1361)	Gold Coast Limited set, *83*	700	900	___
(1362)	Lionel Leisure BN Express set, *83 u*		NRS	___
(1380)	U.S. Steel Industrial Switcher set, *73–75*	60	75	___
(1381)	Cannonball set, *73–75*	60	75	___

		Exc	New	Cond/$
(1382)	Yardmaster set, *73–74*	100	125	_____
(1383)	Santa Fe Freight set, *73–75*	100	130	_____
(1384)	Southern Express set, *73–76*	75	125	_____
(1385)	Blue Streak Freight set, *73–74*	100	125	_____
(1386)	Rock Island Express set, *73–74*	125	150	_____
(1387)	Milwaukee Road Special set, *73*	200	275	_____
(1388)	Golden State Arrow set, *73–75*	200	225	_____
(1390)	Sears 7-unit set, *73 u*		NRS	_____
(1392)	79C95224C Sears 8-unit set, *73 u*		NRS	_____
(1393)	79C95223C Sears 6-unit set, *73 u*		NRS	_____
(1395)	JCPenney set, *73 u*		NRS	_____
(1400)	Happy Huff n' Puff Junior, *75 u*		NRS	_____
(1402)	Chessie System set, *84–85*	125	150	_____
(1403)	Redwood Valley Express set, *84–85*	190	225	_____
(1450)	D&RGW set, *74 (SSS)*	400	500	_____
(1451)	Erie-Lackawanna Limited set, *84*	600	700	_____
(1460)	Grand National set, *74*	275	300	_____
(1461)	Black Diamond set, *74 u, 75*	100	125	_____
(1463)	Coca-Cola Special set, *74 u, 75*	225	290	_____
(1487)	Broadway Limited set, *74–75*	225	285	_____
(1489)	Santa Fe Double Diesel set, *74–76*	150	175	_____
(1492)	79N96185C Sears 7-unit set, *74 u*		NRS	_____
(1493)	79N96185C Sears 7-unit set, *74 u*		NRS	_____
(1499)	JCPenney Great Express set, *74 u*		NRS	_____
(1501)	Midland Freight set, *85–86*	75	100	_____
(1502)	Yard Chief set, *85–86*	200	225	_____
(1506)	Sears Chessie System set, *85 u*		NRS	_____
(1512)	JCPenney Midland Freight set, *85 u*		NRS	_____
(1549)	Toys "R" Us Heavy Iron set, *85–89 u*	200	250	_____
(1552)	Burlington Northern Limited set, *85*	500	675	_____
(1560)	North American Express set, *75*	225	275	_____
(1562)	Fast Freight Flyer set, *85 u*	125	150	_____
(1577)	Liberty Special set, *75 u*	200	240	_____
(1579)	Milwaukee Road set, *75 (SSS)*	400	475	_____
(1581)	Thunderball Freight set, *75–76*	75	100	_____
(1582)	Yard Chief set, *75–76*	120	165	_____
(1584)	Norfolk & Western "Spirit of America" set, *75*	250	275	_____
(1585)	75th Anniversary Special set, *75–77*	215	250	_____
(1586)	Chesapeake Flyer set, *75–77*	150	175	_____

MPC MODERN ERA (1970–1986)

		Exc	New	Cond/$
(1587)	Capitol Limited set, *75*	250	275	_____
(1594)	Sears set, *75 u*		NRS	_____
(1595)	79C9716C Sears 6-unit set, *75 u*		NRS	_____
(1602)	Nickel Plate Special set, *86–91*	150	175	_____
(1606)	Sears Nickel Plate Special set, *86 u*		NRS	_____
(1608)	American Express General set, *86 u*	250	300	_____
(1615)	Cannonball Express set, *86–90*	85	95	_____
(1632)	Santa Fe Work Train set, *86 (SSS)*	275	320	_____
(1652)	B&O Freight set, *86*	225	290	_____
(1658)	Town House set, *86 u*	80	100	_____
(1660)	Yard Boss set, *76*	100	120	_____
(1661)	Rock Island Line set, *76–77*	95	125	_____
(1662)	Black River Freight set, *76–78*	100	125	_____
(1663)	Amtrak Lake Shore Limited set, *76–77*	200	275	_____
(1664)	Illinois Central Freight set, *76–77*	300	350	_____
(1665)	NYC Empire State Express set, *76*	450	600	_____
(1672)	Northern Pacific set, *76 (SSS)*	350	390	_____
(1685)	True Value Freight Flyer set, *86–87 u*	80	100	_____
(1686)	Kay Bee Toys Freight Flyer set, *86 u*		NRS	_____
(1693)	Toys "R" Us Rock Island Line set, *76 u*		NRS	_____
(1694)	Toys "R" Us Black River Freight set, *76 u*		NRS	_____
(1696)	Sears set, *76 u*		NRS	_____
(1698)	True Value Rock Island Line set, *76 u*		NRS	_____
(1760)	Trains n' Truckin' Steel Hauler set, *77–78*	90	100	_____
(1761)	Trains n' Truckin' Cargo King set, *77–78*	100	175	_____
(1762)	Wabash Cannonball set, *77*	125	175	_____
(1764)	Heartland Express set, *77*	225	275	_____
(1765)	Rocky Mountain Special set, *77*	250	300	_____
(1766)	B&O Budd Car set, *77 (SSS)*	400	450	_____
1776	Seaboard U36B, *74–76*	100	125	_____
1776	(See 8559, 8665, 9170)			
(1790)	Lionel Leisure Steel Hauler set, *77 u*		NRS	_____
(1791)	Toys "R" Us Steel Hauler set, *77 u*		NRS	_____
(1792)	True Value Rock Island Line set, *77 u*		NRS	_____
(1793)	Toys "R" Us Black River Freight set, *77 u*		NRS	_____
(1796)	JCPenney Cargo Master set, *77 u*		NRS	_____
(1860)	Workin' on the Railroad Timberline set, *78*	60	75	_____
(1862)	Workin' on the Railroad Logging Empire set, *78*	75	100	_____

MPC MODERN ERA (1970–1986)

		Exc	New	Cond/$
(1864)	Santa Fe Double Diesel set, *78–79*	150	175	_____
(1865)	Chesapeake Flyer set, *78–79*	150	175	_____
(1866)	Great Plains Express set, *78–79*	275	300	_____
(1867)	Milwaukee Road Limited set, *78*	300	375	_____
(1868)	M&St L set, *78 (SSS)*	225	275	_____
(1892)	JCPenney Logging Empire set, *78 u*		NRS	_____
(1893)	Toys "R" Us Logging Empire set, *78 u*		NRS	_____
(1960)	Midnight Flyer set, *79–81*	60	80	_____
(1962)	Wabash Cannonball set, *79*	90	110	_____
(1963)	Black River Freight set, *79–81*	75	90	_____
(1964)	Radio Control Express set, *79 u*		NM	
(1965)	Smokey Mountain Line set, *79*		NRS	_____
(1970)	Southern Pacific Limited set, *79 u*	550	650	_____
1970	(See 8615)			
(1971)	Quaker City Limited set, *79*	450	500	_____
[1971-1976]	Rocky Mountain TCA Reefer, *76 u*		NRS	_____
1973	TCA Bicentennial Observation Car (O27), *76 u*	40	60	_____
1973	(See 9123)			
1974	TCA Bicentennial Passenger Car (O27), *76 u*	40	60	_____
1975	TCA Bicentennial Passenger Car (O27), *76 u*	40	60	_____
1976	TCA Seaboard U36B, *76 u*	150	200	_____
[1976]	Southern TCA Florida East Coast F-3 ABA, shells only, *76 u*		NRS	_____
[1979]	IETCA Boxcar, *79 u*	—	15	_____
[1980]	IETCA SP-Type Caboose, *80 u*	—	15	_____
[1980]	Atlantic TCA Flatcar w/ trailers, *80 u*	25	30	_____
1980	(See 8068, 9544)			
[1981]	IETCA Quad Hopper, *81 u*	—	15	_____
[1981]	LCOL Boxcar, *81 u*	—	25	_____
1981	(See 0511)			
[1982]	IETCA 3-D Tank Car, *82 u*	—	15	_____
1982	(See 7205)			
[1983]	IETCA Reefer, *83 u*	—	15	_____
[1983]	TTOS Phoenix 3-D Tank Car, *83 u*		NRS	_____
[1983]	Great Lakes TCA Churchill Downs Boxcar, *83 u*		NRS	_____
[1983]	Great Lakes TCA Churchill Downs Reefer, *83 u*		NRS	_____
1983	(See 7206)			
[1984]	TTOS Sacramento Northern Boxcar, *84 u*	80	100	_____
[1984]	Ft. Pitt TCA Iron City Boxcar, *84 u*	—	170	_____

		Exc	New	Cond/$
[1984]	Ft. Pitt TCA Iron City Reefer, *84 u*	—	170	____
[1984]	Ft. Pitt TCA Heinz Pickles Boxcar, *84 u*		NRS	____
1984	(See 7212)			
[1984-30X]	Ft. Pitt TCA Heinz Ketchup Boxcar, *84 u*	—	200	____
[1985]	TTOS Snowbird Covered Quad Hopper, *85 u*	40	50	____
[1986]	IETCA Bunk Car, *86 u*	—	15	____
[1986]	Southern TCA Bunk Car, *86 u*	—	30	____
[1986]	LCOL Work Caboose, shell only, *86 u*	—	18	____
(1990)	Mystery Glow Midnight Flyer set, *79 u*		NRS	____
(1991)	JCPenney Wabash Cannonball Deluxe Express set, *79 u*		NRS	____
(1993)	Toys "R" Us Midnight Flyer set, *79 u*		NRS	____
2110	Graduated Trestle set (22), *70–88*	10	15	____
2111	Elevated Trestle set (10), *70–88*	10	15	____
(2113)	Tunnel Portals (2), *84–87*	10	15	____
(2115)	Dwarf Signal, *84–87*	13	15	____
(2117)	Block Target Signal, *84–87*	20	25	____
(2122)	Extension Bridge w/ rock piers, *76–87*	30	40	____
2125	Whistling Freight Shed, *71*	40	50	____
2126	Whistling Freight Shed, *76–87*	25	30	____
2127	Diesel Horn Shed, *76–87*	25	30	____
(2128)	Operating Switchman, *83–86*	30	35	____
2129	Illuminated Freight Station, *83–86*	30	35	____
(2133)	Lighted Freight Station, *72–78, 80–84*	30	40	____
2140	Automatic Banjo Signal, *70–84*	20	25	____
(2145)	Automatic Gateman, *72–84*	35	45	____
(2151)	Operating Semaphore, *78–82*	20	25	____
(2152)	Automatic Crossing Gate, *70–84*	25	30	____
2154	Automatic Highway Flasher, *70–87*	20	25	____
2156	Illuminated Station Platform, *70–71*	30	40	____
2162	Automatic Crossing Gate and Signal, *70–87, 94, 96*		CP	____
(2163)	Block Target Signal, *70–78*	20	25	____
(2170)	Street Lamps (3), *70–87*	15	20	____
(2171)	Gooseneck Street Lamps (2), *80–81, 83–84*	20	25	____
(2175)	Sandy Andy Gravel Loader kit, *76–79*	40	60	____
(2180)	Road Signs (16), *77–95*		CP	____
(2181)	Telephone Poles (10), *77–95*		CP	____
(2195)	Floodlight Tower, *70–71*	45	60	____

		Exc	New	Cond/$
(2199)	Microwave Tower, *72–75*	30	40	_____
(2214)	Girder Bridge, *70–71, 72 u, 73–87*	5	10	_____
2256	Station Platform, *73–81*	15	20	_____
[2256]	TCA Station Platform, *75 u*	25	35	_____
(2260)	Illuminated Bumper, *70–71, 72 u, 73*	25	40	_____
(2280)	Non-Illuminated Bumpers (3), *73–84*	3	5	_____
2282	Die-cast Bumpers (2), *83 u*	20	25	_____
2283	Die-cast Bumpers (2), *84–95*		CP	_____
(2290)	Illuminated Bumpers (2), *75 u, 76–86*	10	12	_____
(2292)	Station Platform, *85–87*	6	10	_____
(2300)	Operating Oil Drum Loader, *83–87*	100	140	_____
(2301)	Operating Sawmill, *80–84*	90	115	_____
2302	Union Pacific Manual Gantry Crane, *80–82*	20	25	_____
2303	Santa Fe Manual Gantry Crane, *80–81, 83 u*	20	25	_____
2305	Getty Operating Oil Derrick, *81–84*	145	165	_____
(2306)	Operating Ice Station w/ 6700 PFE Ice Car, *82–83*	175	220	_____
(2307)	Lighted Billboard, *82–86*	20	25	_____
2308	Animated Newsstand, *82–83*	145	165	_____
(2309)	Mechanical Crossing Gate, *82–92*	4	8	_____
(2310)	Mechanical Crossing Gate, *73–77*	3	5	_____
(2311)	Mechanical Semaphore, *82–92*	4	8	_____
(2312)	Mechanical Semaphore, *73–77*	3	5	_____
(2313)	Floodlight Tower, *75–86*	20	25	_____
(2314)	Searchlight Tower, *75–84*	20	25	_____
(2315)	Operating Coaling Station, *83–84*	125	175	_____
2316	N&W Operating Gantry Crane, *83–84*	145	170	_____
2317	Operating Drawbridge, *75 u, 76–81*	100	125	_____
(2318)	Operating Control Tower, *83–86*	75	95	_____
2319	Illuminated Watchtower, *75–78, 80*	30	35	_____
2320	Flagpole kit, *83–87*	10	15	_____
2321	Operating Sawmill, *84, 86–87*	100	125	_____
2323	Operating Freight Station, *84–87*	80	100	_____
2324	Operating Switch Tower, *84–87*	70	85	_____
(2390)	Lionel Mirror, *82 u*	65	100	_____
2494	Rotary Beacon, *72–74*	40	50	_____
(2709)	Rico Station kit, *81–95*		CP	_____
2710	Billboards (5), *70–84*	3	5	_____
(2714)	Tunnel, *75 u, 76–77*	40	50	_____

		Exc	New	Cond/$
(2717)	Short Extension Bridge, *77–87*	3	5	_____
(2718)	Barrel Platform kit, *77–84*	3	5	_____
(2719)	Watchman's Shanty kit, *77–87*	3	5	_____
(2720)	Lumber Shed kit, *77–84, 87*	3	5	_____
(2721)	Operating Log Mill kit, *78*	3	5	_____
(2722)	Barrel Loader kit, *78*	3	5	_____
(2729)	Water Tower kit, *85*		NM	
(2783)	Freight Station kit, *84*	7	12	_____
(2784)	Freight Platform kit, *81–90*	6	9	_____
(2785)	Engine House kit, *73–77*	40	50	_____
(2786)	Freight Platform kit, *73–77*	4	7	_____
(2787)	Freight Station kit, *73–77, 83*	7	10	_____
(2788)	Coal Station kit, *75 u, 76–77*	20	40	_____
(2789)	Water Tower kit, *75–77, 80*	20	25	_____
(2791)	Cross Country set, *70–71*	25	35	_____
(2792)	Whistle Stop set, *70–71*	25	35	_____
(2792)	Layout Starter Pak, *80–84*	10	25	_____
(2793)	Alamo Junction set, *70–71*	25	35	_____
(2796)	Grain Elevator kit, *76 u, 77*	60	70	_____
(2797)	Rico Station kit, *76–77*	30	45	_____
(2900)	Lockon, *70–95*		CP	_____
(2901)	Track Clips (12) (O27), *71–95*		CP	_____
(2905)	Lockon and Wire, *74–95*		CP	_____
2909	Smoke Fluid, *70–95*		CP	_____
2910	OTC Contactor, *84–86, 88*	4	8	_____
(2911)	Smoke Pellets, *70–73*	10	15	_____
2925	Lubricant, *70–71, 72 u, 73–75*	—	2	_____
(2927)	Maintenance kit, *70, 78–95*		CP	_____
2928	Oil, *71*	—	2	_____
2951	Track Layout Book, *70–86*	1	2	_____
2952	Train and Accessory Manual, *70–74*	1	2	_____
2953	Train and Accessory Manual, *75–86*	1	2	_____
(2960)	Lionel 75th Anniversary Book, *75 u, 76*	10	20	_____
(2980)	Magnetic Conversion Coupler, *70–71*	1	2	_____
(2985)	The Lionel Train Book, *86–95*		CP	_____
3100	Great Northern 4-8-4 (FARR #3), *81*	475	575	_____
[3764]	LOTS Kahn Boxcar, *81 u*	60	75	_____
4044	Transformer, 45-watt, *70–71*	3	5	_____
4045	Safety Transformer, *70–71*	3	4	_____

		Exc	New	Cond/$
4050	Safety Transformer, *72–79*	3	4	_____
4060	AC/DC Power Master Transformer, *80–93*	15	25	_____
4065	DC Hobby Transformer, *81–83*	3	4	_____
4090	Power Master Transformer, *70–84*	40	55	_____
4125	Transformer, 25-watt, *72*	3	4	_____
4150	Trainmaster Transformer, *72–73, 75–77*	6	12	_____
4250	Trainmaster Transformer, *74*	6	12	_____
4449	(See 8307)			
4501	(See 8309)			
4651	Trainmaster Transformer, *78–79*	2	3	_____
4690	MW Transformer, *86–89*	75	95	_____
4851	DC Transformer, *85–91, 94–95*		CP	_____
4870	DC Hobby Transformer and Throttle Controller, *77–78*	3	4	_____
4935	(See 8150)			
(5012)	Curved Track 27", card of 4 (O27), *70–95*		CP	_____
(5013)	Curved Track 27" (O27), *70–78*	.50	.55	_____
(5014)	Half-Curved Track 27" (O27), *70–95*		CP	_____
(5017)	Straight Track, card of 4 (O27), *70–95*		CP	_____
(5018)	Straight Track (O27), *70–78*	.50	.75	_____
(5019)	Half-Straight Track (O27), *70–95*		CP	_____
5020	90° Crossover (O27), *70–95*		CP	_____
(5021)	Left Manual Switch 27" (O27), *70–95*		CP	_____
(5022)	Right Manual Switch 27" (O27), *70–95*		CP	_____
(5023)	45° Crossover (O27), *70–95*		CP	_____
(5025)	Manumatic Uncoupler, *71–72*	1	2	_____
(5027)	Pair Manual Switches 27" (O27), *74–84*	15	25	_____
(5030)	Track Expander set (O27), *71–84*	20	30	_____
(5031)	Ford-Autolite Layout Expander set, *71 u*		NRS	_____
(5033)	Curved Track 27" (O27), *79–95*		CP	_____
(5038)	Straight Track (O27), *79–95*		CP	_____
(5041)	Insulator Pins (12) (O27), *70–95*		CP	_____
(5042)	Steel Pins (12) (O27), *70–95*		CP	_____
(5090)	Three Pair Manual Switches 27" (O27), *78–84*	60	80	_____
(5113)	Curved Track 54" (O27), *79–95*		CP	_____
5121	Left Remote Switch 27" (O27), *70–95*		CP	_____
5122	Right Remote Switch 27" (O27), *70–95*		CP	_____
(5125)	Pair Remote Switches 27" (O27), *71–83*	25	35	_____
5132	Right Remote Switch 31" (O), *80–94*	30	40	_____

		Exc	New	Cond/$
5133	Left Remote Switch 31" (O), *80–94*	30	40	____
(5149)	Remote Uncoupling Section (O27), *70–95*		CP	____
(5193)	Three Pair Remote Switches 27" (O27), *78–83*	90	110	____
5484	(See 8476)			
(5500)	Straight Track (O), *71–95*		CP	____
(5501)	Curved Track 31" (O), *71–95*		CP	____
(5502)	Remote Uncoupling Section (O), *71–72*	8	10	____
(5504)	Half-Curved Track 31" (O), *83–95*		CP	____
(5505)	Half-Straight Track (O), *83–95*		CP	____
5520	90° Crossover (O), *71–72*	7	10	____
5530	Remote Uncoupling Section (O), *81–95*		CP	____
5540	90° Crossover (O), *81–95*		CP	____
(5543)	Insulator Pins (12) (O), *70–95*		CP	____
5545	45° Crossover (O), *83–95*		CP	____
(5551)	Steel Pins (12) (O), *70–95*		CP	____
(5572)	Curved Track 72" (O), *79–95*		CP	____
5600	Curved Track (TT), *73–74*	1	2	____
5601	Curved Track, card of 4 (TT), *73–74*	6	10	____
5602	Curved Track Ballast, card of 4 (TT), *73–74*	6	10	____
5605	Straight Track (TT), *73–74*	1	2	____
5606	Straight Track, card of 4 (TT), *73–74*	6	10	____
5607	Straight Track Ballast, card of 4 (TT), *73–74*	6	10	____
5620	Left Manual Switch (TT), *73–74*	5	15	____
5625	Left Remote Switch (TT), *73–74*	10	20	____
5630	Right Manual Switch (TT), *73–74*	5	15	____
5635	Right Remote Switch (TT), *73–74*	10	20	____
5640	Left Switch Ballast, card of 2 (TT), *73–74*	6	10	____
5650	Right Switch Ballast, card of 2 (TT), *73–74*	6	10	____
5655	Lockon (TT), *73–74*	1	2	____
5660	Terminal Track w/ lockon (TT), *74*	2	4	____
5700	Oppenheimer Reefer, *81*	40	50	____
[5700]	Ozark TCA Oppenheimer Reefer, *81 u*	50	100	____
5701	Dairymen's League Reefer, *81*	30	35	____
5702	National Dairy Despatch Reefer, *81*	30	35	____
5703	North American Despatch Reefer, *81*	30	75	____
5704	Budweiser Reefer, *81–82*	50	80	____
5705	Ball Glass Jars Reefer, *81–82*	40	45	____
5706	Lindsay Brothers Reefer, *81–82*	30	40	____

		Exc	New	Cond/$
5707	American Refrigerator Reefer, *81–82*	30	35	____
5708	Armour Reefer, *82–83*	20	25	____
5709	REA Reefer, *82–83*	35	45	____
5710	Canadian Pacific Reefer, *82–83*	25	30	____
[5710]	NETCA CP Reefer, *82 u*	25	30	____
[5710]	LCAC CP Reefer, *83 u*		NRS	____
5711	Commercial Express Reefer, *82–83*	20	25	____
5712	Lionel Lines Reefer, *82 u*	225	275	____
5713	Cotton Belt Reefer, *83–84*	20	25	____
5714	Michigan Central Reefer, *83–84*	20	30	____
[5714]	LCAC Michigan Central Reefer, *85 u*		NRS	____
5715	Santa Fe Reefer, *83–84*	25	35	____
5716	Central Vermont Reefer, *83–84*	25	30	____
[5716]	NETCA Central Vermont Reefer, *83 u*	25	30	____
5717	Santa Fe Bunk Car, *83*	30	40	____
5718	(See 9849)			
5719	Canadian National Reefer, *84*	25	30	____
5720	Great Northern Reefer, *84*	150	165	____
5721	Soo Line Reefer, *84*	25	30	____
5722	NKP Reefer, *84*	20	25	____
5724	PRR Bunk Car, *84*	25	35	____
[5724]	LCOL PRR Bunk Car, *84 u*	30	40	____
5726	Southern Bunk Car, *84 u*	30	35	____
5727	U.S. Marines Bunk Car, *84–85*	25	30	____
5728	Canadian Pacific Bunk Car, *86*	20	25	____
5730	Strasburg RR Reefer, *85–86*	20	30	____
5731	L&N Reefer, *85–86*	20	25	____
[5731]	TCA Museum L&N Reefer, *90 u*	100	150	____
5732	Jersey Central Reefer, *85–86*	20	25	____
5733	Lionel Lines Bunk Car, *86 u*	40	45	____
5734	TCA REA Reefer, *85 u*	125	150	____
5735	NYC Bunk Car, *85–86*	40	45	____
5739	B&O Tool Car, *86*	45	50	____
5745	Santa Fe Bunk Car, *86 (SSS)*	50	75	____
5760	Santa Fe Tool Car, *86 (SSS)*	50	75	____
5900	AC/DC Converter, *79–83*	4	6	____
[6014-900]	LCCA Frisco Boxcar (027), *75–76 u*	25	40	____
6076	TTOS Santa Fe Hopper (027), *70 u*		NRS	____
6076	LV Hopper (027), *70 u*	20	25	____

		Exc	New	Cond/$
6100	Ontario Northland Covered Quad Hopper, *81–82*	30	40	_____
[6100]	LCAC Ontario Northland Covered Quad Hopper, *82 u*		NRS	_____
6101	Burlington Northern Covered Quad Hopper, *81–82*	20	35	_____
[6101]	Atlantic TCA Burlington Northern Covered Quad Hopper, *82 u*	20	25	_____
6102	GN Covered Quad Hopper (FARR #3), *81*	50	60	_____
6103	Canadian National Covered Quad Hopper, *81*	40	50	_____
6104	Southern Quad Hopper w/ coal load (FARR #4), *83*	75	95	_____
6105	Reading Operating Hopper, *82*	60	65	_____
6106	N&W Covered Quad Hopper, *82*	40	50	_____
6107	Shell Covered Quad Hopper, *82*	25	30	_____
6109	C&O Operating Hopper, *83*	40	60	_____
6110	Missouri Pacific Covered Quad Hopper, *83–84*	15	25	_____
6111	L&N Covered Quad Hopper, *83–84*	20	30	_____
[6111]	LOTS L&N Covered Quad Hopper, *83 u*	40	60	_____
[6111]	Southern TCA L&N Covered Quad Hopper, *83 u*	25	30	_____
6112	LCCA Commonwealth Edison Quad Hopper w/ coal load, *83 u*	75	90	_____
6113	Illinois Central Hopper (O27), *83–85*	10	15	_____
6114	C&NW Covered Quad Hopper, *83*	125	150	_____
6115	Southern Hopper (O27), *83–86*	15	20	_____
6116	Soo Line Ore Car, *84*	30	40	_____
6117	Erie Operating Hopper, *84*	40	45	_____
6118	Erie Covered Quad Hopper, *84*	50	55	_____
6122	Penn Central Ore Car, *84*	30	35	_____
6123	PRR Covered Quad Hopper (FARR #5), *84–85*	60	70	_____
6124	D&H Covered Quad Hopper, *84*	20	30	_____
[6124]	NETCA D&H Covered Quad Hopper, *84 u*	25	30	_____
6126	Canadian National Ore Car, *86*	25	30	_____
6127	Northern Pacific Ore Car, *86*	30	35	_____
6127	(See 5735)			
6131	Illinois Terminal Covered Quad Hopper, *85–86*	20	25	_____
6134	Burlington Northern 2-bay ACF Hopper (Std. O), *86 u*	150	190	_____

		Exc	New	Cond/$
6135	C&NW 2-bay ACF Hopper (Std. O), *86 u*	150	190	_____
6137	Nickel Plate Road Hopper (O27), *86–91*	15	20	_____
6138	B&O Quad Hopper w/ coal load, *86*	30	40	_____
6150	Santa Fe Hopper (O27), *85–86, 92 u*	12	18	_____
6177	Reading Hopper (O27), *86–90*	15	20	_____
6200	FEC Gondola w/ canisters, *81–82*	15	25	_____
6200	(See 8404)			
6201	Union Pacific Animated Gondola, *82–83*	25	35	_____
6202	WM Gondola w/ coal load, *82*	40	45	_____
(6203)	Black Cave Gondola (O27), *82*	3	5	_____
6205	CP Gondola w/ canisters, *83*	30	35	_____
6206	C&IM Gondola w/ canisters, *83–85*	20	30	_____
6207	Southern Gondola w/ canisters (O27), *83–85*	6	8	_____
6208	Chessie System Gondola w/ canisters, *83 u*	35	40	_____
6209	NYC Gondola w/ coal load (Std. O), *84–85*	55	60	_____
6210	Erie-Lackawanna Gondola w/ canisters, *84*	30	40	_____
6211	C&O Gondola w/ canisters, *84–85*	—	12	_____
[6211]	LOTS C&O Gondola w/ canisters, *86 u*	55	80	_____
6214	Lionel Lines Gondola w/ canisters, *84 u*	40	50	_____
6230	Erie-Lackawanna Reefer (Std. O), *86 u*	125	145	_____
6231	Railgon Gondola w/ coal load (Std. O), *86 u*	150	165	_____
6232	Illinois Central Boxcar (Std. O), *86 u*	105	125	_____
6233	Canadian Pacific Flatcar w/ stakes (Std. O), *86 u*	125	150	_____
6234	Burlington Northern Boxcar (Std. O), *85*	45	60	_____
6235	Burlington Northern Boxcar (Std. O), *85*	45	60	_____
6236	Burlington Northern Boxcar (Std. O), *85*	45	60	_____
6237	Burlington Northern Boxcar (Std. O), *85*	45	60	_____
6238	Burlington Northern Boxcar (Std. O), *85*	45	60	_____
6239	Burlington Northern Boxcar (Std. O), *86 u*	60	75	_____
6251	NYC Coal Dump Car, *85*	15	20	_____
6254	NKP Gondola w/ canisters, *86–91*	10	12	_____
6258	Santa Fe Gondola w/ canisters (O27), *85–86, 92 u*	—	6	_____
X6260	NYC Gondola w/ canisters, *85–86*	15	18	_____
6272	Santa Fe Gondola w/ cable reels, *86 (SSS)*	20	25	_____
6300	Corn Products 3-D Tank Car, *81–82*	25	35	_____
6301	Gulf 1-D Tank Car, *81*	20	25	_____
6302	Quaker State 3-D Tank Car, *81*	40	45	_____

		Exc	New	Cond/$
6304	GN 1-D Tank Car (FARR #3), *81*	60	70	____
6305	British Columbia 1-D Tank Car, *81*	50	70	____
6306	Southern 1-D Tank Car (FARR #4), *83*	60	75	____
6307	PRR 1-D Tank Car (FARR #5), *84–85*	75	90	____
6308	Alaska 1-D Tank Car (O27), *82–83*	25	30	____
6310	Shell 2-D Tank Car (O27), *83–84*	20	25	____
6312	C&O 2-D Tank Car (O27), *84–85*	20	30	____
6313	Lionel Lines 1-D Tank Car, *84 u*	50	65	____
6314	B&O 3-D Tank Car, *86*	45	50	____
6315	TCA Pittsburgh 1-D Tank Car, *72 u*	65	70	____
6317	Gulf 2-D Tank Car (O27), *84–85*	20	25	____
6323	LCCA Virginia Chemicals 1-D Tank Car, *86 u*	50	60	____
6325	(See 6579)			
6357	Frisco 1-D Tank Car, *83*	65	95	____
6401	Virginian B/W Caboose, *81*	45	60	____
[6401]	Sacramento-Sierra TCA Virginian B/W Caboose, *84 u*	—	40	____
6403	Amtrak Vista Dome Car (O27), *76–77*	50	60	____
6404	Amtrak Passenger Car (O27), *76–77*	50	60	____
6405	Amtrak Passenger Car (O27), *76–77*	50	60	____
6406	Amtrak Observation Car (O27), *76–77*	50	60	____
6410	Amtrak Passenger Car (O27), *77*	40	60	____
6411	Amtrak Passenger Car (O27), *77*	30	50	____
6412	Amtrak Vista Dome Car (O27), *77*	30	50	____
6420	Reading Transfer Caboose, *81–82*	15	20	____
6421	Joshua L. Cowen B/W Caboose, *82*	40	50	____
6422	DM&IR B/W Caboose, *81*	30	40	____
6425	Erie-Lackawanna B/W Caboose, *83–84*	35	40	____
6426	Reading Transfer Caboose, *82–83*	10	18	____
6427	Burlington Northern Transfer Caboose, *83–84*	10	20	____
6428	C&NW Transfer Caboose, *83–85*	20	25	____
6430	Santa Fe SP-Type Caboose, *83–89*	6	10	____
6431	Southern B/W Caboose (FARR #4), *83*	50	60	____
6432	Union Pacific SP-Type Caboose, *81–82*	10	12	____
6433	Canadian Pacific B/W Caboose, *81*	60	75	____
6435	U.S. Transfer Caboose, *83–84*	10	20	____
6438	GN B/W Caboose (FARR #3), *81*	50	60	____
6439	Reading B/W Caboose, *84–85*	20	30	____
6441	Alaska B/W Caboose, *82–83*	40	50	____

MPC MODERN ERA (1970–1986)

		Exc	New	Cond/$
6446-25	N&W Covered Quad Hopper, *70 u*	175	200	_____
6449	Wendy's N5C Caboose, *81–82*	50	65	_____
6464-500	Timken Boxcar, *70 u*	150	200	_____
6464-1970	TCA Chicago Boxcar, *70 u*	125	160	_____
6464-1971	TCA Disneyland Boxcar, *71 u*	200	225	_____
(6476-135)	Lehigh Valley Hopper "25000" (O27), *70–71 u*		NRS	_____
(6478)	Black Cave SP-Type Caboose, *82*	5	10	_____
6482	Nibco Express SP-Type Caboose, *82 u*	30	40	_____
6483	LCCA Jersey Central SP-Type Caboose, *82 u*	30	40	_____
6485	Chessie System SP-Type Caboose, *84–85*	5	10	_____
6486	Southern SP-Type Caboose, *83–85*	6	8	_____
6490	NKP N5C Caboose, *84 u*		NRS	_____
6491	Erie-Lackawanna Transfer Caboose, *85–86*	8	15	_____
6493	L&C B/W Caboose, *86–87*	25	40	_____
6494	Santa Fe Bobber Caboose, *85–86*	8	10	_____
6496	Santa Fe Work Caboose, *86 (SSS)*	25	35	_____
(6504)	L.A.S.E.R. Flatcar w/ helicopter (O27), *81–82*	20	30	_____
(6505)	L.A.S.E.R. Radar Car, *81–82*	20	30	_____
(6506)	L.A.S.E.R. Security Car, *81–82*	20	30	_____
(6507)	L.A.S.E.R. Flatcar w/ cruise missile, *81–82*	20	30	_____
6508	Canadian Pacific Crane Car, *81*	60	80	_____
[6508]	LCOL Canadian Pacific Crane Car, *83 u*	—	45	_____
(6509)	Depressed Flatcar w/ girders, *81*	75	90	_____
6510	Union Pacific Crane Car, *82*	75	80	_____
6515	Union Pacific Flatcar (O27), *83–84, 86*	5	10	_____
6521	NYC Flatcar w/ stakes (Std. O), *84–85*	60	75	_____
6522	C&NW Searchlight Car, *83–85*	30	35	_____
6524	Erie Crane Car, *84*	75	85	_____
6526	U.S. Marines Searchlight Car, *84–85*	30	35	_____
6529	NYC Searchlight Car, *85–86*	20	25	_____
6531	Express Mail Flatcar w/ trailers, *85–86*	30	40	_____
6560	Bucyrus Erie Crane Car, *71*	150	175	_____
(6561)	Flatcar w/ cruise missile (O27), *83–84*	15	30	_____
(6562)	Flatcar w/ fences (O27), *83–84*	15	25	_____
(6564)	Flatcar w/ two U.S.M.C. tanks (O27), *83–84*	15	25	_____
(6567)	LCCA ICG Crane Car "100408", *85 u*	60	75	_____
(6573)	Redwood Valley Express Flatcar w/ dump bin (O27), *84–85*	8	15	_____

		Exc	New	Cond/$
(6574)	Redwood Valley Express Flatcar w/ crane (027), 84–85	8	15	_____
(6575)	Redwood Valley Express Flatcar w/ fences (027), 84–85	8	15	_____
6576	Santa Fe Flatcar w/ crane (027), 85–86	8	12	_____
6576	Santa Fe Flatcar w/ fences (027), 92 u	8	12	_____
6579	NYC Crane Car, 85–86	40	50	_____
6582	TTOS Portland Flatcar w/ wood load, 86 u	75	100	_____
6585	PRR Flatcar w/ fences (027), 86–90	5	10	_____
6587	W&ARR Flatcar w/ horses, 86 u	20	30	_____
6593	Santa Fe Crane Car, 86 (SSS)	50	60	_____
6670	(See 9378)			
6700	PFE Ice Car (See 2306)			
6900	N&W E/V Caboose, 82	90	120	_____
6901	Ontario Northland E/V Caboose, 82 u	60	75	_____
6903	Santa Fe E/V Caboose, 83	150	200	_____
6904	Union Pacific E/V Caboose, 83	125	150	_____
6905	NKP E/V Caboose, 83 u	75	95	_____
6906	Erie-Lackawanna E/V Caboose, 84	100	125	_____
6907	NYC Woodside Caboose (Std. O), 86 u	125	150	_____
6908	PRR N5C Caboose (FARR #5), 84–85	90	100	_____
6910	NYC E/V Caboose, 84 u	90	100	_____
(6912)	Redwood Valley Express SP-Type Caboose, 84–85	10	20	_____
6913	Burlington Northern E/V Caboose, 85	100	125	_____
6916	NYC Work Caboose, 85–86	15	18	_____
6917	Jersey Central E/V Caboose, 86	60	75	_____
6918	B&O SP-Type Caboose, 86	10	15	_____
6919	NKP SP-Type Caboose, 86–91	5	10	_____
6920	B&A Woodside Caboose (Std. O), 86 u	115	130	_____
6921	PRR SP-Type Caboose, 86–90	5	10	_____
6926	TCA New Orleans E/V Caboose, 86 u	45	65	_____
7200	Quicksilver Passenger Car (027), 82–83	50	60	_____
7201	Quicksilver Passenger Car (027), 82–83	50	60	_____
7202	Quicksilver Observation Car (027), 82–83	50	60	_____
(7203)	N&W Dining Car "491", 82 u	350	465	_____
(7204)	Southern Pacific Dining Car, 82 u	350	450	_____
(7205)	TCA Denver Combination Car "1982", 82 u	50	80	_____
(7206)	TCA Louisville Passenger Car "1983", 83 u	50	80	_____

		Exc	New	Cond/$
7207	NYC Dining Car, *83 u*	175	265	_____
(7208)	PRR Dining Car, *83 u*	175	195	_____
7210	Union Pacific Dining Car, *84*	100	125	_____
(7211)	Southern Pacific Vista Dome Car, *83 u*	300	400	_____
(7212)	TCA Pittsburgh Passenger Car "1984", *84 u*	60	80	_____
7215	B&O Passenger Car, *83–84*	50	60	_____
7216	B&O Passenger Car, *83–84*	50	60	_____
7217	B&O Baggage Car, *83–84*	50	60	_____
7220	Illinois Central Baggage Car, *85, 87*	100	125	_____
7221	Illinois Central Combination Car, *85, 87*	100	125	_____
7222	Illinois Central Passenger Car, *85, 87*	100	125	_____
7223	Illinois Central Passenger Car, *85, 87*	100	125	_____
7224	Illinois Central Dining Car, *85, 87*	100	125	_____
7225	Illinois Central Observation Car, *85, 87*	100	125	_____
7227	Wabash Dining Car (FF #1), *86–87*	100	115	_____
7228	Wabash Baggage Car (FF #1), *86–87*	100	115	_____
7229	Wabash Combination Car (FF #1), *86–87*	100	115	_____
7230	Wabash Passenger Car (FF #1), *86–87*	100	115	_____
7231	Wabash Passenger Car (FF #1), *86–87*	100	115	_____
7232	Wabash Observation Car (FF #1), *86–87*	100	115	_____
7241	W&ARR Passenger Car, *86 u*	50	60	_____
7242	W&ARR Baggage Car, *86 u*	50	60	_____
7301	Norfolk & Western Stock Car, *82*	40	50	_____
7302	Texas & Pacific Stock Car (O27), *83–84*	15	20	_____
7303	Erie Stock Car, *84*	50	65	_____
7304	Southern Stock Car (FARR #4), *83 u*	60	70	_____
7309	Southern Stock Car (O27), *85–86*	15	20	_____
7312	W&ARR Stock Car (O27), *86 u*	25	30	_____
7401	Chessie System Stock Car (O27), *84–85*	15	20	_____
7403	LCCA LNAC Boxcar, *84 u*	30	45	_____
7404	Jersey Central Boxcar, *86*	55	70	_____
(7500)	Lionel 75th Anniversary U36B, *75–77*	125	150	_____
7501	Lionel 75th Anniversary Boxcar, *75–77*	25	35	_____
7502	Lionel 75th Anniversary Reefer, *75–77*	25	35	_____
7503	Lionel 75th Anniversary Reefer, *75–77*	25	35	_____
7504	Lionel 75th Anniversary Covered Quad Hopper, *75–77*	30	40	_____
7505	Lionel 75th Anniversary Boxcar, *75–77*	25	35	_____
7506	Lionel 75th Anniversary Boxcar, *75–77*	25	35	_____

		Exc	New	Cond/$
7507	Lionel 75th Anniversary Reefer, *75–77*	25	35	____
7508	Lionel 75th Anniversary N5C Caboose, *75–77*	30	40	____
7509	Kentucky Fried Chicken Reefer, *81–82*	25	30	____
7510	Red Lobster Reefer, *81–82*	25	30	____
7511	Pizza Hut Reefer, *81–82*	25	30	____
7512	Arthur Treacher's Reefer, *82*	25	30	____
7513	Bonanza Reefer, *82*	25	30	____
7514	Taco Bell Reefer, *82*	25	30	____
7515	Denver Mint Car, *81*	65	80	____
7517	Philadelphia Mint Car, *82*	60	65	____
7518	Carson City Mint Car, *83*	40	50	____
[7518]	IETCA Carson City Mint Car, *84 u*	—	40	____
7519	Toy Fair Reefer, *82 u*	75	100	____
7520	Nibco Express Boxcar, *82 u*	350	500	____
7521	Toy Fair Reefer, *83 u*	75	100	____
7522	New Orleans Mint Car, *84 u*	40	50	____
[7522]	Lone Star TCA New Orleans Mint Car w/ coin, *86 u*	—	275	____
7523	Toy Fair Reefer, *84 u*	100	120	____
7524	Toy Fair Reefer, *85 u*	100	120	____
7525	Toy Fair Boxcar, *86 u*	100	120	____
7530	Dahlonega Mint Car, *86 u*	75	80	____
7600	Frisco "Spirit of '76" N5C Caboose, *74–76*	40	45	____
[7600]	Midwest TCA Frisco "Spirit of '76" N5C Caboose "00003", *76 u*	—	50	____
7601	Delaware Boxcar, *74–76*	20	25	____
7602	Pennsylvania Boxcar, *74–76*	25	30	____
7603	New Jersey Boxcar, *74–76*	25	30	____
7604	Georgia Boxcar, *74 u, 75–76*	25	30	____
7605	Connecticut Boxcar, *74 u, 75–76*	25	30	____
7606	Massachusetts Boxcar, *74 u, 75–76*	25	30	____
7607	Maryland Boxcar, *74 u, 75–76*	25	30	____
7608	South Carolina Boxcar, *75 u, 76*	30	40	____
7609	New Hampshire Boxcar, *75 u, 76*	50	60	____
7610	Virginia Boxcar, *75 u, 76*	175	225	____
7611	New York Boxcar, *75 u, 76*	75	100	____
7612	North Carolina Boxcar, *75 u, 76*	25	50	____
7613	Rhode Island Boxcar, *75 u, 76*	25	65	____
[7679]	VTC Boxcar, *79 u*	—	20	____

MPC MODERN ERA (1970–1986)

		Exc	New	Cond/$
[7681]	VTC N5C Caboose, *81 u*	—	25	____
[7682]	VTC Covered Quad Hopper, *82 u*	—	28	____
[7683]	VTC Virginia Fruit Express Reefer, *83 u*	—	28	____
[7684]	VTC Vitraco Oil 3-D Tank Car, *84 u*	—	28	____
[7685]	VTC Boxcar, *85 u*	—	30	____
[7686]	VTC GP-7, *86 u*	—	125	____
7700	Uncle Sam Boxcar, *75 u*	60	65	____
7701	Camel Boxcar, *76–77*	15	22	____
7702	Prince Albert Boxcar, *76–77*	15	22	____
7703	Beechnut Boxcar, *76–77*	15	22	____
7704	Toy Fair Boxcar, *76 u*	125	135	____
7705	Canadian Toy Fair Boxcar, *76 u*	175	225	____
7706	Sir Walter Raleigh Boxcar, *77–78*	20	30	____
7707	White Owl Boxcar, *77–78*	20	30	____
7708	Winston Boxcar, *77–78*	20	30	____
7709	Salem Boxcar, *78*	20	30	____
7710	Mail Pouch Boxcar, *78*	20	30	____
7711	El Producto Boxcar, *78*	20	30	____
7712	Santa Fe Boxcar (FARR #1), *79*	40	45	____
[7780]	TCA Museum Boxcar, *80 u*	—	30	____
[7781]	TCA Hafner Boxcar, *81 u*	—	30	____
[7782]	TCA Carlisle & Finch Boxcar, *82 u*	—	30	____
[7783]	TCA Ives Boxcar, *83 u*	—	30	____
[7784]	TCA Voltamp Boxcar, *84 u*	—	30	____
[7785]	TCA Hoge Boxcar, *85 u*	—	30	____
7800	Pepsi Boxcar, *76 u, 77*	50	60	____
7801	A&W Boxcar, *76 u, 77*	20	30	____
7802	Canada Dry Boxcar, *76 u, 77*	20	30	____
7803	Trains n' Truckin' Boxcar, *77 u*	25	35	____
7806	Season's Greetings Boxcar, *76 u*	100	125	____
7807	Toy Fair Boxcar, *77 u*	100	125	____
7808	Northern Pacific Stock Car, *77*	50	65	____
7809	Vernors Boxcar, *77 u, 78*	20	30	____
7810	Orange Crush Boxcar, *77 u, 78*	20	30	____
7811	Dr Pepper Boxcar, *77 u, 78*	20	30	____
7812	TCA Houston Stock Car, *77 u*	20	30	____
7813	Season's Greetings Boxcar, *77 u*	100	125	____
7814	Season's Greetings Boxcar, *78 u*	100	125	____
7815	Toy Fair Boxcar, *78 u*	100	125	____

		Exc	New	Cond/$
7816	Toy Fair Boxcar, *79 u*	100	115	_____
7817	Toy Fair Boxcar, *80 u*	125	150	_____
7900	D&RGW Operating Cowboy Car (O27), *82–83*	25	30	_____
7901	Lionel Lines Cop and Hobo Car (O27), *82–83*	40	45	_____
7902	Santa Fe Boxcar (O27), *82–85*	6	10	_____
7903	Rock Island Boxcar (O27), *83*	6	10	_____
7904	San Diego Zoo Giraffe Car (O27), *83–84*	40	50	_____
(7905)	Black Cave Boxcar (O27), *82*	7	10	_____
7908	Tappan Boxcar (O27), *82 u*	50	65	_____
7909	L&N Boxcar (O27), *83–84*	40	50	_____
7910	Chessie System Boxcar (O27), *84–85*	20	25	_____
7912	Toys "R" Us Giraffe Car (O27), *82–84 u*	75	100	_____
7913	Turtleback Zoo Giraffe Car (O27), *85–86*	35	40	_____
7914	Toys "R" Us Giraffe Car (O27), *85–89 u*	75	100	_____
7920	Sears Centennial Boxcar (O27), *85–86 u*	40	50	_____
7925	Erie-Lackawanna Boxcar (O27), *86–90*	8	12	_____
7926	NKP Boxcar (O27), *86–91*	8	11	_____
7930	True Value Boxcar (O27), *86–87 u*	40	60	_____
7931	Town House TV and Appliances Boxcar (O27), *86 u*	40	50	_____
7932	Kay Bee Toys Boxcar (O27), *86–87 u*	40	50	_____
8001	NKP 2-6-4, *80 u*	60	75	_____
8002	Union Pacific 2-8-4 (FARR #2), *80*	500	600	_____
8003	Chessie System 2-8-4, *80*	550	600	_____
8004	Rock Island 4-4-0, *80–82*	150	170	_____
8005	Santa Fe 4-4-0, *80–82*	60	75	_____
8006	ACL 4-6-4, *80 u*	600	700	_____
8007	NYNH&H 2-6-4, *80–81*	60	75	_____
8008	Chessie System 4-4-2, *80*	75	85	_____
8010	Santa Fe NW-2, *70, 71 u*	60	75	_____
8020	Santa Fe Alco A Unit, *70–72, 74–76*	75	100	_____
8020	Santa Fe Alco A Unit Dummy, *70*	50	70	_____
8021	Santa Fe Alco B Unit, *71–72, 74–76*	60	75	_____
8022	Santa Fe Alco A Unit, *71 u*	100	125	_____
8025	CN Alco A Unit, *71–73 u*	100	125	_____
8025	CN Alco A Unit Dummy, *71–73 u*	50	75	_____
8030	Illinois Central GP-9, *70–72*	80	125	_____
8031	Canadian National GP-7, *71–73 u*	70	120	_____

		Exc	New	Cond/$
8031	Illinois Central GP-9 Dummy, *70*		NM	
8040	NKP 2-4-2, *70–72*	30	40	_____
8040	Canadian National 2-4-2, *71 u*	50	100	_____
8041	NYC 2-4-2, *70*	60	75	_____
8041	PRR 2-4-2, *71 u*	60	75	_____
8042	GTW 2-4-2, *70, 71–73 u*	30	40	_____
8043	NKP 2-4-2, *70 u*	50	75	_____
8050	D&H U36C, *80*	125	175	_____
8051	D&H U36C Dummy, *80*	100	125	_____
[8051]	NETCA Hood's Milk Boxcar, *86 u*	45	55	_____
8054/ 8055	Burlington F-3 AA set, *80*	400	500	_____
8056	C&NW FM Trainmaster, *80*	300	350	_____
8057	Burlington NW-2, *80*	135	175	_____
8059	Pennsylvania F-3 B Unit, *80 u*	375	500	_____
8060	Pennsylvania F-3 B Unit, *80 u*	400	550	_____
8061	Chessie System U36C, *80*	160	190	_____
8062	Burlington F-3 B Unit, *80 u*	200	275	_____
8062	Great Northern 4-6-4, *70*		NM	
8063	Seaboard SD-9, *80*	125	175	_____
8064	Florida East Coast GP-9, *80*	115	150	_____
8065	Florida East Coast GP-9 Dummy, *80*	80	100	_____
8066	TP&W GP-20, *80–81, 83 u*	100	125	_____
8067	Texas & Pacific Alco A Unit, *80*		NM	
(8068)	LCCA Rock Island GP-20 "1980", *80 u*	100	140	_____
8071	Virginian SD-18, *80 u*	140	175	_____
8072	Virginian SD-18 Dummy, *80 u*	95	125	_____
(8100)	Norfolk & Western 4-8-4 "611", *81*	700	900	_____
(8101)	Chicago & Alton 4-6-4 "659", *81*	450	550	_____
8102	Union Pacific 4-4-2, *81–82*	60	75	_____
[8103]	LCAC Toronto, Hamilton & Buffalo Boxcar, *81 u*		NRS	_____
(8104)	Union Pacific 4-4-0 "3", *81 u*	275	325	_____
8111	DT&I NW-2, *71–74*	50	75	_____
8140	Southern 2-4-0, *71 u*	25	35	_____
8141	PRR 2-4-2, *71–72*	40	60	_____
8142	C&O 4-4-2, *71–72*	55	65	_____
(8150)	PRR GG-1 "4935", *81*	575	750	_____
8151	Burlington SD-28, *81*	150	195	_____
8152	Canadian Pacific SD-24, *81*	180	215	_____
8153	Reading NW-2, *81–82*	125	150	_____

		Exc	New	Cond/$
8154	Alaska NW-2, *81–82*	125	170	____
8155	Monon U36B, *81–82*	100	125	____
8156	Monon U36B Dummy, *81–82*	60	75	____
8157	Santa Fe FM Trainmaster, *81*	400	450	____
8158	DM&IR GP-35, *81–82*	75	125	____
8159	DM&IR GP-35 Dummy, *81–82*	60	75	____
8160	Burger King GP-20, *81–82*	100	125	____
8161	L.A.S.E.R. Diesel Switcher, *81–82*	30	75	____
8162	Ontario Northland SD-18, *81 u*	125	150	____
8163	Ontario Northland SD-18 Dummy, *81 u*	100	125	____
8164	Pennsylvania F-3 B Unit, *81 u*	450	600	____
8182	Nibco Express NW-2, *82 u*	100	150	____
(8190)	Diesel Horn kit, *81 u*	—	45	____
8200	"Kickapoo" Dockside 0-4-0T, *72*	30	40	____
8203	PRR 2-4-2, *72, 74 u, 75*	30	40	____
8204	C&O 4-4-2, *72*	60	70	____
[8204]	LCAC Algoma Central Boxcar, *82 u*		NRS	____
8206	NYC 4-6-4, *72–75*	175	210	____
8209	"Pioneer" Dockside 0-4-0T w/ tender, *72*	50	75	____
8209	"Pioneer" Dockside 0-4-0T w/o tender, *73–76*	45	60	____
8210	Joshua L. Cowen 4-6-4, *82*	350	400	____
8212	Black Cave 0-4-0, *82*	30	50	____
8213	D&RGW 2-4-2, *82–83, 84–91 u*	60	70	____
8214	Pennsylvania 2-4-2, *82–83*	60	75	____
(8215)	Nickel Plate Road 2-8-4 "779", *82 u*	550	600	____
8250	Santa Fe GP-9, *72, 74–75*	90	120	____
(8251-50)	Horn/Whistle Controller, *72–74*	2	3	____
8252	D&H Alco A Unit, *72*	75	100	____
8253	D&H Alco B Unit, *72*	50	75	____
8254	Illinois Central GP-9 Dummy, *72*	60	75	____
8255	Santa Fe GP-9 Dummy, *72*	75	90	____
8258	Canadian National GP-7 Dummy, *72–73 u*	65	80	____
8260/ 8262	Southern Pacific F-3 AA set, *82*	675	700	____
8261	Southern Pacific F-3 B Unit, *82 u*	700	900	____
8263	Santa Fe GP-7, *82*	75	100	____
8264	CP Vulcan Switcher w/ snowplow, *82*	125	150	____
8265	Santa Fe SD-40, *82*	375	410	____
8266	Norfolk & Western SD-24, *82*	150	200	____
8268	Quicksilver Alco A Unit, *82–83*	100	125	____

		Exc	New	Cond/$
8269	Quicksilver Alco A Unit Dummy, *82–83*	60	75	_____
8272	Pennsylvania EP-5, *82 u*	275	325	_____
8300	Santa Fe 2-4-0, *73–74*	20	25	_____
8302	Southern 2-4-0, *73–76*	25	30	_____
8303	Jersey Central 2-4-2, *73–74*	40	50	_____
8304	Rock Island 4-4-2, *73–75*	100	125	_____
8304	Pennsylvania 4-4-2, *74–75*	90	125	_____
8304	B&O 4-4-2, *75*	90	125	_____
8304	C&O 4-4-2, *75–77*	90	125	_____
8305	Milwaukee Road 4-4-2, *73*	100	125	_____
(8307)	Southern Pacific 4-8-4 "4449", *83*	1000	1300	_____
8308	Jersey Central 2-4-2, *73–74 u*	40	50	_____
(8309)	Southern 2-8-2 "4501" (FARR #4), *83*	450	500	_____
8310	Nickel Plate Road 2-4-0, *73 u*	30	60	_____
8310	Santa Fe 2-4-0, *74–75 u*	30	40	_____
8310	Jersey Central 2-4-0, *74–75 u*	30	60	_____
8311	Southern 0-4-0, *73 u*	30	40	_____
8313	Santa Fe 0-4-0, *83–84*	15	20	_____
8314	Southern 2-4-0, *83–85*	20	25	_____
8315	B&O 4-4-0, *83–84*	85	120	_____
8350	U.S. Steel Diesel Switcher, *73–75*	20	30	_____
8351	Santa Fe Alco A Unit, *73–75*	60	70	_____
8352	Santa Fe GP-20, *73–75*	60	100	_____
8353	Grand Trunk GP-7, *73–75*	60	100	_____
8354	Erie NW-2, *73, 75*	90	120	_____
8355	Santa Fe GP-20 Dummy, *73–74*	80	125	_____
8356	Grand Trunk GP-7 Dummy, *73–75*	60	75	_____
8357	PRR GP-9, *73–75*	125	150	_____
8358	PRR GP-9 Dummy, *73–75*	60	100	_____
(8359)	Chessie System GP-7 "GM50", *73*	100	150	_____
8360	Long Island GP-20, *73–74*	75	100	_____
8361	Western Pacific Alco A Unit, *73–75*	75	100	_____
8362	Western Pacific Alco B Unit, *73–75*	50	75	_____
8363	B&O F-3 A Unit, *73–75*	250	300	_____
8364	B&O F-3 A Unit Dummy, *73–75*	150	200	_____
8365/ 8366	CP F-3 AA set, *73 (SSS)*	450	600	_____
8367	Long Island GP-20 Dummy, *73–75*	100	125	_____
8368	Alaska Vulcan Switcher, *83*	125	175	_____
8369	Erie-Lackawanna GP-20, *83–85*	125	140	_____

MPC MODERN ERA (1970–1986)		Exc	New	Cond/$
8370/ 8372	NYC F-3 AA set, *83*	400	550	_____
8371	NYC F-3 B Unit, *83*	150	225	_____
8374	Burlington Northern NW-2, *83–85*	125	150	_____
8375	C&NW GP-7, *83–85*	125	150	_____
8376	Union Pacific SD-40, *83*	400	450	_____
8377	U.S. Diesel Switcher, *83–84*	60	75	_____
(8378)	Wabash FM Trainmaster "550", *83 u*	1000	1200	_____
8379	PRR Fire Car, *83 u*	150	175	_____
8380	Lionel Lines SD-28, *83 u*	175	245	_____
8402	Reading 4-4-2, *84–85*	60	75	_____
8403	Chessie System 4-4-2, *84–85*	60	75	_____
(8404)	PRR 6-8-6 "6200" (FARR #5), *84–85*	425	525	_____
(8406)	NYC 4-6-4 "783", *84*	700	800	_____
8410	Redwood Valley Express 4-4-0, *84–85*	40	60	_____
8452	Erie Alco A Unit, *74–75*	80	100	_____
8453	Erie Alco B Unit, *74–75*	50	75	_____
8454	D&RGW GP-7, *74–75*	100	125	_____
8455	D&RGW GP-7 Dummy, *74–75*	50	80	_____
8458	Erie-Lackawanna SD-40, *84*	345	390	_____
8459	D&RGW Vulcan Rotary Snowplow, *84*	155	200	_____
8460	MKT NW-2, *74–75*	50	75	_____
8463	Chessie System GP-20, *74 u*	125	150	_____
8464/ 8465	D&RGW F-3 AA set, *74 (SSS)*	290	400	_____
8466	Amtrak F-3 A Unit, *74–76*	200	290	_____
8467	Amtrak F-3 A Unit Dummy, *74–76*	100	125	_____
8468	B&O F-3 B Unit, *74–75 (SSS)*	125	150	_____
8469	CP F-3 B Unit, *74 (SSS)*	135	190	_____
8470	Chessie System U36B, *74*	100	150	_____
8471	Pennsylvania NW-2, *74–76*	200	250	_____
8473	Coca-Cola NW-2, *74 u, 75*	100	125	_____
8474	D&RGW F-3 B Unit, *74 (SSS)*	100	125	_____
8475	Amtrak F-3 B Unit, *74 (SSS)*	100	125	_____
(8476)	TCA 4-6-4 "5484", *85 u*	300	350	_____
8477	NYC GP-9, *84 u*	300	350	_____
8480/ 8482	Union Pacific F-3 AA set, *84*	325	425	_____
8481	Union Pacific F-3 B Unit, *84*	180	200	_____
8485	U.S. Marines NW-2, *84–85*	100	145	_____
8490	(See 8690)			
8500	Pennsylvania 2-4-0, *75–76*	20	25	_____

		Exc	New	Cond/$
8502	Santa Fe 2-4-0, *75*	20	25	_____
8506	PRR 0-4-0, *75–77*	95	125	_____
8507	Santa Fe 2-4-0, *75 u*	25	30	_____
[8507]/ [8508]	LCAC CN F-3 AA set, shells only, *85 u*		NRS	_____
8512	Santa Fe 0-4-0T, *85–86*	25	35	_____
8516	NYC 0-4-0, *85–86*	125	150	_____
8550	Jersey Central GP-9, *75–76*	100	125	_____
8551	Pennsylvania EP-5, *75–76*	175	200	_____
8552/ 8553/ 8554	Southern Pacific Alco ABA set, *75–76*	200	250	_____
8555/ 8557	Milwaukee Road F-3 AA set, *75 (SSS)*	300	400	_____
8556	Chessie System NW-2, *75–76*	200	225	_____
8558	Milwaukee Road EP-5, *76–77*	175	200	_____
(8559)	N&W GP-9 "1776", *75*	100	130	_____
8560	Chessie System U36B Dummy, *75*	75	100	_____
8561	Jersey Central GP-9 Dummy, *75–76*	60	80	_____
8562	Missouri Pacific GP-20, *75–76*	100	125	_____
8563	Rock Island Alco A Unit, *75–76 u*	75	100	_____
8564	Union Pacific U36B, *75*	125	175	_____
8565	Missouri Pacific GP-20 Dummy, *75–76*	60	75	_____
8566	Southern F-3 A Unit, *75–77*	250	350	_____
8567	Southern F-3 A Unit Dummy, *75–77*	125	175	_____
8568	Preamble Express F-3 A Unit, *75 u*	125	175	_____
8569	Soo Line NW-2, *75–77*	60	75	_____
8570	Liberty Special Alco A Unit, *75 u*	100	125	_____
8571	Frisco U36B, *75–76*	75	100	_____
8572	Frisco U36B Dummy, *75–76*	60	75	_____
8573	Union Pacific U36B Dummy, *75 u*	175	225	_____
8575	Milwaukee Road F-3 B Unit, *75 (SSS)*	100	175	_____
8576	Penn Central GP-7, *75 u, 76–77*	125	150	_____
8578	NYC Ballast Tamper, *85, 87*	120	130	_____
8580/ 8582	Illinois Central F-3 AA set, *85, 87*	400	450	_____
8581	Illinois Central F-3 B Unit, *85, 87*	175	200	_____
8585	Burlington Northern SD-40, *85*	350	400	_____
(8587)	Wabash GP-9 "484", *85 u*	300	350	_____
8600	NYC 4-6-4, *76*	200	250	_____
8601	Rock Island 0-4-0, *76–77*	20	25	_____
8602	D&RGW 2-4-0, *76–78*	25	30	_____
8603	C&O 4-6-4, *76–77*	175	250	_____
8604	Jersey Central 2-4-2, *76 u*	40	45	_____

MPC MODERN ERA (1970–1986)		Exc	New	Cond/$
(8606)	B&A 4-6-4 "784", *86 u*	1100	1400	_____
(8610)	Wabash 4-6-2 "672", *86–87*	500	600	_____
(8615)	L&N 2-8-4 "1970", *86 u*	900	1100	_____
8616	Santa Fe 4-4-2, *86*	65	75	_____
8617	Nickel Plate Road 4-4-2, *86–91*	65	75	_____
8625	Pennsylvania 2-4-0, *86–90*	25	40	_____
(8630)	W&ARR 4-4-0 "3", *86 u*	125	150	_____
8635	Santa Fe 0-4-0, *86 (SSS)*	125	150	_____
8650	Burlington Northern U36B, *76–77*	125	150	_____
8651	Burlington Northern U36B Dummy, *76–77*	90	100	_____
8652	Santa Fe F-3 A Unit, *76–77*	300	400	_____
8653	Santa Fe F-3 A Unit Dummy, *76–77*	175	200	_____
8654	Boston & Maine GP-9, *76–77*	115	150	_____
8655	Boston & Maine GP-9 Dummy, *76–77*	80	100	_____
8656	Canadian National Alco A Unit, *76*	150	200	_____
8657	Canadian National Alco B Unit, *76*	75	100	_____
8658	Canadian National Alco A Unit Dummy, *76*	100	200	_____
8659	Virginian Rectifier, *76–77*	150	200	_____
8660	CP Rail NW-2, *76–77*	100	125	_____
8661	Southern F-3 B Unit, *76 (SSS)*	200	225	_____
8662	B&O GP-7, *86*	125	140	_____
8664	Amtrak Alco A Unit, *76–77*	100	150	_____
8665	BAR "Jeremiah O'Brien" GP-9 "1776", *76 u*	100	160	_____
8666	Northern Pacific GP-9, *76 (SSS)*	125	150	_____
8667	Amtrak Alco B Unit, *76–77*	75	100	_____
8668	Northern Pacific GP-9 Dummy, *76 (SSS)*	100	125	_____
8669	Illinois Central Gulf U36B, *76–77*	125	150	_____
8670	Chessie System Diesel Switcher, *76*	35	65	_____
8679	Northern Pacific GP-20, *86*	100	125	_____
8687	Jersey Central FM Trainmaster, *86*	350	400	_____
8690	Lionel Lines Trolley, *86*	125	175	_____
(8701)	W&ARR 4-4-0 "3", *77–79*	175	225	_____
8702	Southern 4-6-4, *77–78*	400	475	_____
8703	Wabash 2-4-2, *77*	25	35	_____
8750	Rock Island GP-7, *77–78*	100	125	_____
8751	Rock Island GP-7 Dummy, *77–78*	50	75	_____
8753	Pennsylvania GG-1, *77 u*	475	550	_____
8754	New Haven Rectifier, *77–78*	175	225	_____
8755	Santa Fe U36B, *77–78*	160	190	_____

MPC MODERN ERA (1970–1986)

		Exc	New	Cond/$
8756	Santa Fe U36B Dummy, *77–78*	90	100	___
8757	Conrail GP-9, *76 u, 77–78*	100	175	___
8758	Southern GP-7 Dummy, *77 u, 78*	80	100	___
8759	Erie-Lackawanna GP-9, *77–79*	120	150	___
8760	Erie-Lackawanna GP-9 Dummy, *77–79*	100	125	___
8761	GTW NW-2, *77–78*	125	175	___
8762	Great Northern EP-5, *77–78*	225	250	___
8763	Norfolk & Western GP-9, *76 u, 77–78*	100	125	___
8764	B&O Budd RDC Passenger, *77 (SSS)*	145	160	___
8765	B&O Budd RDC Baggage Dummy, *77 (SSS)*	75	100	___
8766	B&O Budd RDC Baggage, *77 (SSS)*	200	250	___
8767	B&O Budd RDC Passenger Dummy, *77 (SSS)*	100	125	___
8768	B&O Budd RDC Passenger Dummy, *77 (SSS)*	100	125	___
8769	Republic Steel Diesel Switcher, *77–78*	20	40	___
8770	EMD NW-2, *77–78*	75	100	___
8771	Great Northern U36B, *77*	100	120	___
8772	GM&O GP-20, *77*	100	120	___
8773	Mickey Mouse U36B, *77–78*	300	400	___
8774	Southern GP-7, *77 u, 78*	125	150	___
8775	Lehigh Valley GP-9, *77 u, 78*	125	150	___
8776	C&NW GP-20, *77 u, 78*	125	175	___
8777	Santa Fe F-3 B Unit, *77 (SSS)*	200	225	___
8778	Lehigh Valley GP-9 Dummy, *77 u, 78*	80	100	___
8779	C&NW GP-20 Dummy, *77 u, 78*	100	125	___
8800	Lionel Lines 4-4-2, *78–81*	100	125	___
8801	Blue Comet 4-6-4, *78–80*	400	475	___
8803	Santa Fe 0-4-0, *78*	15	25	___
8850	Penn Central GG-1, *78 u, 79*	375	425	___
8851/ 8852	New Haven F-3 AA set, *78 u, 79*	300	400	___
8854	CP Rail GP-9, *78–79*	100	150	___
8855	Milwaukee Road SD-18, *78*	150	175	___
8857	Northern Pacific U36B, *78–80*	100	125	___
8858	Northern Pacific U36B Dummy, *78–80*	55	85	___
8859	Conrail Rectifier, *78–82*	175	250	___
8860	Rock Island NW-2, *78–79*	100	130	___
8861	Santa Fe Alco A Unit, *78–79*	75	100	___
8862	Santa Fe Alco B Unit, *78–79*	40	50	___

		Exc	New	Cond/$
8864	New Haven F-3 B Unit, *78 (SSS)*	125	150	____
8866	M&St L GP-9, *78 (SSS)*	85	110	____
8867	M&St L GP-9 Dummy, *78 (SSS)*	60	90	____
8868	Amtrak Budd RDC Baggage, *78, 80*	150	200	____
8869	Amtrak Budd RDC Passenger Dummy, *78, 80*	75	100	____
8870	Amtrak Budd RDC Passenger Dummy, *78, 80*	75	100	____
8871	Amtrak Budd RDC Baggage Dummy, *78, 80*	75	100	____
8872	Santa Fe SD-18, *78 u, 79*	100	150	____
8873	Santa Fe SD-18 Dummy, *78 u, 79*	75	100	____
8900	Santa Fe 4-6-4 (FARR #1), *79*	350	425	____
8902	ACL 2-4-0, *79–82, 86–90*	15	20	____
8903	D&RGW 2-4-2, *79–81*	20	25	____
8904	Wabash 2-4-2, *79, 81 u*	35	40	____
8905	"Smokey Mountain" Dockside 0-4-0T, *79*	10	20	____
8950	Virginian FM Trainmaster, *79*	375	400	____
8951	Southern Pacific FM Trainmaster, *79*	500	600	____
8952/ 8953	PRR F-3 AA set, *79*	600	650	____
8955	Southern U36B, *79*	125	175	____
8956	Southern U36B Dummy, *79*	100	125	____
8957	Burlington Northern GP-20, *79*	125	150	____
[8957]	Detroit-Toledo TCA Burlington Northern GP-20, *80 u*		NRS	____
8958	Burlington Northern GP-20 Dummy, *79*	100	125	____
[8958]	Detroit-Toledo TCA Burlington Northern GP-20 Dummy, *80 u*		NRS	____
8960	Southern Pacific U36C, *79 u*	90	110	____
8961	Southern Pacific U36C Dummy, *79 u*	70	90	____
8962	Reading U36B, *79*	125	150	____
8970/ 8971	PRR F-3 AA set, *79 u, 80*	400	500	____
9001	Conrail Boxcar (O27), *86–87 u, 88–90*	5	10	____
9010	GN Hopper (O27), *70–71*	6	8	____
9011	GN Hopper (O27), *70 u, 75–76, 78–83*	6	8	____
9012	TA&G Hopper (O27), *71–72*	5	7	____
9013	Canadian National Hopper (O27), *72–76*	5	7	____
9014	Trailer Train Flatcar (O27), *78–79*		NRS	____
9015	Reading Hopper (O27), *73–75*	20	25	____

		Exc	New	Cond/$
9016	Chessie System Hopper (027), *75–79, 87–88, 89 u*	5	7	_____
[9016]	LCCA Chessie System Hopper (027), *79–80 u*	20	25	_____
9017	Wabash Gondola w/ canisters (027), *78–82*	4	5	_____
9018	DT&I Hopper (027), *78–79, 81–82*	5	7	_____
(9019)	Unlettered Flatcar (027), *78*	3	4	_____
9020	Union Pacific Flatcar (027), *70–77*	4	5	_____
9021	Santa Fe Work Caboose, *70–71, 73–75*	10	15	_____
9022	Santa Fe Bulkhead Flatcar (027), *70–72, 75–79*	8	15	_____
9023	MKT Bulkhead Flatcar (027), *73–74*	8	12	_____
9024	C&O Flatcar (027), *73–75*	4	6	_____
9025	DT&I Work Caboose, *71–74, 77–78*	8	10	_____
9026	Republic Steel Flatcar (027), *75–82*	6	8	_____
9027	Soo Line Work Caboose, *75–76*	8	10	_____
(9030)	"Kickapoo" Gondola (027), *72, 79*	5	10	_____
9031	NKP Gondola w/ canisters (027), *73–75, 82–83, 84–91 u*	5	7	_____
9032	Southern Pacific Gondola w/ canisters (027), *75–78*	3	4	_____
9033	PC Gondola w/ canisters (027), *76–78, 82, 86 u, 87–90, 92 u*	3	4	_____
9034	Lionel Leisure Hopper (027), *77 u*	30	40	_____
9035	Conrail Boxcar (027), *78–82*	4	8	_____
9036	Mobilgas 1-D Tank Car (027), *78–82*	6	12	_____
[9036]	LCCA Mobilgas 1-D Tank Car (027), *78–79 u*	20	25	_____
9037	Conrail Boxcar (027), *78 u, 80*	4	8	_____
9038	Chessie System Hopper (027), *78 u, 80*	15	20	_____
9039	Mobilgas 1-D Tank Car (027), *78 u, 80*	10	15	_____
9040	General Mills Wheaties Boxcar (027), *70–72*	7	10	_____
9041	Hershey's Boxcar (027), *70–71, 73–76*	10	15	_____
9042	Ford-Autolite Boxcar (027), *71 u, 72, 74–76*	10	15	_____
9043	Erie-Lackawanna Boxcar (027), *73–75*	10	15	_____
9044	D&RGW Boxcar (027), *75–76*	6	8	_____
9045	Toys "R" Us Boxcar (027), *75 u*	40	50	_____
9046	True Value Boxcar (027), *76 u*	40	50	_____
9047	Toys "R" Us Boxcar (027), *76 u*	35	50	_____
9048	Toys "R" Us Boxcar (027), *76 u*	35	50	_____
(9049)	Toys "R" Us Boxcar (027), *78 u*		NRS	_____
9050	Sunoco 1-D Tank Car (027), *70–71*	20	25	_____

		Exc	New	Cond/$
9051	Firestone 1-D Tank Car (O27), *74–75, 78*	15	20	____
9052	Toys "R" Us Boxcar (O27), *77 u*	30	40	____
9053	True Value Boxcar (O27), *77 u*	35	50	____
9054	JCPenney Boxcar (O27), *77 u*	30	45	____
9055	Republic Steel Gondola w/ canisters, *78 u*	10	12	____
9057	CP Rail SP-Type Caboose, *78–79*	10	15	____
9058	Lionel Lines SP-Type Caboose, *78–79, 83*	6	8	____
9059	Lionel Lines SP-Type Caboose, *79 u, 81 u*	8	10	____
9060	Nickel Plate Road SP-Type Caboose, *70–72*	6	8	____
9061	Santa Fe SP-Type Caboose, *70–76*	5	8	____
9062	Penn Central SP-Type Caboose, *70–72, 74–76*	5	9	____
9063	GTW SP-Type Caboose, *70, 71–73 u*	15	20	____
9064	C&O SP-Type Caboose, *71–72, 75–77*	7	10	____
9065	Canadian National SP-Type Caboose, *71–73 u*	20	25	____
9066	Southern SP-Type Caboose, *73–76*	8	10	____
(9067)	Kickapoo Valley Bobber Caboose, *72*	7	10	____
9068	Reading Bobber Caboose, *73–76*	6	8	____
[9068]	Gateway TCA Reading Bobber Caboose, *76 u*	—	25	____
9069	Jersey Central SP-Type Caboose, *73–74, 75–76 u*	6	8	____
9070	Rock Island SP-Type Caboose, *73–74*	10	15	____
9071	Santa Fe Bobber Caboose, *74 u, 77–78*	8	10	____
9073	Coca-Cola SP-Type Caboose, *74 u, 75*	15	20	____
9075	Rock Island SP-Type Caboose, *75–76 u*	15	20	____
9076	"We The People" SP-Type Caboose, *75 u*	20	30	____
9077	D&RGW SP-Type Caboose, *76–83, 84–91 u*	6	8	____
9078	Rock Island Bobber Caboose, *76–77*	6	8	____
9079	GTW Hopper (O27), *77*	20	30	____
9080	Wabash SP-Type Caboose, *77*	10	12	____
9085	Santa Fe Work Caboose, *79–82*	5	6	____
9090	General Mills Mini-Max Car, *71*	30	40	____
9106	Miller Vat Car, *84–85*	25	35	____
9107	Dr Pepper Vat Car, *86–87*	25	35	____
9110	B&O Quad Hopper, *71*	25	30	____
9111	N&W Quad Hopper, *72–75*	20	25	____
9112	D&RGW Covered Quad Hopper, *73–75*	20	25	____
9113	Norfolk & Western Quad Hopper, *73 (SSS)*	30	35	____
[9113]	Three Rivers TCA N&W Quad Hopper, *76 u*	30	35	____
9114	Morton Salt Covered Quad Hopper, *74–76*	20	25	____

		Exc	New	Cond/$
9115	Planter's Covered Quad Hopper, *74–76*	20	25	_____
9116	Domino Sugar Covered Quad Hopper, *74–76*	20	25	_____
9117	Alaska Covered Quad Hopper, *74 (SSS), 75–76*	25	35	_____
9118	LCCA Corning Covered Quad Hopper, *74 u*	75	100	_____
9119	Detroit & Mackinac Covered Quad Hopper, *75 (SSS)*	25	30	_____
[9119]	Detroit-Toledo TCA Detroit & Mackinac Covered Quad Hopper, *77 u*	25	35	_____
[9119]	North Texas TCA Detroit & Mackinac Covered Quad Hopper, *78 u*	25	35	_____
9120	Northern Pacific Flatcar w/ trailers, *70–71*	35	45	_____
9121	L&N Flatcar w/ bulldozer and scraper, *71–79*	40	50	_____
9122	Northern Pacific Flatcar w/ trailers, *72–75*	30	40	_____
9123	C&O Auto Carrier (3-tier), *72 u, 73–74*	20	30	_____
(9123)	TCA Dearborn Auto Carrier "1973" (3-tier), *73 u*	30	40	_____
9124	P&LE Flatcar w/ log load, *73–74*	15	20	_____
9125	Norfolk & Western Auto Carrier (2-tier), *73–77*	25	30	_____
9126	C&O Auto Carrier (3-tier), *73–75*	20	30	_____
9128	Heinz Vat Car, *74–76*	25	35	_____
9129	N&W Auto Carrier (3-tier), *75–76*	25	30	_____
9130	B&O Quad Hopper, *70*	20	25	_____
9131	D&RGW Gondola w/ canisters, *73–77*	5	8	_____
9132	Libby's Vat Car, *75 (SSS), 76–77*	20	25	_____
9133	Burlington Northern Flatcar w/ trailers, *76–77, 80*	30	40	_____
9134	Virginian Covered Quad Hopper, *76–77*	25	30	_____
9135	N&W Covered Quad Hopper, *70 u, 71, 75*	20	25	_____
9136	Republic Steel Gondola w/ canisters, *72–76, 79*	8	10	_____
9138	Sunoco 3-D Tank Car, *78 (SSS)*	50	55	_____
9139	PC Auto Carrier (3-tier), *76–77*	20	30	_____
9140	Burlington Gondola w/ canisters, *70, 73–82, 87–89*	6	8	_____
9141	Burlington Northern Gondola w/ canisters, *70–72*	8	10	_____
9142	Republic Steel Gondola w/ canisters, *71*	6	8	_____
[9142]	LCCA Republic Steel Gondola w/ canisters, *77–78 u*	15	20	_____

		Exc	New	Cond/$
9143	Canadian National Gondola w/ canisters, *71–73 u*	40	45	____
9144	D&RGW Gondola w/ canisters, *74 (SSS), 75–76*	8	12	____
9145	ICG Auto Carrier (3-tier), *77–80*	20	30	____
9146	Mogen David Vat Car, *77–81*	20	25	____
9147	Texaco 1-D Tank Car, *77–78*	35	50	____
9148	Du Pont 3-D Tank Car, *77–81*	20	25	____
9149	CP Rail Flatcar w/ trailers, *77–78*	25	40	____
9150	Gulf 1-D Tank Car, *70 u, 71*	20	25	____
9151	Shell 1-D Tank Car, *72*	30	35	____
9152	Shell 1-D Tank Car, *73–76*	25	30	____
9153	Chevron 1-D Tank Car, *74–76*	20	30	____
9154	Borden 1-D Tank Car, *75–76*	40	55	____
9155	LCCA Monsanto 1-D Tank Car, *75 u*	60	70	____
9156	Mobilgas 1-D Tank Car, *76–77*	30	40	____
9157	C&O Flatcar w/ crane, *76–78, 81–82*	50	60	____
9158	PC Flatcar w/ shovel, *76–77, 80*	45	55	____
9159	Sunoco 1-D Tank Car, *76*	45	50	____
9160	Illinois Central N5C Caboose, *70–72*	20	30	____
9161	CN N5C Caboose, *72–74*	15	30	____
9162	PRR N5C Caboose, *72 (SSS), 73–76*	35	45	____
9163	Santa Fe N5C Caboose, *73–76*	15	25	____
9165	Canadian Pacific N5C Caboose, *73 (SSS)*	25	40	____
9166	D&RGW SP-Type Caboose, *74 (SSS), 75*	20	25	____
9167	Chessie System N5C Caboose, *74–76*	30	40	____
9168	Union Pacific N5C Caboose, *75–77*	20	25	____
9169	Milwaukee Road SP-Type Caboose, *75 (SSS)*	20	25	____
(9170)	N&W N5C Caboose "1776", *75*	30	35	____
9171	Missouri Pacific SP-Type Caboose, *75 u, 76–77*	20	25	____
9172	Penn Central SP-Type Caboose, *75 u, 76–77*	25	35	____
9173	Jersey Central SP-Type Caboose, *75 u, 76–77*	20	25	____
9174	NYC P&E B/W Caboose, *76*	75	90	____
9175	Virginian N5C Caboose, *76–77*	30	35	____
9176	BAR N5C Caboose, *76 u*	20	35	____
9177	Northern Pacific B/W Caboose, *76 (SSS)*	25	35	____
9178	ICG SP-Type Caboose, *76–77*	20	25	____
9179	Chessie System Bobber Caboose, *76*	6	10	____

		Exc	New	Cond/$
9180	Rock Island N5C Caboose, *77–78*	20	40	_____
9181	B&M N5C Caboose, *76 u, 77*	30	35	_____
[9181]	NETCA B&M N5C Caboose, *77 u*	25	30	_____
9182	N&W N5C Caboose, *76 u, 77–80*	25	35	_____
9183	Mickey Mouse N5C Caboose, *77–78*	45	75	_____
9184	Erie B/W Caboose, *77–78*	25	35	_____
[9184]	North Texas TCA Erie B/W Caboose, *77 u*	20	25	_____
[9184]	LCOL Erie B/W Caboose, *82 u*	20	25	_____
9185	GTW N5C Caboose, *77*	25	35	_____
9186	Conrail N5C Caboose, *76 u, 77–78*	30	40	_____
[9186]	Atlantic TCA Conrail N5C Caboose, *79 u*	25	35	_____
9187	GM&O SP-Type Caboose, *77*	15	30	_____
9188	GN B/W Caboose, *77*	30	45	_____
9189	Gulf 1-D Tank Car, *77*	50	60	_____
9193	Budweiser Vat Car, *83–84*	125	150	_____
[9193]	Atlantic TCA Budweiser Vat Car, *84 u*	75	100	_____
9200	Illinois Central Boxcar, *70–71*	20	24	_____
9201	Penn Central Boxcar, *70*	20	28	_____
9202	Santa Fe Boxcar, *70*	30	35	_____
9203	Union Pacific Boxcar, *70*	30	35	_____
9204	Northern Pacific Boxcar, *70*	25	30	_____
9205	Norfolk & Western Boxcar, *70*	20	25	_____
9206	Great Northern Boxcar, *70–71*	18	20	_____
9207	Soo Line Boxcar, *71*	15	20	_____
9208	CP Rail Boxcar, *71*	20	22	_____
9209	Burlington Northern Boxcar, *71–72*	20	25	_____
9210	B&O DD Boxcar, *71*	20	25	_____
9211	Penn Central Boxcar, *71*	25	28	_____
9212	LCCA SCL Flatcar w/ trailers, *76 u*	35	40	_____
9213	M&St L Covered Quad Hopper, *78 (SSS)*	25	35	_____
9214	Northern Pacific Boxcar, *71–72*	25	30	_____
9215	Norfolk & Western Boxcar, *71*	20	25	_____
9216	Great Northern Auto Carrier (3-tier), *78*	25	40	_____
9217	Soo Line Operating Boxcar, *82–84*	30	35	_____
9218	Monon Operating Boxcar, *81*	30	40	_____
9219	Missouri Pacific Operating Boxcar, *83*	30	40	_____
9220	Borden Milk Car, *83–86*	100	110	_____
9221	Poultry Dispatch Operating Chicken Car, *83–85*	65	80	_____

		Exc	New	Cond/$
9222	L&N Flatcar w/ trailers, *83–84*	25	40	____
9223	Reading Operating Boxcar, *84*	30	35	____
9224	Churchill Downs Operating Horse Car, *84–86*	125	150	____
9225	Conrail Operating Barrel Car, *84*	70	75	____
9226	Delaware & Hudson Flatcar w/ trailers, *84–85*	30	35	____
9228	Canadian Pacific Operating Boxcar, *86*	20	33	____
9229	Express Mail Operating Boxcar, *85–86*	30	45	____
9230	Monon Boxcar, *71 (SSS), 72 u*	15	24	____
9231	Reading B/W Caboose, *79*	30	40	____
9232	Allis-Chalmers Condenser Car, *80–81, 83 u*	50	60	____
9233	Depressed Flatcar w/ transformer, *80*	75	95	____
9234	Lionel Radioactive Waste Car, *80*	40	60	____
9235	Union Pacific Derrick Car, *83–84*	15	20	____
9236	C&NW Derrick Car, *83–85*	25	35	____
9237	UPS Operating Boxcar, *84*		NM	
9238	Northern Pacific Log Dump Car, *84*	15	20	____
9239	Lionel Lines N5C Caboose, *83 u*	50	60	____
9240	NYC Operating Hopper, *86*	40	45	____
9240	NYC Hopper (O27), *87 u*	20	25	____
9241	PRR Log Dump Car, *85–86*	15	20	____
9245	Illinois Central Derrick Car, *85*		NM	
9247	(See 6529)			
9250	WaterPoxy 3-D Tank Car, *70–71*	30	35	____
X9259	LCCA Southern B/W Caboose, *77 u*	35	40	____
9260	Reynolds Aluminum Covered Quad Hopper, *75–76*	20	25	____
9261	Sun-maid Raisins Covered Quad Hopper, *75 u, 76*	20	30	____
9262	Ralston Purina Covered Quad Hopper, *75 u, 76*	60	75	____
9263	PRR Covered Quad Hopper, *75 u, 76–77*	35	50	____
9264	Illinois Central Covered Quad Hopper, *75 u, 76–77*	30	35	____
[9264]	Midwest TCA Museum Express Illinois Central Covered Quad Hopper, *78 u*	25	30	____
9265	Chessie System Covered Quad Hopper, *75 u, 76–77*	30	35	____

		Exc	New	Cond/$
9266	Southern "Big John" Covered Quad Hopper, *76*	60	75	____
9267	Alcoa Covered Quad Hopper, *76 (SSS)*	30	40	____
9268	Northern Pacific B/W Caboose, *77 u*	30	40	____
9269	Milwaukee Road B/W Caboose, *78*	35	50	____
9270	Northern Pacific N5C Caboose, *78*	15	25	____
9271	M&St L B/W Caboose, *78 (SSS), 79*	20	35	____
9272	New Haven B/W Caboose, *78–80*	20	30	____
[9272]	Detroit-Toledo TCA New Haven B/W Caboose, *79 u*	25	30	____
[9272]	METCA New Haven B/W Caboose, *79 u*	25	30	____
9273	Southern B/W Caboose, *78 u*	40	50	____
9274	Santa Fe B/W Caboose, *78 u*	60	75	____
9276	Peabody Quad Hopper, *78*	30	40	____
9277	Cities Service 1-D Tank Car, *78*	50	60	____
9278	Life Savers 1-D Tank Car, *78–79*	125	175	____
9279	Magnolia 3-D Tank Car, *78, 79 u*	20	25	____
9280	Santa Fe Operating Stock Car (O27), *77–81*	25	30	____
9281	Santa Fe Auto Carrier (3-tier), *78–80*	20	25	____
9282	Great Northern Flatcar w/ trailers, *78–79, 81–82*	40	60	____
9283	Union Pacific Gondola w/ canisters, *77*	15	20	____
9284	Santa Fe Gondola w/ canisters, *77*	20	25	____
9285	ICG Flatcar w/ trailers, *77*	50	65	____
9286	B&LE Covered Quad Hopper, *77*	15	25	____
9287	Southern N5C Caboose, *77 u, 78*	15	25	____
[9287]	Southern TCA Southern N5C Caboose, *77 u*	20	25	____
9288	Lehigh Valley N5C Caboose, *77 u, 78, 80*	20	30	____
9289	C&NW N5C Caboose, *77 u, 78, 80*	30	50	____
[9289]	Midwest TCA Museum Express C&NW N5C Caboose, *80 u*	40	50	____
9290	Union Pacific Operating Barrel Car, *83*	75	95	____
9300	PC Log Dump Car, *70–75, 77*	15	20	____
9301	U.S. Mail Operating Boxcar, *73–84*	30	40	____
[9301]	Sacramento-Sierra TCA U.S. Mail Operating Boxcar, *76 u*	30	45	____
9302	L&N Searchlight Car, *72 u, 73–78*	15	25	____
9303	Union Pacific Log Dump Car, *74–78, 80*	10	20	____

		Exc	New	Cond/$
9304	C&O Coal Dump Car, *74–78*	10	20	____
9305	Santa Fe Operating Cowboy Car (O27), *80–82*	20	30	____
9306	Santa Fe Flatcar w/ horses, *80–82*	20	30	____
9307	Erie Animated Gondola, *80–84*	60	90	____
9308	Aquarium Car, *81–84*	165	200	____
9309	TP&W B/W Caboose, *80–81, 83 u*	25	35	____
9310	Santa Fe Log Dump Car, *78 u, 79–83*	10	20	____
9311	Union Pacific Coal Dump Car, *78 u, 79–82*	10	20	____
9312	Conrail Searchlight Car, *78 u, 79–83*	20	25	____
9313	Gulf 3-D Tank Car, *79 u*	50	60	____
9315	Southern Pacific Gondola w/ canisters, *79 u*	20	30	____
9316	Southern Pacific B/W Caboose, *79 u*	80	100	____
9317	Santa Fe B/W Caboose, *79*	35	50	____
9319	TCA Silver Jubilee Mint Car, *79 u*	200	250	____
9320	Fort Knox Mint Car, *79 u*	200	230	____
9321	Santa Fe 1-D Tank Car (FARR #1), *79*	40	55	____
9322	Santa Fe Covered Quad Hopper (FARR #1), *79*	60	75	____
9323	Santa Fe B/W Caboose (FARR #1), *79*	45	60	____
9324	Tootsie Roll 1-D Tank Car, *79–81*	50	95	____
9325	Norfolk & Western Flatcar w/ fences, *79–81 u*	5	10	____
9325	(See 9363, 9364)			
9326	Burlington Northern B/W Caboose, *79–80*	25	30	____
[9326]	TTOS Burlington Northern B/W Caboose, *82 u*		NRS	____
9327	Bakelite 3-D Tank Car, *80*	20	30	____
9328	Chessie System B/W Caboose, *80*	40	55	____
9329	Chessie System Crane Car, *80*	60	75	____
(9330)	"Kickapoo" Dump Car, *72, 79*	3	8	____
9331	Union 76 1-D Tank Car, *79*	50	60	____
9332	Reading Crane Car, *79*	50	75	____
9333	Southern Pacific Flatcar w/ trailers, *79–80*	40	50	____
9334	Humble 1-D Tank Car, *79*	25	35	____
9335	B&O Log Dump Car, *86*	15	20	____
9336	CP Rail Gondola w/ canisters, *79*	20	30	____
9338	Penn Power Quad Hopper, *79*	60	75	____
9339	Great Northern Boxcar (O27), *79–83, 85 u, 86*	7	10	____
9340	Illinois Central Gondola w/ canisters (O27), *79–81, 82 u, 83*	5	10	____
9341	ACL SP-Type Caboose, *79–82, 86 u, 87–90*	6	8	____
9344	Citgo 3-D Tank Car, *80*	40	50	____

		Exc	New	Cond/$
9345	Reading Searchlight Car, *84–85*	20	25	_____
9346	Wabash SP-Type Caboose, *79*	6	10	_____
9347	TTOS Niagara Falls 3-D Tank Car, *79 u*	40	50	_____
9348	Santa Fe Crane Car (FARR #1), *79 u*	60	70	_____
9349	San Francisco Mint Car, *80*	100	150	_____
9351	PRR Auto Carrier (3-tier), *80*	20	40	_____
9352	Trailer Train Flatcar w/ C&NW trailers, *80*	65	75	_____
[9352]	Trailer Train Flatcar w/ Circus trailers, *80 u*	30	40	_____
9353	Crystal Line 3-D Tank Car, *80*	20	30	_____
9354	Pennzoil 1-D Tank Car, *80, 81 u*	40	50	_____
9355	Delaware & Hudson B/W Caboose, *80*	30	40	_____
[9355]	TTOS D&H B/W Caboose, *82 u*		NRS	_____
9356	Life Savers Stik-O-Pep 1-D Tank Car, *80 u*		NM	
9357	Smokey Mountain Bobber Caboose, *79*	8	10	_____
9358	LCCA Sands of Iowa Covered Quad Hopper, *80 u*	30	40	_____
9359	National Basketball Association Boxcar (O27), *79–80 u*	20	25	_____
9360	National Hockey League Boxcar (O27), *79–80 u*	20	25	_____
9361	C&NW B/W Caboose, *80*	55	65	_____
[9361]	TTOS C&NW B/W Caboose, *82 u*		NRS	_____
9362	Major League Baseball Boxcar (O27), *79–80 u*	20	25	_____
(9363)	N&W Flatcar w/ dump bin "9325" (O27), *79*	5	8	_____
(9364)	N&W Flatcar w/ crane "9325" (O27), *79*	8	10	_____
9365	Toys "R" Us Boxcar (O27), *79 u*	40	50	_____
9366	Union Pacific Covered Quad Hopper (FARR #2), *80*	30	40	_____
9367	Union Pacific 1-D Tank Car (FARR #2), *80*	35	45	_____
9368	Union Pacific B/W Caboose (FARR #2), *80*	40	50	_____
9369	Sinclair 1-D Tank Car, *80*	50	60	_____
9370	Seaboard Gondola w/ canisters, *80*	20	25	_____
9371	Atlantic Sugar Covered Quad Hopper, *80*	30	45	_____
9372	Seaboard B/W Caboose, *80*	30	45	_____
9373	Getty 1-D Tank Car, *80–81, 83 u*	40	50	_____
9374	Reading Covered Quad Hopper, *80–81, 83 u*	50	65	_____
9375	Union Pacific Flatcar w/ fences (O27), *80*		NM	
9376	Soo Line Boxcar (O27), *81 u*		NRS	_____
9376	Texas & Pacific SP-Type Caboose, *80*		NM	
9377	Missouri Pacific Boxcar (O27), *80*		NM	

		Exc	New	Cond/$
9378	Lionel Derrick Car, *80–82*	25	30	_____
9379	Santa Fe Gondola w/ canisters, *80–81, 83 u*	25	35	_____
9380	NYNH&H SP-Type Caboose, *80–81*	10	12	_____
9381	Chessie System SP-Type Caboose, *80*	8	10	_____
9382	Florida East Coast B/W Caboose, *80*	30	40	_____
[9382]	TTOS Florida East Coast B/W Caboose, *82 u*		NRS	_____
9383	Union Pacific Flatcar w/ trailers (FARR #2), *80 u*	45	55	_____
9384	Great Northern Operating Hopper, *81*	65	75	_____
9385	Alaska Gondola w/ canisters, *81*	50	60	_____
9386	Pure Oil 1-D Tank Car, *81*	45	55	_____
9387	Burlington B/W Caboose, *81*	45	60	_____
9388	Toys "R" Us Boxcar (O27), *81 u*	40	50	_____
9389	Lionel Radioactive Waste Car, *81–82*	35	50	_____
9398	PRR Coal Dump Car, *83–84*	20	25	_____
9399	C&NW Coal Dump Car, *83–85*	15	20	_____
9400	Conrail Boxcar, *78*	15	20	_____
[9400]	NETCA Conrail Boxcar, *78 u*	25	30	_____
9401	Great Northern Boxcar, *78*	15	20	_____
[9401]	Detroit-Toledo TCA GN Boxcar, *78 u*	—	30	_____
9402	Susquehanna Boxcar, *78*	30	35	_____
9403	Seaboard Coast Line Boxcar, *78*	15	20	_____
[9403]	Southern TCA SCL Boxcar, *78 u*	—	30	_____
9404	NKP Boxcar, *78*	30	35	_____
9405	Chattahoochee Boxcar, *78*	15	20	_____
[9405]	Southern TCA Chattahoochie Boxcar, *79 u*	—	30	_____
9406	D&RGW Boxcar, *78–79*	15	20	_____
9407	Union Pacific Stock Car, *78*	30	35	_____
9408	Lionel Lines Circus Stock Car, *78 (SSS)*	40	55	_____
9411	Lackawanna "Phoebe Snow" Boxcar, *78*	50	60	_____
9412	RF&P Boxcar, *79*	20	30	_____
[9412]	WB&A TCA RF&P Boxcar, *79 u*	—	30	_____
9413	Napierville Junction Boxcar, *79*	15	20	_____
[9413]	LCAC Napierville Junction Boxcar, *80 u*		NRS	_____
9414	Cotton Belt Boxcar, *79*	20	25	_____
[9414]	LOTS Cotton Belt Boxcar, *80 u*	—	35	_____
[9414]	Sacramento-Sierra TCA Cotton Belt Boxcar, *80 u*	—	45	_____
9415	Providence & Worcester Boxcar, *79*	15	20	_____
[9415]	NETCA Providence & Worcester Boxcar, *79 u*	25	30	_____

		Exc	New	Cond/$
9416	MD&W Boxcar, *79, 81*	15	20	_____
9417	CP Rail Boxcar, *79*	35	45	_____
9418	FARR Boxcar, *79 u*	65	75	_____
9419	Union Pacific Boxcar (FARR #2), *80*	30	37	_____
9420	B&O "Sentinel" Boxcar, *80*	25	30	_____
9421	Maine Central Boxcar, *80*	12	20	_____
9422	EJ&E Boxcar, *80*	15	25	_____
9423	NYNH&H Boxcar, *80*	15	30	_____
[9423]	NETCA NYNH&H Boxcar, *80 u*	25	30	_____
9424	TP&W Boxcar, *80*	20	25	_____
9425	British Columbia DD Boxcar, *80*	25	35	_____
9426	Chesapeake & Ohio Boxcar, *80*	25	40	_____
9427	Bay Line Boxcar, *80–81*	15	20	_____
[9427]	Sacramento-Sierra TCA Bay Line Boxcar, *81 u*	—	45	_____
9428	TP&W Boxcar, *80–81, 83 u*	35	40	_____
9429	"The Early Years" Boxcar, *80*	30	35	_____
9430	"The Standard Gauge Years" Boxcar, *80*	25	30	_____
9431	"The Prewar Years" Boxcar, *80*	25	30	_____
9432	"The Postwar Years" Boxcar, *80*	80	100	_____
9433	"The Golden Years" Boxcar, *80*	80	100	_____
9434	Joshua Lionel Cowen "The Man" Boxcar, *80 u*	60	75	_____
9435	LCCA Central of Georgia Boxcar, *81 u*	40	50	_____
9436	Burlington Boxcar, *81*	45	55	_____
9437	Northern Pacific Stock Car, *81*	36	60	_____
9438	Ontario Northland Boxcar, *81*	20	30	_____
9439	Ashley Drew & Northern Boxcar, *81*	10	20	_____
9440	Reading Boxcar, *81*	50	75	_____
9441	Pennsylvania Boxcar, *81*	65	85	_____
9442	Canadian Pacific Boxcar, *81*	15	18	_____
9443	Florida East Coast Boxcar, *81*	15	18	_____
[9443]	Southern TCA Florida East Coast Boxcar, *81 u*	—	30	_____
9444	Louisiana Midland Boxcar, *81*	15	20	_____
[9444]	Sacramento-Sierra TCA Louisiana Midland Boxcar, *82 u*	—	45	_____
9445	Vermont Northern Boxcar, *81*	15	20	_____
[9445]	NETCA Vermont Northern Boxcar, *81 u*	25	30	_____

		Exc	New	Cond/$
9446	Sabine River & Northern Boxcar, *81*	15	20	____
9447	Pullman Standard Boxcar, *81*	20	25	____
9448	Santa Fe Stock Car, *81–82*	50	60	____
9449	Great Northern Boxcar (FARR #3), *81*	40	50	____
9450	Great Northern Stock Car (FARR #3), *81 u*	90	110	____
9451	Southern Boxcar (FARR #4), *83*	40	50	____
9452	Western Pacific Boxcar, *82–83*	15	20	____
[9452]	Sacramento-Sierra TCA WP Boxcar, *83 u*	—	45	____
9453	MPA Boxcar, *82–83*	15	20	____
9454	New Hope & Ivyland Boxcar, *82–83*	15	20	____
9455	Milwaukee Road Boxcar, *82–83*	15	20	____
9456	PRR DD Boxcar (FARR #5), *84–85*	45	55	____
9460	LCCA D&TS DD Boxcar, *82 u*	35	45	____
9461	Norfolk & Southern Boxcar, *82*	35	60	____
9462	Southern Pacific Boxcar, *83–84*	20	25	____
9463	Texas & Pacific Boxcar, *83–84*	15	20	____
9464	NC&St L Boxcar, *83–84*	15	20	____
9465	Santa Fe Boxcar, *83–84*	15	25	____
9466	Wanamaker Boxcar, *82 u*	80	100	____
[9466]	Atlantic TCA Wanamaker Boxcar, *83 u*		NRS	____
9467	Tennessee World's Fair Boxcar, *82 u*	45	60	____
9468	Union Pacific DD Boxcar, *83*	50	65	____
9469	NYC "Pacemaker" Boxcar (Std. O), *84–85*	75	100	____
9470	Chicago Beltline Boxcar, *84*	15	20	____
9471	Atlantic Coast Line Boxcar, *84*	15	20	____
[9471]	Southern TCA Atlantic Coast Line Boxcar, *84 u*	—	30	____
9472	Detroit & Mackinac Boxcar, *84*	20	25	____
9473	Lehigh Valley Boxcar, *84*	20	25	____
9474	Erie-Lackawanna Boxcar, *84*	40	50	____
9475	D&H "I Love NY" Boxcar, *84 u*	25	40	____
[9475]	LCOL D&H "I Love New York" Boxcar, *85 u*	—	30	____
9476	PRR Boxcar (FARR #5), *84–85*	50	60	____
9480	MN&S Boxcar, *85–86*	15	20	____
9481	Seaboard System Boxcar, *85–86*	15	20	____
9482	Norfolk & Southern Boxcar, *85–86*	15	20	____
[9482]	Southern TCA Norfolk & Southern Boxcar, *85 u*	—	30	____
9483	Manufacturers Railway Boxcar, *85–86*	15	20	____
9484	Lionel 85th Anniversary Boxcar, *85*	30	35	____

		Exc	New	Cond/$
9486	GTW "I Love Michigan" Boxcar, *86*	15	25	_____
9486	Artrain GTW "I Love Michigan" Boxcar, *87 u*	—	400	_____
9490	Christmas Boxcar for Lionel Employees, *85 u*	—	1800	_____
9491	Christmas Boxcar, *86 u*	50	70	_____
9492	Lionel Lines Boxcar, *86*	35	40	_____
9500	Milwaukee Road Passenger Car, *73*	40	60	_____
9501	Milwaukee Road Passenger Car, *73 u, 74–76*	30	40	_____
9502	Milwaukee Road Observation Car, *73*	40	60	_____
9503	Milwaukee Road Passenger Car, *73*	40	60	_____
9504	Milwaukee Road Passenger Car, *73 u, 74–76*	30	40	_____
9505	Milwaukee Road Passenger Car, *73 u, 74–76*	30	40	_____
9506	Milwaukee Road Combination Car, *74 u, 75–76*	25	40	_____
9507	PRR Passenger Car, *74–75*	40	60	_____
9508	PRR Passenger Car, *74–75*	40	60	_____
9509	PRR Observation Car, *74–75*	50	75	_____
9510	PRR Combination Car, *74 u, 75–76*	30	40	_____
9511	Milwaukee Road Passenger Car, *74 u*	30	55	_____
9512	TTOS Summerdale Junction Passenger Car, *74 u*	40	50	_____
9513	PRR Passenger Car, *75–76*	30	50	_____
9514	PRR Passenger Car, *75–76*	30	50	_____
9515	PRR Passenger Car, *75–76*	30	50	_____
9516	B&O Passenger Car, *76*	30	50	_____
9517	B&O Passenger Car, *75*	50	75	_____
9518	B&O Observation Car, *75*	50	75	_____
9519	B&O Combination Car, *75*	50	75	_____
9520	TTOS Phoenix Combination Car, *75 u*	40	50	_____
9521	PRR Baggage Car, *75 u, 76*	100	125	_____
9522	Milwaukee Road Baggage Car, *75 u, 76*	100	125	_____
9523	B&O Baggage Car, *75 u, 76*	75	90	_____
9524	B&O Passenger Car, *76*	40	60	_____
9525	B&O Passenger Car, *76*	40	60	_____
9526	TTOS Snowbird Observation Car, *76 u*	40	50	_____
(9527)	Milwaukee Road Campaign Observation Car, *76 u*	50	60	_____
(9528)	PRR Campaign Observation Car, *76 u*	50	60	_____
(9529)	B&O Campaign Observation Car, *76 u*	50	60	_____

		Exc	New	Cond/$
9530	Southern Baggage Car, *77–78*	45	70	___
9531	Southern Combination Car, *77–78*	45	70	___
9532	Southern Passenger Car, *77–78*	45	70	___
9533	Southern Passenger Car, *77–78*	45	70	___
9534	Southern Observation Car, *77–78*	45	70	___
9535	TTOS Columbus Baggage Car, *77 u*	30	40	___
9536	Blue Comet Baggage Car, *78–80*	45	70	___
9537	Blue Comet Combination Car, *78–80*	45	70	___
9538	Blue Comet Passenger Car, *78–80*	45	70	___
9539	Blue Comet Passenger Car, *78–80*	45	70	___
9540	Blue Comet Observation Car, *78–80*	45	70	___
9541	Santa Fe Baggage Car, *80–82*	20	30	___
(9544)	TCA Chicago Observation Car "1980", *80 u*	—	75	___
9545	Union Pacific Baggage Car, *84*	100	125	___
9546	Union Pacific Combination Car, *84*	100	125	___
9547	Union Pacific Observation Car, *84*	100	125	___
(9548)	Union Pacific "Placid Bay" Passenger Car, *84*	100	125	___
(9549)	Union Pacific "Ocean Sunset" Passenger Car, *84*	100	125	___
9551	W&ARR Baggage Car, *77 u, 78–80*	45	60	___
9552	W&ARR Passenger Car, *77 u, 78–80*	45	60	___
9553	W&ARR Flatcar w/ horses, *77 u, 78–80*	30	50	___
(9554)	Chicago & Alton Baggage Car, *81*	50	75	___
(9555)	Chicago & Alton Combination Car, *81*	50	75	___
(9556)	Chicago & Alton "Wilson" Passenger Car, *81*	60	90	___
(9557)	Chicago & Alton "Webster Groves" Passenger Car, *81*	60	90	___
(9558)	Chicago & Alton Observation Car, *81*	50	75	___
9559	Rock Island Baggage Car, *81–82*	40	60	___
9560	Rock Island Passenger Car, *81–82*	40	60	___
9561	Rock Island Passenger Car, *81–82*	40	60	___
(9562)	Norfolk & Western Baggage Car "577", *81*	90	125	___
(9563)	Norfolk & Western Combination Car "578", *81*	90	125	___
(9564)	Norfolk & Western Passenger Car "579", *81*	110	150	___
(9565)	Norfolk & Western Passenger Car "580", *81*	110	150	___

		Exc	New	Cond/$
9566)	Norfolk & Western Observation Car "581", *81*	90	125	_____
9567)	Norfolk & Western Vista Dome Car "582", *81 u*	350	525	_____
9569)	PRR Combination Car, *81 u*	125	150	_____
9570)	PRR Baggage Car, *79*	125	150	_____
9571)	PRR Passenger Car, *79*	140	175	_____
9572)	PRR Passenger Car, *79*	140	175	_____
9573)	PRR Vista Dome Car, *79*	125	150	_____
9574)	PRR Observation Car, *79*	125	150	_____
9575)	PRR Passenger Car, *79–80 u*	135	175	_____
9576	Burlington Baggage Car, *80*	100	125	_____
9577	Burlington Passenger Car, *80*	100	125	_____
9578	Burlington Passenger Car, *80*	100	125	_____
9579	Burlington Vista Dome Car, *80*	100	125	_____
9580	Burlington Observation Car, *80*	100	125	_____
9581	Chessie System Baggage Car, *80*	60	75	_____
9582	Chessie System Combination Car, *80*	60	75	_____
9583	Chessie System Passenger Car, *80*	60	75	_____
9584	Chessie System Passenger Car, *80*	60	75	_____
9585	Chessie System Observation Car, *80*	60	75	_____
9586	Chessie System Dining Car, *86 u*	100	125	_____
9588	Burlington Vista Dome Car, *80 u*	125	175	_____
(9589)	Southern Pacific Baggage Car, *82–83*	100	125	_____
(9590)	Southern Pacific Combination Car, *82–83*	100	125	_____
(9591)	Southern Pacific "Pullman" Passenger Car, *82–83*	100	125	_____
(9592)	Southern Pacific "Chair" Passenger Car, *82–83*	100	125	_____
(9593)	Southern Pacific Observation Car, *82–83*	100	125	_____
9594	NYC Baggage Car, *83–84*	100	125	_____
9595	NYC Combination Car, *83–84*	100	125	_____
(9596)	NYC "Wayne County" Passenger Car, *83–84*	100	125	_____
(9597)	NYC "Hudson River" Passenger Car, *83–84*	100	125	_____
(9598)	NYC Observation Car, *83–84*	100	125	_____
(9599)	Chicago & Alton Dining Car, *86 u*	90	125	_____
9600	Chessie System Hi-cube Boxcar, *75 u, 76–77*	20	23	_____
9601	ICG Hi-cube Boxcar, *75 u, 76–77*	20	23	_____
[9601]	Gateway TCA ICG Hi-cube Boxcar, *77 u*	—	25	_____
9602	Santa Fe Hi-cube Boxcar, *75 u, 76–77*	20	23	_____

		Exc	New	Cond/$
9603	Penn Central Hi-cube Boxcar, *76–77*	20	23	____
9604	Norfolk & Western Hi-cube Boxcar, *76–77*	20	23	____
9605	NH Hi-cube Boxcar, *76–77*	20	35	____
9606	Union Pacific Hi-cube Boxcar, *76 u, 77*	20	23	____
9607	Southern Pacific Hi-cube Boxcar, *76 u, 77*	20	23	____
9608	Burlington Northern Hi-cube Boxcar, *76 u, 77*	20	23	____
9610	Frisco Hi-cube Boxcar, *77*	30	45	____
9611	TCA Boston Hi-cube Boxcar, *78 u*	35	40	____
9620	NHL Wales Boxcar, *80*	20	25	____
9621	NHL Campbell Boxcar, *80*	20	25	____
9622	NBA Western Boxcar, *80*	20	25	____
9623	NBA Eastern Boxcar, *80*	20	25	____
9624	National League Baseball Boxcar, *80*	20	25	____
9625	American League Baseball Boxcar, *80*	20	25	____
9626	Santa Fe Hi-cube Boxcar, *82–84*	15	20	____
9627	Union Pacific Hi-cube Boxcar, *82–83*	15	20	____
9628	Burlington Northern Hi-cube Boxcar, *82–84*	10	15	____
9629	Chessie System Hi-cube Boxcar, *83–84*	20	30	____
9660	Mickey Mouse Hi-cube Boxcar, *77–78*	40	50	____
9661	Goofy Hi-cube Boxcar, *77–78*	40	45	____
9662	Donald Duck Hi-cube Boxcar, *77–78*	40	50	____
9663	Dumbo Hi-cube Boxcar, *77 u, 78*	40	70	____
9664	Cinderella Hi-cube Boxcar, *77 u, 78*	55	90	____
9665	Peter Pan Hi-cube Boxcar, *77 u, 78*	50	90	____
9666	Pinocchio Hi-cube Boxcar, *78*	125	185	____
9667	Snow White Hi-cube Boxcar, *78*	350	475	____
9668	Pluto Hi-cube Boxcar, *78*	150	200	____
9669	Bambi Hi-cube Boxcar, *78 u*	60	100	____
9670	Alice In Wonderland Hi-cube Boxcar, *78 u*	50	75	____
9671	Fantasia Hi-cube Boxcar, *78 u*	50	60	____
9672	Mickey Mouse 50th Anniversary Hi-cube Boxcar, *78 u*	395	495	____
9678	TTOS Hollywood Hi-cube Boxcar, *78 u*	25	30	____
9700	Southern Boxcar, *72–73*	20	25	____
9700-1976 (See 9779)				
9701	B&O DD Boxcar, *72*	15	20	____
9701	TCA B&O DD Boxcar, *72 u*	75	100	____

		Exc	New	Cond/$
[9701]	LCCA B&O DD Boxcar, *72 u*		NRS	_____
9702	Soo Line Boxcar, *72–73*	15	20	_____
9703	CP Rail Boxcar, *72*	40	50	_____
9704	Norfolk & Western Boxcar, *72*	10	20	_____
9705	D&RGW Boxcar, *72*	12	25	_____
[9705]	Sacramento-Sierra TCA D&RGW Boxcar, *75 u*	—	50	_____
9706	C&O Boxcar, *72*	20	23	_____
9707	MKT Stock Car, *72–75*	15	23	_____
9708	U.S. Mail Boxcar, *72–75*	15	23	_____
9708	U.S. Mail Toy Fair Boxcar, *73 u*	85	100	_____
9709	BAR "State of Maine" Boxcar, *72 (SSS),* *73–74*	35	40	_____
9710	Rutland Boxcar, *72 (SSS), 73–74*	30	35	_____
9711	Southern Boxcar, *74–75*	20	23	_____
9712	B&O DD Boxcar, *73–74*	30	35	_____
9713	CP Rail Boxcar, *73–74*	20	25	_____
9713	CP Rail Season's Greetings Boxcar, *74 u*	100	125	_____
9714	D&RGW Boxcar, *73–74*	20	25	_____
9715	C&O Boxcar, *73–74*	20	23	_____
9716	Penn Central Boxcar, *73–74*	20	25	_____
9717	Union Pacific Boxcar, *73–74*	20	25	_____
9718	Canadian National Boxcar, *73–74*	20	23	_____
[9718]	LCAC Canadian National Boxcar, *79 u*		NRS	_____
9719	New Haven DD Boxcar, *73 u*	25	30	_____
9723	Western Pacific Boxcar, *73 (SSS), 74*	30	35	_____
9723	Western Pacific Toy Fair Boxcar, *74 u*	100	125	_____
[9723]	Sacramento-Sierra TCA WP Boxcar, *73 u*		NRS	_____
9724	Missouri Pacific Boxcar, *73 (SSS), 74*	32	37	_____
9725	MKT Stock Car, *73 (SSS), 74–75*	20	23	_____
[9725]	Midwest TCA Stock Car "00002", *75 u*		NRS	_____
9726	Erie-Lackawanna Boxcar, *78 (SSS)*	25	30	_____
[9726]	Sacramento-Sierra TCA Erie-Lack. Boxcar, *79 u*	—	45	_____
9727	LCCA TA&G Boxcar, *73 u*	175	195	_____
9728	LCCA Union Pacific Stock Car, *78 u*	35	40	_____
9729	CP Rail Boxcar, *78*	30	37	_____
9730	CP Rail Boxcar, *74–75*	25	30	_____
[9730]	Western Michigan TCA CP Rail Boxcar, *74 u*		NRS	_____
[9730]	Detroit-Toledo TCA CP Rail Boxcar, *76 u*	—	35	_____

		Exc	New	Cond/$
[9730]	Sacramento-Sierra TCA CP Rail Boxcar, *77 u*	—	40	___
9731	Milwaukee Road Boxcar, *74–75*	15	20	___
9732	Southern Pacific Boxcar, *79 u*	30	40	___
9733	LCCA Airco Boxcar w/ tank, *79 u*	50	65	___
9734	Bangor & Aroostook Boxcar, *79*	30	40	___
9735	Grand Trunk Boxcar, *74–75*	15	20	___
9737	Central Vermont Boxcar, *74–76*	20	23	___
9738	Illinois Terminal Boxcar, *82*	50	60	___
9739	D&RGW Boxcar, *74 (SSS), 75–76*	20	25	___
[9739]	LCCA D&RGW Boxcar, *78 u*		NRS	___
[9739]	North Texas TCA D&RGW Boxcar, *76 u*	—	25	___
9740	Chessie System Boxcar, *74–75*	15	20	___
[9740]	Great Lakes TCA Chessie System Boxcar, *76 u*	—	25	___
[9740]	WB&A TCA Chessie System Boxcar, *76 u*	—	30	___
9742	M&St L Boxcar, *73 u*	25	30	___
9742	M&St L Season's Greetings Boxcar, *73 u*	100	125	___
9743	Sprite Boxcar, *74 u, 75*	15	23	___
9744	Tab Boxcar, *74 u, 75*	15	23	___
9745	Fanta Boxcar, *74 u, 75*	15	23	___
9747	Chessie System DD Boxcar, *75–76*	25	30	___
9748	CP Rail Boxcar, *75–76*	20	23	___
9749	Penn Central Boxcar, *75–76*	15	20	___
9750	DT&I Boxcar, *75–76*	10	20	___
9751	Frisco Boxcar, *75–76*	20	25	___
9752	L&N Boxcar, *75–76*	15	20	___
9753	Maine Central Boxcar, *75–76*	15	23	___
[9753]	NETCA Maine Central Boxcar, *75 u*	25	35	___
9754	NYC "Pacemaker" Boxcar, *75 (SSS), 76–77*	30	45	___
[9754]	METCA NYC "Pacemaker" Boxcar, *76 u*	—	35	___
9755	Union Pacific Boxcar, *75–76*	20	25	___
9757	Central of Georgia Boxcar, *74 u*	20	25	___
9758	Alaska Boxcar, *75 (SSS), 76–77*	30	40	___
9759	Paul Revere Boxcar, *75 u*	40	50	___
9760	Liberty Bell Boxcar, *75 u*	40	50	___
9761	George Washington Boxcar, *75 u*	40	50	___
(9762)	Toy Fair Boxcar, *75 u*	150	200	___
9763	D&RGW Stock Car, *76–77*	20	25	___
9764	GTW DD Boxcar, *76–77*	20	23	___
9767	Railbox Boxcar, *76–77*	25	30	___

		Exc	New	Cond/$
[9767]	Gateway TCA Railbox Boxcar, *78 u*	—	30	_____
9768	B&M Boxcar, *76–77*	20	23	_____
[9768]	NETCA B&M Boxcar, *76 u*	25	30	_____
9769	B&LE Boxcar, *76–77*	15	20	_____
9770	Northern Pacific Boxcar, *76–77*	15	20	_____
9771	Norfolk & Western Boxcar, *76–77*	15	20	_____
[9771]	LCCA N&W Boxcar, *77 u*		NRS	_____
[9771]	TCA Museum N&W Boxcar, *77 u*	30	40	_____
[9771]	WB&A TCA N&W Boxcar, *78 u*	—	30	_____
9772	Great Northern Boxcar, *76*	70	75	_____
9773	NYC Stock Car, *76*	25	30	_____
9774	TCA Orlando Southern Belle Boxcar, *75 u*	30	45	_____
9775	M&St L Boxcar, *76 (SSS)*	25	35	_____
9776	Southern Pacific "Overnight" Boxcar, *76 (SSS)*	50	60	_____
9777	Virginian Boxcar, *76–77*	20	25	_____
9778	Season's Greetings Boxcar, *75 u*	150	200	_____
(9779)	TCA Philadelphia Boxcar "9700-1976", *76 u*	35	40	_____
9780	Johnny Cash Boxcar, *76 u*	25	35	_____
9781	Delaware & Hudson Boxcar, *77–78*	20	25	_____
9782	Rock Island Boxcar, *77–78*	20	23	_____
9783	B&O "Time-Saver" Boxcar, *77–78*	35	40	_____
[9783]	WB&A TCA B&O "Time-Saver" Boxcar, *77 u*	—	30	_____
9784	Santa Fe Boxcar, *77–78*	25	35	_____
9785	Conrail Boxcar, *77–78*	20	25	_____
[9785]	Midwest TCA Museum Express Conrail Boxcar, *77 u*		NRS	_____
[9785]	NETCA Conrail Boxcar, *78 u*	25	30	_____
[9785]	Sacramento-Sierra TCA Conrail Boxcar, *78 u*	—	35	_____
9786	C&NW Boxcar, *77–79*	20	30	_____
[9786]	Midwest TCA Museum Express C&NW Boxcar, *79 u*		NRS	_____
9787	Jersey Central Boxcar, *77–79*	20	30	_____
9788	Lehigh Valley Boxcar, *77–79*	15	20	_____
[9788]	Atlantic TCA Lehigh Valley Boxcar, *78 u*	20	25	_____
9789	Pickens Boxcar, *77*	30	50	_____
9801	B&O "Sentinel" Boxcar (Std. O), *73–75*	50	60	_____
9802	Miller High Life Reefer (Std. O), *73–75*	45	50	_____
9803	Johnson Wax Boxcar (Std. O), *73–75*	40	45	_____

		Exc	New	Cond/$
9805	Grand Trunk Reefer (Std. O), *73–75*	40	45	_____
9806	Rock Island Boxcar (Std. O), *74–75*	65	95	_____
9807	Stroh's Beer Reefer (Std. O), *74–76*	75	115	_____
9808	Union Pacific Boxcar (Std. O), *75–76*	65	95	_____
9809	Clark Reefer (Std. O), *75–76*	40	45	_____
9811	Pacific Fruit Express Reefer (FARR #2), *80*	30	40	_____
9812	Arm & Hammer Reefer, *80*	20	23	_____
9813	Ruffles Reefer, *80*	20	23	_____
9814	Perrier Reefer, *80*	25	35	_____
9815	NYC "Early Bird" Reefer (Std. O), *84–85*	65	75	_____
9816	Brach's Candy Reefer, *80*	20	23	_____
9817	Bazooka Gum Reefer, *80*	20	23	_____
9818	Western Maryland Reefer, *80*	30	40	_____
9819	Western Fruit Express Reefer (FARR #3), *81*	30	40	_____
9820	Wabash Gondola w/ coal load (Std. O), *73–74*	45	55	_____
9821	Southern Pacific Gondola w/ coal load (Std. O), *73–75*	45	55	_____
9822	Grand Trunk Gondola w/ coal load (Std. O), *74–75*	45	55	_____
9823	Santa Fe Flatcar w/ crates (Std. O), *75–76*	65	95	_____
9824	NYC Gondola w/ coal load (Std. O), *75–76*	55	85	_____
9825	Schaefer Reefer (Std. O), *76–77*	60	80	_____
9826	P&LE Boxcar (Std. O), *76–77*	100	125	_____
9827	Cutty Sark Reefer, *84*	23	27	_____
9828	J&B Reefer, *84*	23	27	_____
9829	Dewar's White Label Reefer, *84*	23	27	_____
9830	Johnnie Walker Red Label Reefer, *84*	23	27	_____
9831	Pepsi Cola Reefer, *82*	50	70	_____
9832	Cheerios Reefer, *82*	100	125	_____
9833	Vlasic Pickles Reefer, *82*	20	25	_____
9834	Southern Comfort Reefer, *83–84*	20	27	_____
9835	Jim Beam Reefer, *83–84*	20	27	_____
9836	Old Grand-Dad Reefer, *83–84*	20	27	_____
9837	Wild Turkey Reefer, *83–84*	20	27	_____
9840	Fleischmann's Gin Reefer, *85*	23	27	_____
9841	Calvert Gin Reefer, *85*	23	27	_____
9842	Seagram's Gin Reefer, *85*	23	27	_____
9843	Tanqueray Gin Reefer, *85*	23	27	_____
9844	Sambuca Reefer, *86*	20	25	_____

		Exc	New	Cond/$
9845	Baileys Irish Cream Reefer, *86*	23	27	_____
9846	Seagram's Vodka Reefer, *86*	20	25	_____
9847	Wolfschmidt Vodka Reefer, *86*	20	25	_____
9849	Lionel Lines Reefer, *83 u*	60	75	_____
9850	Budweiser Reefer, *72 u, 73–75*	30	40	_____
9851	Schlitz Reefer, *72 u, 73–75*	23	27	_____
9852	Miller Reefer, *72 u, 73–77*	23	27	_____
9853	Cracker Jack Reefer, caramel, *72 u, 73–75*	30	35	_____
9853	Cracker Jack Reefer, white, *72 u, 73–75*	15	20	_____
9854	Baby Ruth Reefer, *72 u, 73–76*	15	20	_____
9855	Swift Reefer, *72 u, 73–77*	20	27	_____
9856	Old Milwaukee Reefer, *75–76*	20	27	_____
9858	Butterfinger Reefer, *73 u, 74–76*	25	30	_____
9859	Pabst Reefer, *73 u, 74–75*	25	35	_____
9860	Gold Medal Reefer, *73 u, 74–76*	20	23	_____
9861	Tropicana Reefer, *75–77*	25	35	_____
9862	Hamm's Reefer, *75–76*	25	27	_____
9863	REA Reefer, *74 (SSS), 75–76*	30	35	_____
9864	TCA Seattle Reefer, *74 u*	35	45	_____
9866	Coors Reefer, *76–77*	30	40	_____
9867	Hershey's Reefer, *76–77*	40	50	_____
9868	TTOS Oklahoma City Reefer, *80 u*	40	50	_____
9869	Santa Fe Reefer, *76 (SSS)*	40	50	_____
9870	Old Dutch Cleanser Reefer, *77–78, 80*	15	20	_____
9871	Carlings Black Label Reefer, *77–78, 80*	30	35	_____
9872	Pacific Fruit Express Reefer, *77–79*	25	30	_____
[9872]	Midwest TCA PFE Reefer, *79 u*		NRS	_____
9873	Ralston Purina Reefer, *78*	30	45	_____
9874	Miller Lite Beer Reefer, *78–79*	30	40	_____
9875	A&P Reefer, *78–79*	25	35	_____
9876	Central Vermont Reefer, *78*	40	50	_____
9877	Gerber Reefer, *79–80*	50	60	_____
9878	Good and Plenty Reefer, *79*	20	25	_____
9879	Hills Brothers Reefer, *79–80*	20	25	_____
9879	Kraft Reefer, *79 u*		NM	
9880	Santa Fe Reefer (FARR #1), *79*	40	45	_____
9881	Rath Packing Reefer, *79 u*	35	40	_____
9882	NYC "Early Bird" Reefer, *79*	35	45	_____
9883	Nabisco Oreo Reefer, *79*	60	70	_____

		Exc	New	Cond/$
[9883]	TTOS Phoenix Reefer, *83 u*		NRS	___
9884	Fritos Reefer, *81–82*	20	25	___
9885	Lipton Tea Reefer, *81–82*	20	25	___
9886	Mounds Reefer, *81–82*	20	25	___
9887	Fruit Growers Express Reefer (FARR #4), *83*	45	60	___
9888	Green Bay & Western Reefer, *83*	60	75	___
16800	Lionel Railroader Club Ore Car, *86 u*	80	100	___
25000	(See 6476-135)			
[80948]	LOTS Michigan Central Boxcar, *82 u*	100	175	___
[86009]	LCAC CN Bunk Car, *86 u*	—	130	___
97330	(See 9733)			
100408	(See 6567)			
[121315]	LOTS PRR Hi-cube Boxcar, *84 u*	75	100	___
[830005]	LCAC CN Boxcar, *83 u*		NRS	___
[840006]	LCAC Canadian Wheat Board Covered Quad Hopper, *84 u*	—	160	___
79C95204C	Sears Santa Fe Diesel set, *71 u*		NRS	___
79C97101C	Sears 5-unit set, *71 u*		NRS	___
79C9715C	Sears 4-unit set, *75 u*		NRS	___
79C9717C	Sears 7-unit set, *75 u*		NRS	___
79N9552C	Sears 6-unit set, *72 u*		NRS	___
79N9553C	Sears 6-unit Diesel set, *72 u*		NRS	___
79N95223C	Sears 6-unit set, *74 u*		NRS	___
79N96178C	Sears 4-unit set, *74 u*		NRS	___
79N97082C	Sears set, *70 u*		NRS	___
79N97101C	Sears 5-unit set, *75 u*		NRS	___
79N98765C	Sears Logging Empire set, *78 u*		NRS	___
UCS	Remote Control Track (O), *70*	5	8	___
No Number	B&A Hudson and Standard O cars set, *86 u*	1900	2200	___
No Number	The Blue Comet set, *78–80, 87 u*	700	800	___
No Number	Burlington "Texas Zephyr" set, *80, 80 u*	1300	1500	___
No Number	Jersey Central set, *86*	425	500	___
No Number	Chessie System Special set, *80, 86 u*	750	950	___
No Number	Chicago & Alton Limited set, *81, 86 u*	750	950	___
No Number	Favorite Food Freight set, *81–82*	275	325	___
No Number	The General set, *77–80*	275	300	___
No Number	Great Northern set (FARR #3), *81, 81 u*	800	900	___

	Exc	New	Cond/$
No Number Illinois Central "City of New Orleans" set, *85, 87, 93*	1300	1500	_____
No Number Joshua Lionel Cowen set, *80, 80 u, 82*	700	750	_____
No Number Lionel Lines set, *82–84 u, 86, 86–87 u, 94–95*	650	800	_____
No Number Mickey Mouse Express set, *77–78, 78 u*	1700	2000	_____
No Number The Mint set, *79 u, 80–83, 84 u, 86 u, 87, 91 u, 93*	1200	1400	_____
No Number NYC "20th Century Limited" set, *83, 83 u, 95*	1300	1500	_____
No Number N&W "Powhatan Arrow" set, *81, 81 u, 82 u, 91 u*	2000	2400	_____
No Number PRR set, *79–80, 79–80 u, 81 u, 83 u*	1500	1700	_____
No Number PRR set (FARR #5), *84–85, 89 u*	750	900	_____
No Number Rock Island & Peoria set, *80–82*	250	325	_____
No Number Santa Fe set (FARR #1), *79, 79 u*	600	750	_____
No Number Southern set (FARR #4), *83, 83 u*	850	1000	_____
No Number Southern Crescent Limited set, *77–78, 87 u*	600	700	_____
No Number Southern Pacific Daylight Diesel set, *82–83, 82–83 u, 90 u*	2800	3000	_____
No Number The Spirit of '76 set, *74–76*	625	700	_____
No Number Toys "R" Us Thunderball Freight set, *75 u*		NRS	_____
No Number Union Pacific set (FARR #2), *80, 80 u*	700	800	_____
No Number Union Pacific "Overland Route" set, *84, 92 u*	1000	1400	_____
No Number Wabash set (FF #1), *86, 87*	1000	1200	_____
No Number L.A.S.E.R. Playmat, *81–82*	—	10	_____
No Number Cannonball Freight Playmat, *81–82*	—	10	_____
No Number Station Platform, *83–84*	—	10	_____
No Number Rocky Mountain Platform, *83–84*	—	10	_____
No Number Commando Assault Train Playmat, *83–84*	—	10	_____
No Number Black Cave Flyer Playmat, *82*	—	10	_____
[No Number] Pacific Northwest TCA F-3 AA, shells only, *74 u*	—	75	_____
[No Number] LCCA Lionel Lines Tender only, *76–77 u*	25	30	_____
[No Number] Lone Star TCA Texas Special F-3 A Unit, shell only, *81 u*		NRS	_____

[No Number] Lone Star TCA Texas Special F-3 B Unit,
     shell only, *82 u*   NRS _____
[No Number] Sacramento-Sierra TCA Lionel Lines
     Tender, shell only, *84 u*   NRS _____
[No Number] Atlantic TCA Pennsylvania Reading
     Seashore Bunk Car, *85 u*   65   80 _____

4	(See 18008, 18013)
T-4	(See 12923)
5	(See 18023)
12	(See 16137, 52029)
14	(See 52032)
27	(See 18841)
29	(See 52039)
36	(See 19042)
40	(See 11737)
52	(See 18555)
55-00637	(See 18927)
74	(See 19718)
91	(See 18558)
102	(See 19538)
109	(See 11809)
121	(See 19717)
125	(See 19724)
150	(See 18553)
154	(See 18223)
155	(See 18224)
190	(See 17899)
197	(See 18843)
200	(See 18117/ 18118)
200A	(See 18121)
200B	(See 18122)
0200	(See 18512)
202	(See 18506)
203	(See 18506)
211	(See 19136)
217	(See 19715)
250	(See 18512)
254	(See 18920)
260	(See 19133)
300	(See 17307, 18934/ 18935)
300	(See 19719)
301	(See 16807, 17308)

302	(See 17309)
303	(See 17310)
304	(See 18934/ 18935)
342	(See 11903)
342B	(See 11903)
343	(See 11903)
351C	(See 11724)
366A	(See 11724)
370B	(See 11724)
371	(See 18907)
371B	(See 18108)
400	(See 18505)
401	(See 18505)
425	(See 19135)
469	(See 19132)
483	(See 18306)
484	(See 18310)
485	(See 18310)
490	(See 18043)
494	(See 19140)
495	(See 19141)
501	(See 17213)
504	(See 18504)
507	(See 19128)
537	(See 19143)
538	(See 19142)
539	(See 16539)
576	(See 19108)
577	(See 19139)
582	(See 19144)
600	(See 18824)
601	(See 19111)
612	(See 18040)
618	(See 18042)
619	(See 18041)
638	(See 18638)
639	(See 18639)
672	(See 8610)
680	(See 51229)

		Exc	New	Cond/$
681	(See 51240)			
684	(See 51233)			
685	(See 51245)			
700	(See 18046)			
721	(See 18554)			
725A	(See 11734)			
725B	(See 11734)			
736A	(See 11734)			
785	(See 18002)			
788	(See 19818)			
789	(See 19134)			
858	(See 18116)			
859	(See 18116)			
863	(See 18309)			
868	(See 18842)			
901	(See 19532)			
907	(See 16566, 18024)			
914	(See 17893)			
1017	(See 18921)			
1041	(See 16538)			
1115	(See 19040)			
1116	(See 19041)			
1192	(See 19120)			
1200	(See 19116)			
1201	(See 18022)			
1212	(See 19118)			
1240	(See 19117)			
1289	(See 17875)			
1322	(See 19119)			
1390	(See 18044)			
1403	(See 19145)			
1458	(See 52031)			
1501	(See 18003)			
1538	(See 18838)			
1552	(See 52007)			
1602)	Nickel Plate Special set, *86–91*	150	175	_____
1615)	Cannonball Express set, *86–90*	85	95	_____
1623	(See 19146)			
1685)	True Value Freight Flyer set, *86–87 u*	80	100	_____

		Exc	New	Cond/$
(1687)	Freight Flyer set, *87–90*	50	60	____
1750	(See 52035)			
1754	(See 52037)			
1803	(See 19147)			
1815	(See 18815)			
1818	(See 18931)			
1821	(See 18840)			
1900	(See 18502)			
1905-95	(See 16953)			
1921	(See 52047)			
1947	(See 18830)			
1952	(See 19960)			
1960	(See 18943)			
1987	(See 16205, 16310, 16311, 16507, 18605)			
[1988]	Midwest TCA IC Boxcar, *88 u*		NRS	____
1989	(See 16110, 17879, 18614)			
1990	(See 17883, 18090, 19708)			
1992	(See 18818)			
1993	(See 16655, 18713, 19927)			
1993X	(See 52008)			
1994	(See 52043, 52050)			
1995	(See 19934, 19935, 52062)			
1996	(See (52079, 52085)			
2000	(See 18710, 18711, 18712, 19131)			
2100	(See 18006)			
2101	(See 18011, 18557)			
2110	Graduated Trestle set (22), *70–88*	10	15	____
2111	Elevated Trestle set (10), *70–88*	10	15	____
(2113)	Tunnel Portals (2), *84–87*	10	15	____
(2115)	Dwarf Signal, *84–87*	13	15	____
(2117)	Block Target Signal, *84–87*	20	25	____
(2122)	Extension Bridge w/ rock piers, *76–87*	30	40	____
2126	Whistling Freight Shed, *76–87*	25	30	____
2127	Diesel Horn Shed, *76–87*	25	30	____
2154	Automatic Highway Flasher, *70–87*	20	25	____
2162	Automatic Crossing Gate and Signal, *70–87, 94, 96*		CP	____
(2170)	Street Lamps (3), *70–87*	15	20	____

LTI MODERN ERA (1987–1996)

	Exc	New	Cond/$
(2180) Road Signs (16), *77–95*		CP	_____
(2181) Telephone Poles (10), *77–95*		CP	_____
2184 (See 17218)			
2214 Girder Bridge, *70–71, 72 u, 73–87*	5	10	_____
2283 Die-cast Bumpers (2), *84–95*		CP	_____
2283 (See 52039)			
2292 Station Platform, *85–87*	6	10	_____
(2300) Operating Oil Drum Loader, *83–87*	100	140	_____
(2309) Mechanical Crossing Gate, *82–92*	4	8	_____
(2311) Mechanical Semaphore, *82–92*	4	8	_____
2320 Flagpole kit, *83–87*	10	15	_____
2321 Operating Sawmill, *84, 86–87*	100	120	_____
2323 Operating Freight Station, *84–87*	80	100	_____
2324 Operating Switch Tower, *84–87*	70	85	_____
2400 (See 18305)			
2401 (See 18304)			
2402 (See 18304)			
2403 (See 18305)			
2487 (See 18833)			
2504 (See 19150)			
2601 (See 52023)			
2626 (See 18016)			
(2709) Rico Station kit, *81–95*		CP	_____
(2716) Short Extension Bridge, *88–95*		CP	_____
(2717) Short Extension Bridge, *77–87*	3	5	_____
(2719) Watchman's Shanty kit, *77–87*	3	5	_____
(2720) Lumber Shed kit, *77–84, 87*	3	5	_____
(2784) Freight Platform kit, *81–90*	6	9	_____
2848 (See 12848)			
(2900) Lockon, *70–95*		CP	_____
(2901) Track Clips (12) (O27), *71–95*		CP	_____
2902 (See 12902)			
2903 (See 18630)			
(2905) Lockon and Wire, *74–95*		CP	_____
2909 Smoke Fluid, *70–95*		CP	_____
2910 OTC Contactor, *84–86, 88*	4	8	_____
(2927) Maintenance kit, *70, 78–95*		CP	_____
2930 (See 12930)			
2956 (See 19721)			

		Exc	New	Cond/$
(2985)	The Lionel Train Book, *86–95*		CP	____
3000	(See 18009, 33000)			
3004	(See 33004)			
3005	(See 33005)			
3010	(See 23010)			
3011	(See 23011)			
3158	(See 18034)			
3285	(See 16805)			
3400	(See 19109)			
3500	(See 19110)			
3768	(See 18028)			
4000	(See 18812, 18825)			
4002	(See 18211)			
4004	(See 18218)			
4023	(See 52030)			
04039	(See 16908)			
04040	(See 16939)			
4060	Power Master Transformer, *80–93*	15	25	____
4060	(See 18831)			
4100	(See 18030)			
4124	(See 18514)			
4136	(See 18819)			
4410	(See 18007)			
4501	(See 18018)			
4574	(See 18306)			
4600	(See 18816)			
4690	MW Transformer, *86–89*	75	95	____
4851	DC Transformer, *85–91, 94–95*		CP	____
4866	(See 18308)			
4907	(See 18313)			
(5012)	Curved Track 27", card of 4 (O27), *70–95*		CP	____
(5014)	Half-Curved Track 27" (O27), *70–95*		CP	____
(5016)	36" Straight Track (O27), *87–88*	2	3	____
(5017)	Straight Track, card of 4 (O27), *70–95*		CP	____
5017	(See 51230)			
(5019)	Half-Straight Track (O27), *70–95*		CP	____
5020	90° Crossover (O27), *70–95*		CP	____
5020	(See 51234)			
(5021)	Left Manual Switch 27" (O27), *70–95*		CP	____

		Exc	New	Cond/$
(5022)	Right Manual Switch 27" (027), *70–95*		CP	_____
5023	45° Crossover (027), *70–95*		CP	_____
(5024)	35" Straight Track (027), *88–95*		CP	_____
(5033)	Curved Track 27" (027), *79–95*		CP	_____
(5038)	Straight Track (027), *79–95*		CP	_____
(5041)	Insulator Pins (12) (027), *70–95*		CP	_____
(5042)	Steel Pins (12) (027), *70–95*		CP	_____
(5044)	Curved Track Ballast 42" (027), *88*		NM	
(5045)	Curved Track Ballast 54" (027), *87–88*	1	2	_____
(5046)	Curved Track Ballast 27" (027), *87–88*	1	2	_____
(5047)	Straight Track Ballast (027), *87–88*	1	2	_____
(5049)	Curved Track 42" (027), *88–95*		CP	_____
5100	(See 18001)			
(5113)	Curved Track 54" (027), *79–95*		CP	_____
5121	Left Remote Switch 27" (027), *70–95*		CP	_____
5122	Right Remote Switch 27" (027), *70–95*		CP	_____
5132	Right Remote Switch 31" (O), *80–94*	30	40	_____
5133	Left Remote Switch 31" (O), *80–94*	30	40	_____
(5149)	Remote Uncoupling Section (027), *70–95*		CP	_____
5165	Right Remote Switch 72" (O), *87–95*		CP	_____
5166	Left Remote Switch 72" (O), *87–95*		CP	_____
5167	Right Remote Switch 42" (027), *88–95*		CP	_____
5168	Left Remote Switch 42" (027), *88–95*		CP	_____
5300	(See 18636)			
5340	(See 18005, 18012)			
5366	(See 52078)			
5450	(See 18026, 18027, 18029)			
(5500)	Straight Track (O), *71–95*		CP	_____
5500	(See 18216)			
(5501)	Curved Track 31" (O), *71–95*		CP	_____
(5504)	Half-Curved Track 31" (O), *83–95*		CP	_____
(5505)	Half-Straight Track (O), *83–95*		CP	_____
5512	(See 18221)			
5517	(See 18222)			
(5522)	36" Straight Track (O), *87–88*	3	4	_____
(5523)	40" Straight Track (O), *88–95*		CP	_____
5530	Remote Uncoupling Section (O), *81–95*		CP	_____
5540	90° Crossover (O), *81–95*		CP	_____
(5543)	Insulator Pins (12) (O), *70–95*		CP	_____

LTI MODERN ERA (1987–1996)

		Exc	New	Cond/$
5545	45° Crossover (O), *83–95*		CP	_____
(5551)	Steel Pins (12) (O), *70–95*		CP	_____
(5554)	Curved Track 54" (O), *90–95*		CP	_____
(5560)	Curved Track Ballast 72" (O), *87–88*	1	2	_____
(5561)	Curved Track Ballast 31" (O), *87–88*	1	2	_____
(5562)	Straight Track Ballast (O), *87–88*	1	2	_____
(5572)	Curved Track 72" (O), *79–95*		CP	_____
5658	(See 16559)			
[5731]	TCA Museum L&N Reefer, *90 u*	100	150	_____
5800	(See 18836)			
5808	(See 18826)			
6001	(See 18107)			
6002	(See 18107)			
6003	(See 17611)			
6005	(See 18821)			
6006	(See 18210)			
6007	(See 18217)			
6061	(See 16061)			
6062	(See 16062)			
6063	(See 16063)			
6064	(See 16064)			
6065	(See 16065)			
6066	(See 16066)			
6067	(See 16067)			
6068	(See 16068)			
6069	(See 16069)			
6070	(See 16070)			
6071	(See 16071)			
6072	(See 16072)			
6073	(See 16073)			
6074	(See 16074)			
6080	(See 16080)			
6081	(See 16081)			
6082	(See 16082)			
6083	(See 16083)			
6084	(See 16084)			
6086	(See 16086)			
6087	(See 16087)			
6088	(See 16088)			

		Exc	New	Cond/$
6089	(See 16089)			
6090	(See 16090)			
6108	(See 16108)			
6137	NKP Hopper (027), *86–91*	15	20	____
6150	Santa Fe Hopper (027), *85–86, 92 u*	12	18	____
6177	Reading Hopper (027), *86–90*	15	20	____
6200	(See 18010)			
6226	(See 16226)			
6254	NKP Gondola w/ canisters, *86–91*	10	12	____
6258	Santa Fe Gondola w/ canisters (027), *85–86, 92 u*	—	6	____
6336	(See 16336)			
6408	(See 16408)			
6430	Santa Fe SP-Type Caboose, *83–89*	6	10	____
6464	(See 19248, 19249, 19250, 19258, 19269, 19275)			
6464-095	(See 52051)			
6464-100	(See 19259, 19260)			
6464-125	(See 19267, 52063)			
6464-150	(See 19268, 52064)			
6464-225	(See 19274)			
6464-275	(See 19273)			
6464-555	(See 52081)			
6464-1895	(See 52058)			
6464-1972	(See 52086)			
6464-1993	(See 52009)			
6464-1995	(See 52057)			
6464-1996	(See 52087)			
6493	L&C B/W Caboose, *86–87*	25	40	____
6508	(See 16508)			
6528	(See 16528)			
6576	Santa Fe Flatcar w/ fences (027), *92 u*	8	12	____
6585	PRR Flatcar w/ fences (027), *86–90*	5	10	____
6602	(See 16053)			
6603	(See 16054)			
6609	(See 16079)			
6616	(See 16052, 16077)			
6620	(See 16050, 16075)			
6630	(See 16051, 16076)			
6919	Nickel Plate Road SP-Type Caboose, *86–91*	5	10	____
6921	PRR SP-Type Caboose, *86–90*	5	10	____

		Exc	New	Cond/$
7000	(See 51301)			
7200	(See 19415)			
7220	Illinois Central Baggage Car, *85, 87*	100	125	____
7221	Illinois Central Combination Car, *85, 87*	100	125	____
7222	Illinois Central Passenger Car, *85, 87*	100	125	____
7223	Illinois Central Passenger Car, *85, 87*	100	125	____
7224	Illinois Central Dining Car, *85, 87*	100	125	____
7225	Illinois Central Observation Car, *85, 87*	100	125	____
7227	Wabash Dining Car (FF #1), *86–87*	100	115	____
7228	Wabash Baggage Car (FF #1), *86–87*	100	115	____
7229	Wabash Combination Car (FF #1), *86–87*	100	115	____
7230	Wabash Passenger Car (FF #1), *86–87*	100	115	____
7231	Wabash Passenger Car (FF #1), *86–87*	100	115	____
7232	Wabash Observation Car (FF #1), *86–87*	100	115	____
7420	(See 18513)			
7500	(See 18214)			
7613	(See 17613)			
7643	(See 18215)			
[7692-1]	VTC Baggage Car (O27), *92 u*	30	35	____
[7692-2]	VTC Combination Car (O27), *92 u*	30	35	____
[7692-3]	VTC Dining Car (O27), *92 u*	30	35	____
[7692-4]	VTC Passenger Car (O27), *92 u*	30	35	____
[7692-5]	VTC Vista Dome Car (O27), *92 u*	30	35	____
[7692-6]	VTC Passenger Car (O27), *92 u*	30	35	____
[7692-7]	VTC Observation Car (O27), *92 u*	30	35	____
7694	(See 52060)			
7805	(See 16078)			
7890	(See 17303)			
7914	Toys "R" Us Giraffe Car (O27), *85–89 u*	75	100	____
7925	Erie-Lackawanna Boxcar (O27), *86–90*	8	12	____
7926	NKP Boxcar (O27), *86–91*	8	11	____
7930	True Value Boxcar (O27), *86–87 u*	40	60	____
7932	Kay Bee Toys Boxcar (O27), *86–87 u*	40	50	____
8004	(See 18004)			
8014	(See 18014)			
8100	(See 11711)			
8101	(See 11711)			
8102	(See 11711)			
8103	(See 18103)			

		Exc	New	Cond/$
8119	(See 18119/18120)			
8120	(See 18119/18120)			
8124	(See 51300)			
8200	(See 18200)			
8201	(See 18201)			
8203	(See 18203)			
8204	(See 18204)			
8206	(See 18206)			
8209	(See 18209)			
8212	(See 18212)			
8213	D&RGW 2-4-2, *82–83, 84–91 u*	60	70	_____
8223	(See 18835)			
8300	(See 18300)			
8301	(See 18301)			
8302	(See 18302)			
8303	(See 18303)			
8311	(See 18311)			
[8389]	NLOE Long Island Boxcar, *89 u*	50	60	_____
[8390]	NLOE Long Island Covered Quad Hopper, *90 u*	40	50	_____
[8391A]	NLOE Long Island Bunk Car, *91 u*	30	35	_____
[8391B]	NLOE Long Island Tool Car, *91 u*	30	35	_____
8392	NLOE Long Island 1-D Tank Car, *92 u*	50	60	_____
8393	(See 52019, 52020)			
8394	(See 52026)			
8395	(See 52061)			
8396	(See 52076)			
8400	(See 18400)			
8404	(See 18404)			
8419	(See 18419)			
8446	(See 18832)			
8459	(See 18202)			
8500	(See 18500, 18550)			
8501	(See 18219, 18501)			
8502	(See 18220)			
8503	(See 18503)			
8578	NYC Ballast Tamper, *85, 87*	120	130	_____
8580/ 8582	Illinois Central F-3 AA set, *85, 87*	400	450	_____
8581	Illinois Central F-3 B Unit, *85, 87*	175	200	_____

133

		Exc	New	Cond/$
8586	(See 18208)			
8600	(See 18600)			
8601	(See 18601)			
8602	(See 18602)			
8604	(See 18604)			
8606	(See 18606)			
8607	(See 18607)			
8608	(See 18608)			
8609	(See 18609)			
(8610)	Wabash 4-6-2 "672" (FF #1), *86–87*	500	600	_____
8610	(See 18610)			
8611	(See 18611)			
8612	(See 18612)			
8613	(See 18613)			
8615	(See 18615)			
8616	(See 18616)			
8617	Nickel Plate Road 4-4-2, *86–91*	65	75	_____
8618	(See 18618)			
8620	(See 18620)			
8621	(See 18621)			
8622	(See 18622)			
8623	(See 18623)			
8625	Pennsylvania 2-4-0, *86–90*	25	40	_____
8625	(See 18625, 18635)			
8626	(See 18626)			
8627	(See 18627)			
8628	(See 18628)			
8632	(See 18632)			
8633	(See 18627, 18633, 18637)			
8640	(See 18640)			
8641	(See 18641)			
8642	(See 18642)			
8688	(See 18213)			
8689	(See 18207)			
8699	(See 18307)			
8700	(See 18700)			
8702	(See 18702)			
8704	(See 18704)			
8705	(See 18705)			

		Exc	New	Cond/$
8706	(See 18706)			
8707	(See 18707)			
8716	(See 18716)			
8800	(See 18800)			
8801	(See 18801)			
8802	(See 18802)			
8803	(See 18803)			
8804	(See 18804)			
8805	(See 18805, 18890)			
8806	(See 18806)			
8807	(See 18807)			
8808	(See 18808)			
8809	(See 18551)			
8810	(See 18810)			
8811	(See 18811)			
8813	(See 18552)			
8814	(See 18814)			
8820	(See 18820)			
8827	(See 18827)			
8834	(See 18834)			
8837	(See 18837)			
8900	(See 18900)			
8901	(See 18901/ 18902)			
8902	ACL 2-4-0, *79–82, 86 u, 87–90*	15	20	____
8902	(See 18901/ 18902)			
8903	(See 18903/ 18904)			
8904	(See 18903/ 18904)			
8906	(See 18906)			
8908	(See 18908/ 18909)			
8909	(See 18908/ 18909)			
8910	(See 18910)			
8911	(See 18911)			
[8912]	LCAC Canada Southern Operating Hopper, *89 u*	—	125	____
8912	(See 18912)			
8913	(See 18913)			
8915	(See 18915)			
8916	(See 18916)			
8918	(See 18918)			
8919	(See 18919)			

135

		Exc	New	Cond/$
8922	(See 18922)			
8923	(See 18923)			
8924	(See 18924)			
8925	(See 18925)			
8926	(See 18926)			
8932	(See 18932)			
8933	(See 18933)			
8936	(See 18936)			
8937	(See 18937)			
8977	(See 18000)			
9001	Conrail Boxcar (O27), *86–87 u, 88–90*	5	10	___
9011	(See 19011)			
9015	(See 19015)			
9016	Chessie System Hopper (O27), *75–79, 87–88, 89 u*	5	7	___
9016	(See 19016)			
9017	(See 19017)			
9018	(See 19018)			
9019	(See 19019)			
9023	(See 19023)			
9024	(See 19024)			
9025	(See 19025)			
9026	(See 19026)			
9027	(See 19027)			
9031	NKP Gondola w/ canisters (O27), *73–75, 82–83, 84–91 u*	5	7	___
9031	(See 19031)			
9032	(See 19032)			
9033	PC Gondola w/ canisters (O27), *76–78, 82, 86 u, 87–90, 92 u*	3	4	___
9033	(See 19033)			
9047	(See 19047)			
9048	(See 19048)			
9049	(See 19049)			
9050	(See 19050)			
9077	D&RGW SP-Type Caboose, *76–83, 84–91 u*	6	8	___
9100	(See 18205, 19100)			
9101	(See 19101)			
9102	(See 19102)			
9103	(See 19103)			

		Exc	New	Cond/$
9104	(See 19104)			
9105	(See 19105)			
9106	(See 19106)			
9107	Dr Pepper Vat Car, *86–87*	25	35	_____
9121	(See 19121)			
9129	(See 19129)			
9140	Burlington Gondola w/ canisters, *70, 73–82, 87–89*	6	8	_____
9146	(See 19821)			
9215	(See 52004)			
9240	NYC Hopper (O27), *87 u*	20	25	_____
9288	(See 18844)			
9312	(See 18905)			
8341	ACL SP-Type Caboose, *86 u, 87–90*	6	8	_____
9405	(See 19716)			
9486	Artrain GTW "I Love Michigan" Boxcar, *87 u*	—	400	_____
9517	(See 52005)			
9695	(See 52077)			
9706	(See 19706)			
9790	(See 19243)			
9791	(See 19244)			
10001	(See 19251)			
10009	(See 17008)			
10131	(See 16541)			
(11700)	Conrail Limited set, *87*	550	650	_____
(11701)	Rail Blazer set, *87–88*	—	80	_____
(11702)	Black Diamond set, *87*	175	225	_____
(11703)	Iron Horse Freight set, *88–91*	135	140	_____
(11704)	Southern Freight Runner set, *87 (SSS)*	225	300	_____
(11705)	Chessie System Unit Train set, *88*	500	600	_____
(11706)	Dry Gulch Line set, *88 (SSS)*	225	300	_____
(11707)	Silver Spike set, *88–89*	275	300	_____
(11708)	Midnight Shift set, *88 u, 89*	80	100	_____
(11710)	CP Rail Freight set, *89*	450	525	_____
(11711)	Santa Fe F-3 ABA set "8100", "8101", "8102", *91*	700	800	_____
(11712)	Great Lakes Express set, *90 (SSS)*	300	325	_____
(11713)	Santa Fe Dash 8-40B set, *90*	500	600	_____
(11714)	Badlands Express set, *90–91*	60	75	_____

LTI MODERN ERA (1987–1996)

	Exc	New	Cond/$
(11715) Lionel 90th Anniversary set, *90*	300	375	____
(11716) Lionelville Circus Special set, *90–91*	200	250	____
(11717) CSX Freight set, *90*	250	300	____
(11718) Norfolk Southern Dash 8-40C Unit Train set, *92*	600	700	____
(11719) Coastal Freight set, *91 (SSS)*	275	350	____
(11720) Santa Fe Special set, *91*	60	75	____
(11721) Mickey's World Tour Train set, *91, 92 u*	100	125	____
(11722) Girl's Train set, *91*	500	650	____
(11723) Amtrak Maintenance Train set, *91, 92 u*	275	300	____
(11724) Great Northern F-3 ABA set "366A", "370B", "351C", *92*	600	700	____
(11726) Erie-Lackawanna Freight set, *91 u*	250	300	____
(11727) Coastal Limited set, *92*	100	130	____
(11728) High Plains Runner set, *92*	150	165	____
(11729) L&N Express set, *92*		NM	
11730 Evergreen Intermodal Container (See 12805)			
11731 Maersk Intermodal Container (See 12805)			
11732 American President Lines Intermodal Container (See 12805)			
(11733) Feather River set, *92 (SSS)*	325	400	____
(11734) Erie Alco ABA set "725A", "725B", "736A" (FF #7), *93*	300	375	____
(11735) New York Central Flyer set, *93–95*		CP	____
(11736) Union Pacific Express set, *93–95*		CP	____
(11737) TCA F-3 ABA set "40", *93 u*	450	600	____
(11738) Soo Line set, *93 (SSS)*	300	340	____
(11739) Super Chief set, *93–94*	125	140	____
(11740) Conrail Consolidated set, *93*	275	300	____
(11741) Northwest Express set, *93*	150	175	____
(11742) Coastal Limited set, *93 u*	100	125	____
(11743) Chesapeake & Ohio Freight set, *94*	250	275	____
(11744) NYC Passenger/Freight set, *94 (SSS)*	300	350	____
(11745) U.S. Navy set, *94–95*		CP	____
(11746) Seaboard Freight set, *94, 95 u*		CP	____
(11747) Lionel Lines Steam set, *95*		CP	____
(11748) Amtrak set, *95*		CP	____
(11749) Western Maryland set, *95 (SSS)*		CP	____
(11750) McDonald's Nickel Plate Special set, *87 u*		NRS	____

	Exc	New	Cond/$
(11751) 49C95171C Sears Pennsylvania Passenger set, *87 u*	150	200	_____
(11752) JCPenney Timber Master set, *87 u*	100	150	_____
(11753) Kay Bee Toys Rail Blazer set, *87 u*	100	125	_____
(11754) Key America set, *87 u*		NRS	_____
(11755) Timber Master set, *87 u*		NRS	_____
(11756) Hawthorne Freight Flyer set, *87–88 u*	100	125	_____
(11757) Chrysler Mopar Express set, *87 u*	250	275	_____
(11757) Chrysler Mopar Express set, *88 u*	300	325	_____
(11758) The Desert King set, *89 (SSS)*	250	300	_____
(11759) JCPenney Silver Spike set, *88 u*		NRS	_____
(11761) JCPenney Iron Horse Freight set, *88 u*		NRS	_____
(11761) True Value Cannonball Express set, *88 u*	100	150	_____
(11762) True Value Cannonball Express set, *89 u*	100	150	_____
(11763) United Model Freight Hauler set, *88 u*		NRS	_____
(11764) 49N95178 Sears Iron Horse Freight set, *88 u*	200	250	_____
(11765) Spiegel Silver Spike set, *88 u*		NRS	_____
(11767) Shoprite Freight Flyer set, *88 u*	100	150	_____
(11769) JCPenney Midnight Shift set, *89 u*		NRS	_____
(11770) 49GY95280 Sears Circus set, *89 u*	200	225	_____
(11771) K-Mart Microracers set, *89 u*	100	125	_____
(11772) Macy's Freight Flyer set, *89 u*	150	200	_____
(11773) 49GY95281 Sears NYC Passenger set, *89 u*		NRS	_____
(11774) Ace Hardware Cannonball Express set, *89 u*	150	175	_____
(11775) Anheuser-Busch set, *89–92 u*	200	250	_____
(11776) Pace Iron Horse Freight set, *89 u*	150	175	_____
(11777) 49N95265 Sears Lionelville Circus Special set, *90 u*	225	250	_____
(11778) 49N95264 Sears Badlands Express set, *90 u*	60	75	_____
(11779) 49N95267 Sears CSX Freight set, *90 u*	250	300	_____
(11780) 49N95266 Sears Northern Pacific Passenger set, *90 u*	200	250	_____
(11781) True Value Cannonball Express set, *90 u*	100	150	_____
(11783) Toys "R" Us Heavy Iron set, *90–91 u*	200	250	_____
(11784) Pace Iron Horse Freight set, *90 u*	150	175	_____
(11785) Costco Union Pacific Express set, *90 u*	175	200	_____
(11789) Sears Illinois Central Passenger set, *91 u*	200	225	_____
(11793) Santa Fe set w/ mailer, *91 u*	60	75	_____
(11794) Mickey's World Tour set w/ mailer, *91 u*	100	125	_____

LTI MODERN ERA (1987–1996)

		Exc	New	Cond/$
(11796)	Union Pacific Express set, *91 u*	175	200	____
(11797)	Sears Coastal Limited set w/ mailer, *92 u*	100	130	____
(11800)	Toys "R" Us Heavy Iron Thunder Limited set, *92–93 u*	250	300	____
(11803)	Mall Promotion Nickel Plate Special set, *92 u*		NRS	____
(11804)	K-Mart Coastal Limited set, *92 u*	100	130	____
(11809)	Village Trolley Company set, *95*		CP	____
(11810)	Budweiser Modern Era set, *93–94 u*	225	260	____
(11811)	United Auto Workers set, *93 u*	175	225	____
(11812)	Mall Promotion Coastal Limited set, *93 u*		NRS	____
(11813)	Crayola Activity Train set, *94 u, 95*		CP	____
(11814)	Ford Limited Edition set, *94 u*	200	240	____
(11818)	Chrysler Mopar set, *94 u*	200	240	____
(11819)	Georgia Power set, *95 u*		CP	____
(11820)	Red Wing Shoes NYC Flyer set, *95 u*		CP	____
(11903)	Atlantic Coast Line F-3 ABA set "342", "342B", 343", *96*		CP	____
(11906)	Factory Selection Special set, *95 u*		CP	____
12000	(See 52000)			
12046	(See 52046)			
12700	Erie Magnetic Gantry Crane, *87*	175	200	____
(12701)	Operating Fueling Station, *87*	90	105	____
(12702)	Control Tower, *87*	80	100	____
(12703)	Icing Station, *88–89*	80	100	____
(12704)	Dwarf Signal, *88–93*	15	20	____
(12705)	Lumber Shed kit, *88–95*		CP	____
(12706)	Barrel Loader Building kit, *87–95*		CP	____
(12707)	Billboards (3), *87–95*		CP	____
(12708)	Street Lamps (3), *88–93*	10	15	____
(12709)	Banjo Signal, *87–91, 95*		CP	____
(12710)	Engine House kit, *87–91*	25	30	____
(12711)	Water Tower kit, *87–95*		CP	____
(12712)	Automatic Ore Loader, *87–88*	20	30	____
(12713)	Automatic Gateman, *87–88, 94–95*		CP	____
(12714)	Automatic Crossing Gate, *87–91, 93–95*		CP	____
(12715)	Illuminated Bumpers (2), *87–95*		CP	____
(12716)	Searchlight Tower, *87–89, 91–92*	25	30	____
(12717)	Non-Illuminated Bumpers (3), *87–95*		CP	____
(12718)	Barrel Shed kit, *87–95*		CP	____

		Exc	New	Cond/$
(12719)	Animated Refreshment Stand, *88–89*	70	80	_____
12720	Rotary Beacon, *88–89*	40	50	_____
(12721)	Illuminated Extension Bridge w/ rock piers, *89*	30	45	_____
(12722)	Roadside Diner w/ smoke, *88–89*	40	50	_____
(12723)	Microwave Tower, *88–91, 94–95*		CP	_____
(12724)	Double Signal Bridge, *88–90*	45	60	_____
12725	Lionel Tractor and Trailer, *88–89*	15	20	_____
(12726)	Grain Elevator kit, *88–91, 94–95*		CP	_____
(12727)	Automatic Operating Semaphore, *89–95*		CP	_____
(12728)	Illuminated Freight Station, *89*	30	40	_____
(12729)	Mail Pick-up set, *88–91, 95*		CP	_____
(12730)	Girder Bridge, *88–95*		CP	_____
(12731)	Station Platform, *88–95*		CP	_____
(12732)	Coal Bag, *88–95*		CP	_____
(12733)	Watchman Shanty kit, *88–95*		CP	_____
(12734)	Passenger/Freight Station, *89–95*		CP	_____
(12735)	Diesel Horn Shed, *88–91*	25	30	_____
(12736)	Coaling Station kit, *88–91*	20	30	_____
(12737)	Whistling Freight Shed, *88–95*		CP	_____
(12739)	Lionel Gas Company Tractor and Tanker, *89*	15	20	_____
(12740)	Log Package (3), *88–92, 94–95*		CP	_____
12741	Union Pacific Intermodal Crane, *89*	200	230	_____
(12742)	Gooseneck Street Lamps (2), *89–95*		CP	_____
(12743)	Track Clips (12) (O), *89–95*		CP	_____
(12744)	Rock Piers (2), *89–92, 94–95*		CP	_____
(12745)	Barrel Pack (6), *89–95*		CP	_____
(12746)	Operating/Uncoupling Track (O27), *89–95*		CP	_____
(12748)	Illuminated Station Platform, *89–95*		CP	_____
(12749)	Rotary Radar Antenna, *89–92, 95*		CP	_____
(12750)	Crane kit, *89–91*	8	10	_____
(12751)	Shovel kit, *89–91*	8	10	_____
(12752)	History of Lionel Trains video (VHS), *89–92, 94*	22	25	_____
(12753)	Ore Load (2), *89–91, 95*		CP	_____
(12754)	Graduated Trestle set (22), *89–95*		CP	_____
(12755)	Elevated Trestle set (10), *89–95*		CP	_____
(12756)	The Making of the Scale Hudson video (VHS), *91–94*	22	25	_____
(12759)	Floodlight Tower, *90–95*		CP	_____
(12760)	Automatic Highway Flasher, *90–91*	35	40	_____

LTI MODERN ERA (1987–1996)

		Exc	New	Cond/$
(12761)	Animated Billboard, *90–91, 93, 95*		CP	
(12762)	Freight Station			
	w/ train control and sounds, *90–91*		NM	
(12763)	Single Signal Bridge, *90–91, 93*	30	35	
(12765)	Die-cast Auto Assortment (6), *90*		NM	
(12767)	Steam Clean and Wheel Grind Shop, *92–93, 95*		CP	
(12768)	Burning Switch Tower, *90, 93*	85	100	
(12770)	Arch-Under Bridge, *90–95*		CP	
(12771)	Mom's Roadside Diner w/ smoke, *90–91*	40	60	
(12772)	Illuminated Extension Bridge w/ rock piers, *90–95*		CP	
(12773)	Freight Platform kit, *90–95*		CP	
(12774)	Lumber Loader kit, *90–95*		CP	
12777	Chevron Tractor and Tanker, *90–91*	10	15	
12778	Conrail Tractor and Trailer, *90*	10	15	
12779	Lionelville Grain Company			
	Tractor and Trailer, *90*	10	15	
(12780)	RS-1 50 Watt Transformer, *90–93*	100	150	
12781	N&W Intermodal Crane, *90–91*	210	225	
(12782)	Lift Bridge, *91–92*	500	600	
12783	Monon Tractor and Trailer, *91*	15	20	
(12784)	Intermodal Containers (3), *91*	15	20	
12785	Lionel Gravel Company Tractor and Trailer, *91*	10	15	
12786	Lionel Steel Company Tractor and Trailer, *91*	10	15	
12787	Family Lines Intermodal Container (See 12784)			
12788	UP Intermodal Container (See 12784)			
12789	B&M Intermodal Container (See 12784)			
(12790)	ZW-II Transformer, *91*		NM	
(12791)	Animated Passenger Station, *91*	75	90	
(12794)	Lionel Tractor, *91*	10	15	
(12795)	Cable Reels (2), *91–95*		CP	
(12797)	Crossing Gate and Signal, *91*		NM	
(12798)	Forklift Loader Station, *92–95*		CP	
(12800)	Scale Hudson Replacement Pilot Truck, *91 u*	15	20	
(12802)	"Chat & Chew" Roadside Diner			
	w/ smoke and lights, *92–95*		CP	
(12804)	Highway Lights (4), *92–95*		CP	
(12805)	Intermodal Containers (3), *92*	10	15	
12806	Lionel Lumber Company Tractor and Trailer, *92*	10	15	
(12807)	Little Caesars Tractor and Trailer, *92*	10	15	

		Exc	New	Cond/$
2808	Mobil Tractor and Tanker, *92*	10	15	_____
12809)	Animated Billboard, *92–93*	30	35	_____
12810)	American Flyer Tractor and Trailer "DX26925", *94*	15	18	_____
2811	Alka Seltzer Tractor and Trailer, *92*	10	15	_____
12812)	Illuminated Freight Station, *93–95*		CP	_____
12818)	Animated Freight Station, *92, 94–95*		CP	_____
12819	Inland Steel Tractor and Trailer, *92*	10	15	_____
12821)	Lionel Catalog video (VHS), *92*	15	20	_____
12826)	Intermodal Containers (3), *93*	10	15	_____
12827)	CSX Intermodal Container "610584" (See 12826)			
12828)	NYC Intermodal Container (See 12826)			
12829)	Great Northern Container (See 12826)			
12831)	Rotary Beacon, *93–95*		CP	_____
12832)	Block Target Signal, *93–95*		CP	_____
12833)	RoadRailer Tractor and Trailer, *93*	10	15	_____
12834	Pennsylvania Magnetic Gantry Crane, *93*	135	150	_____
12835)	Operating Fueling Station, *93*	80	100	_____
12836	Santa Fe Quantum Tractor and Trailer, *93*	10	15	_____
12837)	Humble Oil Tractor and Tanker, *93*	10	15	_____
12838)	Crate Load (2), *93–95*		CP	_____
12839)	Grade Crossing (2), *93–95*		CP	_____
12840)	Insulated Straight Track (O), *93–95*		CP	_____
12841)	Insulated Straight Track (O27), *93–95*		CP	_____
12842)	Dunkin' Donuts Tractor and Trailer, *92 u*	30	40	_____
12843)	Die-cast Metal Sprung Trucks (2), *93–95*		CP	_____
12844)	Coil Covers (2) (O), *93–95*		CP	_____
12847)	Icing Station, *94–95*		CP	_____
12848)	Lionel Oil Company Oil Derrick "2848", *94*	100	145	_____
12849)	Lionel Controller w/ wall pack, *94, 95 u*		CP	_____
12852)	Trailer Frame, *94–95*		CP	_____
12853)	Coil Covers (2) (Std. O), *94–95*		CP	_____
12854)	U.S. Navy Tractor and Tanker, *94–95*		CP	_____
12855)	Intermodal Containers (3), *94–95*		CP	_____
12856	CP Rail Intermodal Container (See 12855)			
12857	Frisco Intermodal Container (See 12855)			
12858	Vermont Railways Intermodal Container (See 12855)			
12860)	Lionel Visitor's Center Tractor and Trailer, *94 u*	20	25	_____
12861)	Lionel Leasing Company Tractor, *94*	5	8	_____

LTI MODERN ERA (1987–1996)

	Exc	New	Cond/$
(12862) Oil Drum Loader, *94–95*		CP	___
(12864) Little Caesars Tractor and Trailer, *94*	10	15	___
(12865) Wisk Tractor and Trailer, *94*	10	15	___
(12866) PH-1 Power House, *94 u, 95*		CP	___
(12867) PM-1 Power Master, *94 u, 95*		CP	___
(12868) Cab-1 Remote Controller, *94 u, 95*		CP	___
(12869) Marathon Oil Tractor and Tanker, *94*	10	15	___
(12873) Operating Sawmill, *95–96*		CP	___
(12874) Street Lamps (3), *94–95*		CP	___
(12875) Lionel Railroader Club Tractor and Trailer, *94 u*	20	30	___
(12877) Operating Fueling Station, *95*		CP	___
(12878) Control Tower, *95*		CP	___
(12880) Power Station Transformer, *96*		CP	___
(12881) Chrysler Mopar Tractor and Trailer, *94 u*	40	50	___
(12882) Lighted Billboard, *95*		CP	___
(12883) Dwarf Signal, *95*		CP	___
(12884) Truck Loading Dock kit, *95*		CP	___
(12885) 40-Watt Control System, *94 u, 95*		CP	___
12886 395 Floodlight Tower, *95*		CP	___
(12887) Lionel Conductor Display, *95*		NM	
(12888) Automatic Highway Flasher, *95*		CP	___
(12889) Operating Windmill, *95*		CP	___
(12890) Big Red Button, *94 u, 95*		CP	___
(12891) Lionel Lines Refrigerator Tractor and Trailer, *95*		CP	___
(12892) Automatic Flagman, *95*		CP	___
(12893) Power Master Cable, *94 u, 95*		CP	___
(12894) Single Signal Bridge, *95*		CP	___
(12895) Double Signal Bridge, *95*		CP	___
(12896) Tunnel Portals (2), *95*		CP	___
(12897) Engine House kit, *95*		CP	___
(12898) Flagpole kit, *95*		CP	___
(12899) Searchlight Tower, *95*		CP	___
(12900) Crane kit, *95*		CP	___
(12901) Shovel kit, *95*		CP	___
(12902) Marathon Oil Derrick "2902", *94 u, 95*		CP	___
(12903) Diesel Horn Shed, *95*		CP	___
(12904) Coaling Station kit, *95*		CP	___
(12905) Factory kit, *95*		CP	___

		Exc	New	Cond/$
(12906)	Maintenance Shed kit, *95*		CP	_____
(12907)	Intermodal Containers (3), *95*		CP	_____
(12908)	Western Pacific Intermodal Container (See 12907)			
(12909)	Northern Pacific Intermodal Container "33621" (See 12907)			
(12910)	CP Rail Intermodal Container "680441" (See 12907)			
(12911)	Trainmaster Command Base, *95*		CP	_____
12912	Oil Pumping Station, *95*		CP	_____
(12914)	SC-1 Controller, *95*		CP	_____
(12917)	Operating Switch Tower, *96*		CP	_____
(12921)	LRRC Illuminated Station Platform, *95 u*		CP	_____
12922	NYC Operating Gantry Crane w/ coil covers, *96*		CP	_____
(12923)	Red Wing Shoes Tractor and Trailer "T-4", *95 u*		CP	_____
(12930)	Lionelville Oil Company Oil Derrick "2930", *95 u, 96*		CP	_____
15000	D&RGW Waffle-side Boxcar, *95*		CP	_____
15001	Seaboard Waffle-side Boxcar, *95*		CP	_____
15100	Amtrak Passenger Car (O27), *95*		CP	_____
15101	Reading Baggage Car (O27), *96*		CP	_____
15102	Reading Combination Car (O27), *96*		CP	_____
15103	Reading Passenger Car (O27), *96*		CP	_____
15104	Reading Vista Dome Car (O27), *96*		CP	_____
15105	Reading Full Vista Dome Car (O27), *96*		CP	_____
15106	Reading Observation Car (O27), *96*		CP	_____
15791	(See 17889)			
15906	RailSounds Trigger Button, *90–95*		CP	_____
16000	PRR Vista Dome Car (O27), *87–88*	25	35	_____
16001	PRR Passenger Car (O27), *87–88*	25	35	_____
16002	PRR Passenger Car (O27), *87–88*	25	35	_____
16003	PRR Observation Car (O27), *87–88*	25	35	_____
16009	PRR Combination Car (O27), *88*	30	35	_____
16010	Virginia & Truckee Passenger Car, *88 (SSS)*	40	50	_____
16011	Virginia & Truckee Passenger Car, *88 (SSS)*	40	50	_____
16012	Virginia & Truckee Baggage Car, *88 (SSS)*	40	50	_____
16013	Amtrak Combination Car (O27), *88–89*	25	40	_____
16014	Amtrak Vista Dome Car (O27), *88–89*	25	40	_____
16015	Amtrak Observation Car (O27), *88–89*	25	40	_____
16016	NYC Baggage Car (O27), *89*	25	35	_____
16017	NYC Combination Car (O27), *89*	25	35	_____

LTI MODERN ERA (1987–1996)

		Exc	New	Cond/$
16018	NYC Passenger Car (O27), *89*	25	35	___
16019	NYC Vista Dome Car (O27), *89*	25	35	___
16020	NYC Passenger Car (O27), *89*	25	35	___
16021	NYC Observation Car (O27), *89*	25	35	___
16021	(See 17210)			
16022	Pennsylvania Baggage Car (O27), *89*	25	40	___
16022	(See 17211)			
16023	Amtrak Passenger Car (O27), *89*	25	35	___
16023	(See 17212)			
16024	NP Dining Car (O27), *92*	40	45	___
16027	LL Combination Car (O27), *90 (SSS)*	40	50	___
16028	LL Passenger Car (O27), *90 (SSS)*	40	50	___
16029	LL Passenger Car (O27), *90 (SSS)*	40	50	___
16030	LL Observation Car (O27), *90 (SSS)*	40	50	___
16031	Pennsylvania Dining Car (O27), *90*	35	40	___
16033	Amtrak Baggage Car (O27), *90*	25	35	___
16034	NP Baggage Car (O27), *90–91*	20	30	___
16035	NP Combination Car (O27), *90–91*	20	30	___
16036	NP Passenger Car (O27), *90–91*	20	30	___
16037	NP Vista Dome Car (O27), *90–91*	20	30	___
16038	NP Passenger Car (O27), *90–91*	20	30	___
16039	NP Observation Car (O27), *90–91*	20	30	___
16040	Southern Pacific Baggage Car, *90–91*	25	35	___
16041	NYC Dining Car (O27), *91*	45	55	___
16042	Illinois Central Baggage Car (O27), *91*	25	35	___
16043	Illinois Central Combination Car (O27), *91*	25	35	___
16044	Illinois Central Passenger Car (O27), *91*	25	35	___
16045	Illinois Central Vista Dome Car (O27), *91*	25	35	___
16046	Illinois Central Passenger Car (O27), *91*	25	35	___
16047	Illinois Central Observation Car (O27), *91*	25	35	___
16048	Amtrak Dining Car (O27), *91–92*	40	50	___
16049	Illinois Central Dining Car (O27), *92*	25	35	___
(16050)	C&NW Baggage Car "6620", *93*	45	55	___
(16051)	C&NW Combination Car "6630", *93*	45	55	___
(16052)	C&NW Passenger Car "6616", *93*	45	55	___
(16053)	C&NW Passenger Car "6602", *93*	45	55	___
(16054)	C&NW Observation Car "6603", *93*	45	55	___
16055	Santa Fe Passenger Car (O27), *93–94*	30	40	___
16056	Santa Fe Vista Dome Car (O27), *93–94*	30	40	___

		Exc	New	Cond/$
16057	Santa Fe Passenger Car (O27), *93–94*	30	40	_____
16058	Santa Fe Combination Car (O27), *93–94*	30	40	_____
16059	Santa Fe Vista Dome Car (O27), *93–94*	30	40	_____
16060	Santa Fe Observation Car (O27), *93–94*	30	40	_____
(16061)	N&W Baggage Car "6061", *94*	45	55	_____
(16062)	N&W Combination Car "6062", *94*	45	55	_____
(16063)	N&W Passenger Car "6063", *94*	45	55	_____
(16064)	N&W Passenger Car "6064", *94*	45	55	_____
(16065)	N&W Observation Car "6065", *94*	45	55	_____
(16066)	NYC Combination Car "6066", *94 (SSS)*	45	55	_____
(16067)	NYC Passenger Car "6067", *94 (SSS)*	45	55	_____
(16068)	UP Baggage Car "6068" (O27), *94*	40	50	_____
(16069)	UP Combination Car "6069" (O27), *94*	40	50	_____
(16070)	UP Passenger Car "6070" (O27), *94*	40	50	_____
(16071)	UP Dining Car "6071" (O27), *94*	40	50	_____
(16072)	UP Vista Dome Car "6072" (O27), *94*	40	50	_____
(16073)	UP Passenger Car "6073" (O27), *94*	40	50	_____
(16074)	UP Observation Car "6074" (O27), *94*	40	50	_____
(16075)	Missouri Pacific Baggage Car "6620", *95*		CP	_____
(16076)	Missouri Pacific Combination Car "6630", *95*		CP	_____
(16077)	Missouri Pacific Passenger Car "6616", *95*		CP	_____
(16078)	Missouri Pacific Passenger Car "7805", *95*		CP	_____
(16079)	Missouri Pacific Observation Car "6609", *95*		CP	_____
(16080)	New Haven Baggage Car "6080" (O27), *95*		CP	_____
(16081)	New Haven Combination Car "6081" (O27), *95*		CP	_____
(16082)	New Haven Passenger Car "6082" (O27), *95*		CP	_____
(16083)	New Haven Vista Dome Car "6083" (O27), *95*		CP	_____
(16084)	New Haven Full Vista Dome Car "6084" (O27), *95*		CP	_____
(16086)	New Haven Observation Car "6086" (O27), *95*		CP	_____
(16087)	NYC Baggage Car "6087", *95 (SSS)*		CP	_____
(16088)	NYC Passenger Car "6088", *95 (SSS)*		CP	_____
(16089)	NYC Dining Car "6089", *95 (SSS)*		CP	_____
(16090)	NYC Observation Car "6090", *95 (SSS)*		CP	_____
(16091)	NYC Passenger Cars, set of 4, *95 (SSS)*		CP	_____
16092	Santa Fe Full Vista Dome Car (O27), *95*		CP	_____
16093	Illinois Central Full Vista Dome Car (O27), *95*		CP	_____
16094	Pennsylvania Full Vista Dome Car (O27), *95*		CP	_____
16095	Amtrak Combination Car (O27), *95*		CP	_____
16096	Amtrak Vista Dome Car (O27), *95*		CP	_____

		Exc	New	Cond/$
16097	Amtrak Observation Car (O27), 95		CP	___
16098	Amtrak Passenger Car (O27), 95		CP	___
16099	Amtrak Vista Dome Car (O27), 95		CP	___
16102	Southern 3-D Tank Car, 87 (SSS)	40	50	___
16103	Lehigh Valley 2-D Tank Car (O27), 88	25	30	___
16104	Santa Fe 2-D Tank Car (O27), 89	20	25	___
16105	D&RGW 3-D Tank Car, 89 (SSS)	45	60	___
(16106)	Mopar Express 3-D Tank Car, 88 u	75	125	___
16107	Sunoco 2-D Tank Car (O27), 90	20	25	___
(16108)	Racing Fuel 1-D Tank Car "6108" (O27), 89 u, 92 u	10	15	___
16109	B&O 1-D Tank Car, 91 (SSS)	40	50	___
(16110)	Circus Animals Operating Stock Car "1989" (O27), 89 u	25	35	___
16111	Alaska 1-D Tank Car (O27), 90–91	20	25	___
16112	Dow Chemical 3-D Tank Car, 90	25	35	___
16113	Diamond Shamrock 2-D Tank Car (O27), 91	20	25	___
16114	Hooker Chemicals 1-D Tank Car (O27), 91	15	20	___
16115	MKT 3-D Tank Car, 92	20	25	___
16116	U.S. Army 1-D Tank Car, 91 u	40	50	___
16119	MKT 2-D Tank Car (O27), 92, 93 u	15	20	___
16121	C&NW Stock Car, 92 (SSS)	75	90	___
16123	Union Pacific 3-D Tank Car, 93–95		CP	___
16124	Penn Salt 3-D Tank Car, 93	20	25	___
16125	Virginian Stock Car, 93	20	25	___
16126	Jefferson Lake 3-D Tank Car, 93	25	30	___
16127	Mobil 1-D Tank Car, 93	25	30	___
16128	Alaska 1-D Tank Car, 94	25	30	___
16129	Alaska 1-D Tank Car (O27), 93 u, 94	10	15	___
16130	SP Stock Car (O27), 93 u, 94	8	10	___
16131	T&P Reefer, 94	20	25	___
16132	Deep Rock 3-D Tank Car, 94	25	30	___
16133	Santa Fe Reefer, 94	20	25	___
16134	Reading Reefer, 94	20	25	___
16135	C&O Stock Car, 94	25	30	___
16136	B&O 1-D Tank Car, 94	30	35	___
16137	Ford 1-D Tank Car "12", 94 u	35	40	___
16138	Goodyear 1-D Tank Car, 95		CP	___
16140	Domino Sugar 1-D Tank Car, 95		CP	___

LTI MODERN ERA (1987–1996)

		Exc	New	Cond/$
16141	Erie Stock Car, *95*		CP	____
16142	Santa Fe 1-D Tank Car, *95*		CP	____
16143	Reading Reefer, *95*		CP	____
16144	San Angelo 3-D Tank Car, *95*		CP	____
16146	Dairy Despatch Reefer, *95*		CP	____
(16147)	Clearly Canadian 1-D Tank Car (O27), *94 u*	—	60	____
16149	Zep Chemical 1-D Tank Car (O27), *95 u*		CP	____
16200	Rock Island Boxcar (O27), *87–88*	8	12	____
16201	Wabash Boxcar (O27), *88–91*	8	12	____
16203	Key America Boxcar (O27), *87 u*	50	75	____
16204	Hawthorne Boxcar (O27), *87 u*	60	100	____
(16205)	Mopar Express Boxcar "1987" (O27), *87–88 u*	50	60	____
16206	D&RGW Boxcar, *89 (SSS)*	50	60	____
16207	True Value Boxcar (O27), *88 u*	50	75	____
16208	PRR Auto Carrier w/ autos (3-tier), *89*	35	55	____
16209	Disney Magic Boxcar (O27), *88 u*	75	100	____
16211	Hawthorne Boxcar (O27), *88 u*	50	75	____
16213	Shoprite Boxcar (O27), *88 u*	50	70	____
16214	D&RGW Auto Carrier, *90*	25	30	____
16215	Conrail Auto Carrier, *90*	25	30	____
16217	Burlington Northern Auto Carrier, *92*	25	30	____
16219	True Value Boxcar (O27), *89 u*	50	70	____
(16220)	Ace Hardware Boxcar (O27), *89 u*	50	70	____
(16221)	Macy's Boxcar (O27), *89 u*	50	70	____
16222	Great Northern Boxcar (O27), *90–91*	8	15	____
(16223)	Budweiser Reefer, *89–92 u*	50	60	____
16224	True Value "Lawn Chief" Boxcar (O27), *90 u*	50	70	____
16225	Budweiser Vat Car, *90–91 u*	100	125	____
(16226)	Union Pacific Boxcar "6226" (O27), *90–91 u*	15	20	____
16227	Santa Fe Boxcar (O27), *91*	15	20	____
16228	Union Pacific Auto Carrier, *92*	25	30	____
16229	Erie-Lackawanna Auto Carrier, *91 u*	45	60	____
16232	Chessie System Boxcar, *92, 93 u, 94, 95 u*		CP	____
16233	MKT DD Boxcar, *92*	20	30	____
16234	ACY Boxcar, *92 (SSS)*	40	50	____
16235	Railway Express Agency Reefer, *92*	25	30	____
16236	NYC "Pacemaker" Boxcar, *92 u*	35	40	____
16237	Railway Express Agency Boxcar, *92 u*	30	35	____
16238	NYNH&H Boxcar, *93–95*		CP	____

LTI MODERN ERA (1987–1996)

		Exc	New	Cond/$
16239	Union Pacific Boxcar, *93–95*		CP	____
16241	Toys "R" Us Boxcar, *92–93 u*	50	60	____
16242	Grand Trunk Auto Carrier, *93*	35	40	____
16243	Conrail Boxcar, *93*	30	40	____
16244	Duluth, South Shore & Atlantic Boxcar, *93*	20	25	____
16245	Contadina Boxcar, *93*	20	25	____
16245	(See 52068)			
16247	ACL Boxcar, *94*	20	25	____
16247	(See 52046)			
16248	Budweiser Boxcar, *93–94 u*	25	30	____
16249	United Auto Workers Boxcar, *93 u*		NRS	
16250	Santa Fe Boxcar (O27), *93 u, 94*	8	10	____
16251	Columbus & Greenville Boxcar, *94*	20	25	____
(16252)	Rapid Strike Attack Force Fleet Boxcar "6106888", *94–95*		CP	____
16253	Santa Fe Auto Carrier, *94*	25	30	____
16255	Wabash DD Boxcar, *95*		CP	____
16256	Ford DD Boxcar, *94 u*	35	40	____
(16257)	Crayola Boxcar, *94 u, 95*		CP	____
16258	Lehigh Valley Boxcar, *95*		CP	____
16259	Chrysler Mopar Boxcar, *94 u*	30	35	____
16260	Chrysler Mopar Auto Carrier, *94 u*	50	60	____
16261	Union Pacific DD Boxcar, *95*		CP	____
16264	Red Wing Shoes Boxcar, *95*		CP	____
16265	Georgia Power "Atlanta '96" Boxcar, *95 u*		CP	____
16266	Crayola Boxcar, *95*		CP	____
16300	Rock Island Flatcar w/ fences (O27), *87–88*	8	10	____
16301	Lionel Barrel Ramp Car, *87*	20	25	____
16303	PRR Flatcar w/ trailers, *87*	30	40	____
16304	Rock Island Gondola w/ cable reels (O27), *87–88*	5	10	____
16305	Lehigh Valley Ore Car, *87*	85	120	____
16306	Santa Fe Barrel Ramp Car, *88*	15	20	____
16307	NKP Flatcar w/ trailers, *88*	30	40	____
16308	Burlington Northern Flatcar w/ trailer, *88–89*	40	55	____
16309	Wabash Gondola w/ canisters, *88–91*	10	15	____
(16310)	Mopar Express Gondola w/ canisters "1987", *87–88 u*	30	35	____
(16311)	Mopar Express Flatcar w/ trailers "1987", *87–88 u*	100	150	____

		Exc	New	Cond/$
16313	PRR Gondola w/ cable reels (O27), *88 u, 89*	8	10	_____
16314	Wabash Flatcar w/ trailers, *89*	30	40	_____
16315	PRR Flatcar w/ fences (O27), *88 u, 89*	8	10	_____
16317	PRR Barrel Ramp Car, *89*	20	25	_____
16318	Lionel Lines Depressed Flatcar			
	w/ cable reels, *89*	20	25	_____
16320	Great Northern Barrel Ramp Car, *90*	15	20	_____
16321/ 16322	Sealand TTUX Flatcar set w/ trailers, *90*	85	110	_____
16323	Lionel Lines Flatcar w/ trailers, *90*	30	35	_____
16324	PRR Depressed Flatcar w/ cable reels, *90*	20	25	_____
16325	Microracers Exhibition Ramp Car, *89 u*	25	35	_____
16326	Santa Fe Depressed Flatcar w/ cable reels, *91*	20	25	_____
(16327)	"The Big Top" Circus Gondola			
	w/ canisters, *89 u*	20	25	_____
16328	NKP Gondola w/ cable reels, *90–91*	15	20	_____
16329	SP Flatcar w/ horses (O27), *90–91*	20	25	_____
16330	MKT Flatcar w/ trailers, *91*	25	35	_____
16331	Southern Barrel Ramp Car, *91*		NM	
16332	Lionel Lines Depressed Flatcar			
	w/ transformer, *91*	25	30	_____
16333	Frisco Bulkhead Flatcar w/ wood load, *91*	20	25	_____
(16334)	C&NW TTUX Flatcar set w/ trailers			
	"16337" and "16338", *91*	70	80	_____
16335	NYC "Pacemaker" Flatcar w/ trailer, *91 (SSS)*	75	95	_____
(16336)	UP Gondola w/ canisters "6336", *90–91 u*	20	25	_____
16337/ 16338	C&NW TTUX Flatcars			
	w/ trailers (See 16334)			
16339	Mickey's World Tour Gondola			
	w/ canisters (O27), *91, 92 u*	20	25	_____
16340	Amtrak Flatcar w/ stakes, *91*		NM	
16341	NYC Depressed Flatcar w/ transformer, *92*	25	30	_____
16342	CSX Gondola w/ coil covers, *92*	20	25	_____
16343	Burlington Gondola w/ coil covers, *92*	20	25	_____
16345/ 16346	SP TTUX Flatcar set w/ trailers, *92*	60	75	_____
16347	Ontario Northland Bulkhead Flatcar			
	w/ pulp load, *92*	30	35	_____
16348	Lionel-Erie Liquefied Gas Car, *92*	40	45	_____
16349	Allis Chalmers Condenser Car, *92*	40	50	_____
16350	CP Rail Bulkhead Flatcar w/ wood load, *91 u*	25	35	_____

LTI MODERN ERA (1987–1996)

		Exc	New	Cond/$
16351	Lionel Flatcar w/ U.S.N. submarine, *92*	50	65	____
16352	U.S. Military Flatcar w/ cruise missile, *92*	40	55	____
16353	B&M Gondola w/ coil covers, *91 u*	30	35	____
16355	Burlington Gondola, *92, 93 u, 94–95*		CP	____
16356	MKT Depressed Flatcar w/ cable reels, *92*	20	25	____
16357	L&N Flatcar w/ trailer, *92*	30	40	____
16358	L&N Gondola w/ coil covers, *92*	25	35	____
16359	Pacific Coast Gondola w/ coil covers, *92 (SSS)*	35	40	____
(16360)	N&W Maxi-Stack Flatcar set			
	w/ containers "16361" and "16362", *93*	70	80	____
16361/ 16362	N&W Maxi-Stack Flatcars			
	w/ containers (See 16360)			
(16363)	Southern TTUX Flatcar set			
	w/ trailers "16364" and "16365", *93*	60	75	____
16364/ 16365	Southern TTUX Flatcars			
	w/ trailers (See 16363)			
16367	Clinchfield Gondola w/ coil covers, *93*	20	25	____
16368	MKT Liquid Oxygen Car, *93*	20	25	____
16369	Amtrak Flatcar w/ wheel load, *92 u*	20	30	____
16370	Amtrak Flatcar w/ rail load, *92 u*	20	30	____
16371	BN I-Beam Flatcar w/ load, *92 u*	40	50	____
16372	Southern I-Beam Flatcar w/ load, *92 u*	30	40	____
16373	Erie-Lackawanna Flatcar w/ stakes, *93*	20	25	____
16374	D&RGW Flatcar w/ trailer, *93*	30	35	____
16375	NYC Bulkhead Flatcar, *93–95*		CP	____
16376	UP Flatcar w/ trailer, *93–95*		CP	____
16378	Toys "R" Us Flatcar w/ trailer, *92–93 u*	75	125	____
16379	NP Bulkhead Flatcar w/ pulp load, *93*	20	25	____
16380	UP I-Beam Flatcar w/ load, *93*	30	35	____
16380	(See 52084)			
16381	CSX I-Beam Flatcar w/ load, *93*	30	35	____
16382	Kansas City Southern Bulkhead Flatcar, *93*	20	25	____
16383	Conrail Flatcar w/ trailer, *93*	50	60	____
16384	Soo Line Gondola w/ cable reels, *93*	20	25	____
16385	Soo Line Ore Car, *93*	60	75	____
16386	SP Flatcar w/ wood load, *94*	20	25	____
16387	Kansas City Southern Gondola			
	w/ coil covers, *94*	20	25	____
16388	LV Gondola w/ canisters, *94*	20	25	____

		Exc	New	Cond/$
16389	PRR Flatcar w/ wheel load, *94*	25	30	____
16390	Lionel Flatcar w/ water tank, *94*	30	40	____
16391	Lionel Lines Gondola, *93 u*		NRS	____
16392	Wabash Gondola w/ canisters (O27), *93 u, 94*	8	10	____
16393	Wisconsin Central Bulkhead Flatcar, *94*	15	22	____
16394	Central Vermont Bulkhead Flatcar, *94*	15	22	____
16395	CP Flatcar w/ rail load, *94*	20	25	____
16396	Alaska Bulkhead Flatcar, *94*	15	22	____
16397	Milwaukee Road I-Beam Flatcar w/ load, *94*	40	45	____
16398	C&O Flatcar w/ trailer, *94*	60	70	____
16399	Western Pacific I-Beam Flatcar w/ load, *94*	40	45	____
16400	PRR Hopper (O27), *88 u, 89*	20	25	____
16402	Southern Quad Hopper w/ coal load, *87 (SSS)*	35	50	____
16406	CSX Quad Hopper w/ coal load, *90*	30	40	____
16407	B&M Covered Quad Hopper, *91 (SSS)*	30	40	____
(16408)	Union Pacific Hopper "6408" (O27), *90–91 u*	20	25	____
16410	MKT Hopper (O27), *92, 93 u*	20	25	____
16411	L&N Quad Hopper w/ coal load, *92*	30	35	____
16412	C&NW Covered Quad Hopper, *94*	20	25	____
16413	Clinchfield Quad Hopper w/ coal load, *94*	20	25	____
16413	(See 52059)			
16414	CCC&St L Hopper (O27), *94*	15	20	____
16415	Milwaukee Road Hopper (O27), *94 u*	—	15	____
16416	D&RGW Covered Quad Hopper, *95*		CP	____
16417	Wabash Quad Hopper w/ coal load, *95*		CP	____
16418	C&NW Hopper w/ coal load (O27), *95*		CP	____
16420	Western Maryland Quad Hopper w/ coal load, *95 (SSS)*		CP	____
16421	Western Maryland Quad Hopper w/ coal load, *95 (SSS)*		CP	____
16422	Western Maryland Quad Hopper w/ coal load, *95 (SSS)*		CP	____
16423	Western Maryland Quad Hopper w/ coal load, *95 (SSS)*		CP	____
16424	Western Maryland Covered Quad Hopper, *95 (SSS)*		CP	____
16425	Western Maryland Covered Quad Hopper, *95 (SSS)*		CP	____

		Exc	New	Cond/$
16426	Western Maryland Covered Quad Hopper, 95 (SSS)		CP	___
16427	Western Maryland Covered Quad Hopper, 95 (SSS)		CP	___
(16429)	Western Maryland Quad Hoppers w/ coal loads (2) (See 16422, 16423)			
(16430)	Georgia Power Quad Hopper w/ coal load "82947", 95 u		CP	___
16500	Rock Island Bobber Caboose, 87–88	10	15	___
16501	Lehigh Valley SP-Type Caboose, 87	20	25	___
16503	NYC Transfer Caboose, 87	15	20	___
16504	Southern N5C Caboose, 87 (SSS)	25	45	___
16505	Wabash SP-Type Caboose, 88–91	10	15	___
16506	Santa Fe B/W Caboose, 88	30	35	___
(16507)	Mopar Express SP-Type Caboose "1987", 87–88 u	40	50	___
(16508)	Lionel Lines SP-Type Caboose "6508", 89 u	15	20	___
16509	D&RGW SP-Type Caboose, 89 (SSS)	25	35	___
16510	New Haven B/W Caboose, 89	25	35	___
16511	PRR Bobber Caboose, 88 u, 89	10	15	___
16513	Union Pacific SP-Type Caboose, 89	15	25	___
16515	Lionel Lines RailScope SP-Type Caboose, 89	25	35	___
16516	Lehigh Valley SP-Type Caboose, 90	15	25	___
16517	Atlantic Coast Line B/W Caboose, 90	20	30	___
16518	Chessie System B/W Caboose, 90	35	50	___
16519	Rock Island Transfer Caboose, 90	15	25	___
(16520)	"Welcome To The Show" Circus SP-Type Caboose, 89 u	15	25	___
16521	PRR SP-Type Caboose, 90–91	10	15	___
16522	"Chills & Thrills" Circus N5C Caboose, 90–91	10	15	___
16523	Alaska SP-Type Caboose, 91	30	40	___
(16524)	Anheuser-Busch SP-Type Caboose, 89–92 u	30	40	___
16525	D&H B/W Caboose, 91 (SSS)	35	45	___
16526	Kansas City Southern SP-Type Caboose, 91	20	25	___
16527	Western Pacific Work Caboose, 92		NM	
(16528)	Union Pacific SP-Type Caboose "6528", 90–91 u	20	25	___
(16529)	Santa Fe SP-Type Caboose "16829", 91	10	15	___

		Exc	New	Cond/$
(16530)	Mickey's World Tour SP-Type Caboose "16830", *91, 92 u*	15	20	_____
16531	Texas & Pacific SP-Type Caboose, *92*	20	25	_____
16533	C&NW B/W Caboose, *92*	25	35	_____
16534	Delaware & Hudson SP-Type Caboose, *92*	20	25	_____
16535	Erie-Lackawanna B/W Caboose, *91 u*	35	45	_____
16536	Chessie System SP-Type Caboose, *92, 93 u, 94, 95 u*		CP	_____
16537	MKT SP-Type Caboose, *92, 93 u*	20	25	_____
(16538)	L&N B/W Caboose "1041", *92 u*	35	40	_____
16538	L&N/Family Lines Steelside Caboose w/ smoke (Std. O), *92*		NM	
(16539)	WP Steelside Caboose w/ smoke "539" (Std. O), *92 (SSS)*	60	75	_____
(16541)	Montana Rail Link E/V Caboose w/ smoke "10131", *93*	60	75	_____
(16543)	NYC SP-Type Caboose, *93–95*		CP	_____
16544	Union Pacific SP-Type Caboose, *93–95*		CP	_____
16544	(See 16564)			
16546	Clinchfield SP-Type Caboose, *93*	25	30	_____
16547	Happy Holidays SP-Type Caboose, *93–95*		CP	_____
16548	Conrail SP-Type Caboose, *93*	25	35	_____
16549	Soo Line Work Caboose, *93*	20	30	_____
16550	U.S. Navy Searchlight Caboose, *94–95*		CP	_____
16551	Budweiser SP-Type Caboose, *93–94 u*	30	35	_____
16552	Frisco Searchlight Caboose, *94*	30	35	_____
16553	United Auto Workers SP-Type Caboose, *93 u*		NRS	_____
(16554)	GT E/V Caboose w/ smoke "79052", *94*	50	55	_____
16555	C&O SP-Type Caboose, *94*	25	30	_____
16556	(See 16909)			
16557	Ford SP-Type Caboose, *94 u*	25	30	_____
(16558)	Crayola SP-Type Caboose, *94 u, 95*		CP	_____
(16559)	Seaboard CC Caboose "5658", *95*		CP	_____
16560	Chrysler Mopar Caboose, *94 u*	30	35	_____
(16561)	Union Pacific CC Caboose "25766", *95*		CP	_____
16562	Reading CC Caboose, *95*		CP	_____
(16563)	Lionel Lines SP-Type Caboose, *95*		CP	_____
16564	Western Maryland CC Caboose, *95 (SSS)*		CP	_____
16565	Milwaukee Road B/W Caboose, *95*		CP	_____

LTI MODERN ERA (1987–1996)

		Exc	New	Cond/$
(16566)	U.S. Army SP-Type Caboose "907", 95		CP	____
16570	NdeM E/V Caboose, 96		NM	
(16571)	Georgia Power SP-Type Caboose "52789", 95 u		CP	____
16578	Lionel Lines SP-Type Caboose, 95 u		CP	____
16600	Illinois Central Coal Dump Car, 88	15	25	____
16601	Canadian National Searchlight Car, 88	20	25	____
16602	Erie-Lackawanna Coal Dump Car, 87	15	25	____
16603	Detroit Zoo Giraffe Car (O27), 87	40	50	____
16604	NYC Log Dump Car, 87	15	25	____
16605	Bronx Zoo Giraffe Car (O27), 88	40	45	____
16606	Southern Searchlight Car, 87	15	25	____
[16606]	Southern TCA Southern Searchlight Car, 88 u	20	30	____
(16607)	Southern Coal Dump Car "16707", 87 (SSS)	20	30	____
16608	Lehigh Valley Searchlight Car, 87	25	35	____
16609	Lehigh Valley Derrick Car, 87	25	35	____
16610	Lionel Track Maintenance Car, 87–88	15	25	____
16611	Santa Fe Log Dump Car, 88	15	25	____
16612	Soo Line Log Dump Car, 89	15	25	____
16613	MKT Coal Dump Car, 89	15	25	____
16614	Reading Cop and Hobo Car (O27), 89	25	30	____
16615	Lionel Lines Extension Searchlight Car, 89	20	30	____
16616	D&RGW Searchlight Car, 89 (SSS)	25	35	____
16617	C&NW Boxcar w/ ETD, 89	20	30	____
16618	Santa Fe Track Maintenance Car, 89	15	25	____
16619	Wabash Coal Dump Car, 90	15	25	____
16620	C&O Track Maintenance Car, 90–91	15	25	____
16621	Alaska Log Dump Car, 90	20	25	____
16622	CSX Boxcar w/ ETD, 90–91	20	30	____
16623	MKT DD Boxcar w/ ETD, 91	20	30	____
16624	NH Cop and Hobo Car (O27), 90–91	25	35	____
16625	NYC Extension Searchlight Car, 90	20	30	____
16626	CSX Searchlight Car, 90	20	30	____
16627	CSX Log Dump Car, 90	20	25	____
16628	"Laughter" Circus Animated Gondola, 90–91	40	50	____
16629	"Animal Car" Circus Elephant Car (O27), 90–91	45	60	____
16630	SP Operating Cowboy Car (O27), 90–91	25	30	____
16631	RI Boxcar w/ Steam RailSounds, 90	125	150	____
16632	BN Boxcar w/ Diesel RailSounds, 90	125	150	____

		Exc	New	Cond/$
16633	Great Northern Cop and Hobo Car (O27), 91		NM	
16634	WM Coal Dump Car, 91	20	25	___
16635	CP Rail Track Maintenance Car, 91		NM	
16636	D&RGW Log Dump Car, 91	20	25	___
16637	WP Extension Searchlight Car, 91	30	35	___
16638	Lionelville Circus Operating Animal Car (O27), 91	60	75	___
16639	B&O Boxcar w/ Steam RailSounds, 91	125	150	___
16640	Rutland Boxcar w/ Diesel RailSounds, 91	125	150	___
16641	Toys "R" Us Giraffe Car (O27), 90–91 u	50	75	___
16642	Mickey's World Tour Goofy Car (O27), 91, 92 u	40	50	___
16643	Amtrak Coal Dump Car, 91		NM	
16644	Amtrak Crane Car, 91, 92 u	40	50	___
16645	Amtrak Searchlight Caboose, 91, 92 u	30	35	___
16646	Railbox Boxcar w/ ETD, 92		NM	
16649	Railway Express Agency Boxcar w/ Steam RailSounds, 92	145	155	___
16650	NYC "Pacemaker" Boxcar w/ Diesel RailSounds, 92	145	160	___
16651	Circus Operating Clown Car (O27), 92	35	40	___
16652	Lionel Radar Car, 92	35	45	___
16653	Western Pacific Crane Car, 92 (SSS)	45	60	___
16654	(See 17214)			
(16655)	Steam Tender w/ RailSounds "1993", 93	150	175	___
16656	Burlington Log Dump Car, 92 u	20	25	___
16657	Lehigh Valley Coal Dump Car, 92 u	20	25	___
16658	Erie-Lackawanna Crane Car, 93	50	60	___
16659	Union Pacific Searchlight Car, 93–95		CP	___
16660	Lionel Fire Car w/ ladders, 93–94	55	60	___
16661	Lionel Flatcar w/ boat, 93	40	60	___
16662	Looney Tunes Operating Bugs Bunny and Yosemite Sam Car (O27), 93–94	35	40	___
16663	Missouri Pacific Searchlight Car, 93	25	30	___
16664	L&N Coal Dump Car, 93	25	30	___
16665	Maine Central Log Dump Car, 93	25	30	___
16666	Lionel Toxic Waste Car, 93–94	30	40	___
16667	Conrail Searchlight Car, 93	30	35	___
16668	Ontario Northland Log Dump Car, 93	25	30	___
16669	Soo Line Searchlight Car, 93	20	25	___
16670	Lionel TV Car, 93–94	35	40	___

		Exc	New	Cond/$
(16673)	Lionel Lines Tender w/ whistle, *94–96*		CP	____
16674	Pinkerton Animated Gondola, *94*	30	35	____
16675	Great Northern Log Dump Car, *94*	25	28	____
16676	Burlington Coal Dump Car, *94*	25	28	____
16677	NATO Flatcar w/ Royal Navy submarine, *94*	35	40	____
16678	Rock Island Searchlight Car, *94*	25	28	____
16679	U.S. Mail Operating Boxcar, *94*	45	50	____
16680	Lionel Cherry Picker Car, *94*	30	35	____
16681	Aquarium Car, *95*		CP	____
16682	Lionelville Farms Operating Stock Car (O27), *94*	25	30	____
16683	Los Angeles Zoo Elephant Car (O27), *94*	30	35	____
16684	U.S. Navy Crane Car, *94–95*		CP	____
16685	Erie Extension Searchlight Car, *95*		CP	____
16686	Mickey Mouse and Big Bad Pete Animated Boxcar, *95*		CP	____
16687	U.S. Mail Operating Boxcar, *94*	40	50	____
16688	Lionel Fire Car w/ ladders, *94*	50	70	____
16689	Lionel Toxic Waste Car, *94*	30	35	____
16690	Looney Tunes Operating Bugs Bunny and Yosemite Sam Car (O27), *94*	30	35	____
16701	Southern Tool Car, *87 (SSS)*	50	65	____
16702	Amtrak Bunk Car, *91, 92 u*	30	35	____
16703	NYC Tool Car, *92*	30	35	____
16704	Lionel TV Car, *94*	30	35	____
16705	Chesapeake & Ohio Cop and Hobo Car, *95*		CP	____
16706	Animal Transport Service Giraffe Car, *95*		CP	____
16707	(See 16607)			
16708	C&NW Track Maintenance Car, *95*		CP	____
16709	New York Central Derrick Car, *95*		CP	____
16710	U.S. Army Operating Missle Car, *95*		CP	____
16711	Pennsylvania Searchlight Car, *95*		CP	____
16712	Pinkerton Animated Gondola, *95*		CP	____
16713	Great Northern Log Dump Car, *95*		CP	____
16714	Burlington Coal Dump Car, *95*		CP	____
16717	Jersey Central Crane Car, *96*		CP	____
16718	U.S.M.C. Missle Launching Flatcar, *96*		CP	____
16800	Lionel Railroader Club Ore Car, *86 u*	80	100	____
16801	Lionel Railroader Club Bunk Car, *88 u*	35	50	____
16802	Lionel Railroader Club Tool Car, *89 u*	35	50	____

		Exc	New	Cond/$
16803	Lionel Railroader Club Searchlight Car, *90 u*	30	40	____
16804	Lionel Railroader Club B/W Caboose, *91 u*	30	40	____
(16805)	Budweiser Malt Nutrine Reefer "3285", *91–92 u*	65	80	____
16806	Toys "R" Us Boxcar, *92 u*	40	45	____
(16807)	H.J. Heinz Reefer "301", *93*	35	40	____
16808	Toys "R" Us Boxcar, *93 u*	40	45	____
16829	(See 16529)			
16830	(See 16530)			
(16901)	Lionel Catalog video (VHS), *91 u*	20	25	____
16903	CP Bulkhead Flatcar w/ pulp load, *94 (SSS)*	30	35	____
(16904)	NYC "Pacemaker" TTUX Flatcar set w/ trailers "16905" and "16906", *94*	70	75	____
16905/ 16906	NYC "Pacemaker" TTUX Flatcars w/ trailers (See 16904)			
16907	Lionel Flatcar w/ farm tractors, *94*	35	45	____
(16908)	U.S. Navy Flatcar "04039" w/ submarine "930", *94–95*		CP	____
(16909)	U.S. Navy Gondola w/ canisters "16556", *94–95*		CP	____
16910	Missouri Pacific Flatcar w/ trailer, *94*	25	30	____
16911	B&M Flatcar w/ trailer, *94*	25	30	____
(16912)	CN Maxi-Stack Flatcar set w/ containers "640000" and "640001", *94*	70	75	____
(16913)/ (16914)	CN Maxi-Stack Flatcars w/ containers "640000" and "640001" (See 16912)			
16915	Lionel Lines Gondola (O27), *93–94 u*	8	10	____
16916	Ford Flatcar w/ trailer, *94 u*	50	65	____
(16917)	Crayola Gondola w/ crayons, *94 u, 95*		CP	____
16919	Chrysler Mopar Gondola w/ coil covers, *94 u*	30	35	____
16920	Lionel Flatcar w/ construction block helicopter, *95*		CP	____
16922	Chesapeake & Ohio Flatcar w/ trailer, *95*		CP	____
16923	Lionel Intermodal Service Flatcar w/ wheel chocks, *95*		CP	____
16925	New York Central Flatcar w/ trailer, *95*		CP	____
16926	Frisco Flatcar w/ trailers, *95*		CP	____
16927	New York Central Flatcar w/ gondola, *95*		CP	____
16928	Soo Line Flatcar w/ dump bin (O27), *95*		CP	____
16929	BC Rail Gondola w/ cable reels, *95*		CP	____

		Exc	New	Cond/$
16930	Santa Fe Flatcar w/ wheel load, *95*		CP	____
16932	Erie Flatcar w/ rail load, *95*		CP	____
16933	Lionel Lines Flatcar w/ automobiles, *95*		CP	____
16934	Pennsylvania Flatcar w/ Ertl road grader, *95*		CP	____
16935	UP Depressed Flatcar w/ Ertl bulldozer, *95*		CP	____
(16936)	Susquehanna Maxi-Stack Flatcar set w/ containers "16937" and "16938", *95*		CP	____
16937/ 16938	Susquehanna Maxi-Stack Flatcars w/ containers (See 16936)			
(16939)	U.S. Navy Flatcar w/ boat "04040", *95*		CP	____
16943	Jersey Central Gondola, *96*		CP	____
(16944)	Georgia Power Depressed Flatcar w/ transformer "31438", *95 u*		CP	____
(16945)	Georgia Power Depressed Flatcar w/ cable reels "31950", *95 u*		CP	____
16952	U.S. Navy Flatcar w/ Ertl helicopter, *96*		CP	____
(16953)	NYC Flatcar w/ Red Wing Shoes trailer "1905–95", *95 u*		CP	____
17000	(See 17107)			
17002	Conrail 2-bay ACF Hopper (Std. O), *87*	100	110	____
17003	Du Pont 2-bay ACF Hopper (Std. O), *90*	60	85	____
17004	MKT 2-bay ACF Hopper (Std. O), *91*	30	40	____
17005	Cargill 2-bay ACF Hopper (Std. O), *92*	30	40	____
17006	Soo Line 2-bay ACF Hopper (Std. O), *93 (SSS)*	50	60	____
(17007)	GN 2-bay ACF Hopper "173872" (Std. O), *94*	35	40	____
(17008)	D&RGW 2-bay ACF Hopper "10009" (Std. O), *95*		CP	____
17100	Chessie System 3-bay ACF Hopper (Std. O), *88*	50	60	____
17101	Chessie System 3-bay ACF Hopper (Std. O), *88*	50	60	____
17102	Chessie System 3-bay ACF Hopper (Std. O), *88*	50	60	____
17103	Chessie System 3-bay ACF Hopper (Std. O), *88*	50	60	____
17104	Chessie System 3-bay ACF Hopper (Std. O), *88*	50	60	____
17105	Chessie System 3-bay ACF Hopper (Std. O), *95*		CP	____
17107	Sclair 3-bay ACF Hopper (Std. O), *89*	100	115	____
17108	Santa Fe 3-bay ACF Hopper (Std. O), *90*	60	75	____
17109	N&W 3-bay ACF Hopper (Std. O), *91*	30	40	____
17110	Union Pacific Hopper w/ coal load (Std. O), *91*	30	40	____
17111	Reading Hopper w/ coal load (Std. O), *91*	30	40	____
17112	Erie-Lack. 3-bay ACF Hopper (Std. O), *92*	30	40	____
17113	LV Hopper w/ coal load (Std. O), *92–93*	30	40	____

		Exc	New	Cond/$
17114	Peabody Hopper w/ coal load (Std. O), *92–93*	50	60	___
(17118)	Archer Daniels Midland 3-bay ACF			
	Hopper "60029" (Std. O), *93*	35	45	___
(17120)	CSX Hopper w/ coal load "295110" (Std. O), *94*	30	40	___
(17121)	ICG Hopper w/ coal load "72867" (Std. O), *94*	30	40	___
(17122)	RI 3-bay ACF Hopper "800200" (Std. O), *94*	30	40	___
(17123)	Cargill Covered Grain Hopper "844304"			
	(Std. O), *95*		CP	___
(17124)	Archer Daniels Midland 3-bay ACF Hopper			
	"50224" (Std. O), *95*		CP	___
(17125)	Goodyear 3-bay ACF Hopper (Std. O), *95*		NM	
17200	Canadian Pacific Boxcar (Std. O), *89*	60	75	___
17201	Conrail Boxcar (Std. O), *87*	60	75	___
17202	Santa Fe Boxcar			
	w/ Diesel RailSounds (Std. O), *90*	130	145	___
17203	Cotton Belt DD Boxcar (Std. O), *91*	35	40	___
17204	Missouri Pacific DD Boxcar (Std. O), *91*	35	40	___
17207	C&IM DD Boxcar (Std. O), *92*	35	40	___
17208	Union Pacific DD Boxcar (Std. O), *92*	35	40	___
(17209)	B&O DD Boxcar "296000" (Std. O), *93*	40	50	___
(17210)	Chicago & Illinois Midland Boxcar			
	"16021" (Std. O), *92 u*	30	40	___
(17211)	Chicago & Illinois Midland Boxcar			
	"16022" (Std. O), *92 u*	30	40	___
(17212)	Chicago & Illinois Midland Boxcar			
	"16023" (Std. O), *92 u*	30	40	___
(17213)	Susquehanna Boxcar "501" (Std. O), *93*	35	40	___
17214	Railbox Boxcar			
	w/ Diesel RailSounds (Std. O), *93*	140	155	___
(17216)	PRR DD Boxcar "60155" (Std. O), *94*	40	45	___
(17217)	New Haven "State of Maine" Boxcar			
	"45003" (Std. O), *95*		CP	___
(17218)	BAR "State of Maine" Boxcar			
	"2184" (Std. O), *95*		CP	___
17219	Tazmanian Devil 40th Birthday Boxcar (Std. O), *95*		CP	___
17220	Pennsylvania Boxcar (Std. O), *96*		CP	___
17221	NYC Boxcar (Std. O), *96*		CP	___
17222	Western Pacific Boxcar (Std. O), *96*		CP	___
17300	Canadian Pacific Reefer (Std. O), *89*	60	75	___

LTI MODERN ERA (1987–1996)

		Exc	New	Cond/$
17301	Conrail Reefer (Std. O), *87*	60	75	____
17302	Santa Fe Reefer w/ ETD (Std. O), *90*	60	75	____
(17303)	C&O Reefer "7890" (Std. O), *93*	35	45	____
(17304)	Wabash Reefer "26269" (Std. O), *94*	35	42	____
(17305)	Pacific Fruit Express Reefer "459400" (Std. O), *94*	35	42	____
(17306)	Pacific Fruit Express Reefer "459401" (Std. O), *94*	35	42	____
(17307)	Tropicana Reefer "300" (Std. O), *95*		CP	____
(17308)	Tropicana Reefer "301" (Std. O), *95*		CP	____
(17309)	Tropicana Reefer "302" (Std. O), *95*		CP	____
(17310)	Tropicana Reefer "303" (Std. O), *95*		CP	____
17311	Railway Express Agency Reefer (Std. O), *96*		CP	____
17400	CP Rail Gondola w/ coal load (Std. O), *89*	50	60	____
17401	Conrail Gondola w/ coal load (Std. O), *87*	50	60	____
17402	Santa Fe Gondola w/ coal load (Std. O), *90*	50	60	____
(17403)	Chessie System Gondola w/ coil covers "371629" (Std. O), *93*	35	40	____
(17404)	Illinois Central Gulf Gondola w/ coil covers "245998" (Std. O), *93*	35	40	____
(17405)	Reading Gondola w/ coil covers "24876" (Std. O), *94*	35	40	____
(17406)	PRR Gondola w/ coil covers "385405" (Std. O), *95*		CP	____
17500	CP Flatcar w/ logs (Std. O), *89*	50	60	____
17501	Conrail Flatcar w/ stakes (Std. O), *87*	50	60	____
17502	Santa Fe Flatcar w/ trailer (Std. O), *90*	75	95	____
17503	NS Flatcar w/ trailer (Std. O), *92*	50	65	____
17504	NS Flatcar w/ trailer (Std. O), *92*	50	65	____
17505	NS Flatcar w/ trailer (Std. O), *92*	50	65	____
17506	NS Flatcar w/ trailer (Std. O), *92*	50	65	____
17507	NS Flatcar w/ trailer (Std. O), *92*	50	65	____
17508	BN I-Beam Flatcar w/ load (Std. O), *92*		NM	
17509	Southern I-Beam Flatcar w/ load (Std. O), *92*		NM	
(17510)	NP Flatcar w/ logs "51200" (Std. O), *94*	30	35	____
(17511)	WM Flatcars w/ logs, set of 3 (Std. O), *95*		CP	____
17512	WM Flatcar w/ logs (Std. O), *95*		CP	____
17513	WM Flatcar w/ logs (Std. O), *95*		CP	____
17514	WM Flatcar w/ logs (Std. O), *95*		CP	____

		Exc	New	Cond/$
17515	Norfolk Southern Flatcar w/ tractors (Std. O), *95*		CP	_____
17600	NYC Woodside Caboose (Std. O), *87 u*	70	85	_____
17601	Southern Woodside Caboose (Std. O), *88*	70	85	_____
17602	Conrail Woodside Caboose (Std. O), *87*	100	120	_____
17603	Rock Island Woodside Caboose (Std. O), *88*	40	55	_____
17604	Lackawanna Woodside Caboose (Std. O), *88*	60	65	_____
17605	Reading Woodside Caboose (Std. O), *89*	50	60	_____
17606	NYC Steelside Caboose w/ smoke (Std. O), *90*	60	70	_____
17607	Reading Steelside Caboose w/ smoke (Std. O), *90*	60	70	_____
17608	C&O Steelside Caboose w/ smoke (Std. O), *91*	60	70	_____
17610	Wabash Steelside Caboose w/ smoke (Std. O), *91*	60	70	_____
(17611)	NYC Woodside Caboose "6003" (Std. O), *90 u, 91*	60	70	_____
17612	NKP Steelside Caboose w/ smoke (FF #6) (Std. O), *92*	60	70	_____
(17613)	Southern Steelside Caboose w/ smoke "7613" (Std. O), *92*	60	70	_____
17615	Northern Pacific Woodside Caboose w/ smoke (Std. O), *92*	60	70	_____
17617	D&RGW Steelside Caboose (Std. O), *95*		CP	_____
17618	Frisco Woodside Caboose (Std. O), *95*		CP	_____
17870	LCCA East Camden & Highland Boxcar (Std. O), *87 u*	70	85	_____
(17871)	TTOS NYC Flatcar w/ Kodak and Xerox trailers "81487", *87 u*	300	400	_____
(17872)	TTOS Anaconda Ore Car "81988", *88 u*	70	100	_____
17873	LCCA Ashland Oil 3-D Tank Car, *88 u*	50	70	_____
(17874)	LOTS MILW Log Dump Car "59629", *88 u*	100	140	_____
(17875)	LOTS PHD Boxcar "1289", *89 u*	75	95	_____
17876	LCCA Columbia Newberry & Laurens Boxcar (Std. O), *89 u*	60	75	_____
(17877)	TTOS MKT 1-D Tank Car "3739469", *89 u*	60	75	_____
17878	Gadsden Pacific Magma Ore Car w/ load, *89 u*	60	75	_____
(17879)	TCA Valley Forge Dining Car "1989", *89 u*	65	75	_____
17880	LCCA D&RGW Woodside Caboose (Std. O), *90 u*	65	85	_____

LTI MODERN ERA (1987–1996)

		Exc	New	Cond/$
17881	Gadsden Pacific Phelps-Dodge Ore Car w/ load, *90 u*	50	60	
(17882)	LOTS B&O DD Boxcar w/ ETD "298011", *90 u*	85	100	
(17883)	TCA New Georgia RR Passenger Car "1990", *90 u*	50	65	
17884	TTOS Columbus & Dayton Terminal Boxcar (Std. O), *90 u*	50	70	
17885	Artrain 1-D Tank Car, *90 u*	80	95	
17886	Gadsden Pacific Cyprus Ore Car w/ load, *91 u*	40	50	
17887	LCCA Conrail Flatcar w/ Armstrong Tile trailer (Std. O), *91 u*	55	70	
17888	LCCA Conrail Flatcar w/ Ford New Holland trailer (Std. O), *91 u*	70	90	
(17889)	TTOS SP Flatcar w/ trailer "15791" (Std. O), *91 u*	60	80	
(17890)	LOTS CSX Auto Carrier "151161", *91 u*	95	110	
17891	Artrain Grand Trunk Boxcar, *91 u*	80	100	
(17892)	LCCA Conrail Flatcars w/ trailers (Std. O) (See 17887, 17888)			
[17893]	LCAC BAOC 1-D Tank Car "914", *91 u*	—	100	
(17894)	TTOS Southern Pacific Tractor, *91 u*	20	25	
(17895)	LCCA Tractor, *91 u*	15	20	
(17896)	LCCA Lancaster Lines Tractor, *91 u*	25	30	
[17897]	VTC Passenger Cars (See 7692)			
(17898)	TCA Wabash Reefer "21596", *92 u*	50	60	
(17899)	LCCA NASA Uni-body Tank Car "190" (Std. O), *92 u*	75	95	
17900	Santa Fe Uni-body Tank Car (Std. O), *90*	40	50	
17901	Chevron Uni-body Tank Car (Std. O), *90*	40	50	
17902	NJ Zinc Uni-body Tank Car (Std. O), *91*	40	50	
17903	Conoco Uni-body Tank Car (Std. O), *91*	40	50	
17904	Texaco Uni-body Tank Car (Std. O), *92*	40	50	
17905	Archer Daniels Midland Uni-body Tank Car (Std. O), *92*	40	50	
(17906)	SCM Uni-body Tank Car "78286" (Std. O), *93*	50	60	
17908	Marathon Oil Uni-body Tank Car (Std. O), *95*		CP	
17909	Hooker Chemicals Uni-body Tank Car (Std. O), *96*		CP	
(18000)	PRR 0-6-0 "8977" *89, 91*	525	650	

		Exc	New	Cond/$
(18001)	Rock Island 4-8-4 "5100", *87*	400	485	_____
(18002)	NYC 4-6-4 "785", *87 u*	750	850	_____
(18003)	Delaware Lackawanna & Western 4-8-4 "1501", *88*	425	525	_____
(18004)	Reading 4-6-2 "8004", *89*	300	350	_____
(18005)	NYC 4-6-4 "5340" w/ display case, *90*	1100	1475	_____
(18006)	Reading 4-8-4 "2100", *89 u*	725	800	_____
(18007)	Southern Pacific 4-8-4 "4410", *91*	475	575	_____
(18008)	Disneyland 35th Anniversary 4-4-0 "4" w/ display case, *90*	250	300	_____
(18009)	NYC 4-8-2 "3000", *90 u, 91*	850	950	_____
(18010)	Pennsylvania 6-8-6 "6200", *91–92*	1100	1400	_____
(18011)	Chessie System 4-8-4 "2101", *91*	600	700	_____
(18012)	NYC 4-6-4 "5340", *90*	1000	1250	_____
(18013)	Disneyland 35th Anniversary 4-4-0 "4", *90*	200	250	_____
(18014)	Lionel Lines 2-6-4 "8014", *91*	130	180	_____
(18016)	Northern Pacific 4-8-4 "2626", *92*	500	600	_____
(18018)	Southern 2-8-2 "4501", *92*	850	950	_____
18021	(See 18030)			
(18022)	Pere Marquette 2-8-4 "1201", *93*	500	600	_____
(18023)	Western Maryland Shay "6", *92*	1000	1200	_____
(18024)	Sears T&P 4-8-2 "907" w/ display case, *92 u*	900	1000	_____
(18025)	T&P 4-8-2 "907", *92 u* (See 18024)			
(18026)	Smithsonian NYC Dreyfuss 4-6-4 "5450" (2-rail), *92 u*		NRS	_____
(18027)	NYC Dreyfuss 4-6-4 "5450" (3-rail), *93 u*		NRS	_____
(18028)	Smithsonian Pennsylvania 4-6-2 "3768" (2-rail), *93 u*		NRS	_____
(18029)	NYC Dreyfuss 4-6-4 "5454" (3-rail) w/ operating roller base, *93 u*		NRS	_____
(18030)	Frisco 2-8-2 "4100", *93 u*	725	800	_____
(18031)	Bundesbahn BR-50 2-10-0 (2-rail), *93 u*		NRS	_____
(18034)	Santa Fe 2-8-2 "3158", *94*	650	700	_____
(18035)	Reichsbahn BR-50 2-10-0 (2-rail), *93 u*		NRS	_____
(18036)	French BR-50 2-10-0 (2-rail), *93 u*		NRS	_____
(18040)	N&W 4-8-4 "612", *95*		CP	_____
(18041)	Boston & Albany 4-6-4 "619", *95*		NM	

LTI MODERN ERA (1987–1996)

	Exc	New	Cond/$
(18042) Boston & Albany 4-6-4 "618", *95*		CP	___
(18043) Chesapeake & Ohio 4-6-4 "490", *95*		CP	___
(18044) Southern 4-6-2 "1390", *96*		CP	___
(18046) Wabash 4-6-4 "700", *96*		CP	___
(18090) LCCA D&RGW 4-6-2 "1990", *90 u*	350	425	___
(18100) Santa Fe F-3 A Unit "8100" (See 11711)			
(18101) Santa Fe F-3 B Unit "8101" (See 11711)			
(18102) Santa Fe F-3 A Unit Dummy "8102" (See 11711)			
(18103) Santa Fe F-3 B Unit Dummy "8103", *91 u*	325	375	___
(18104) Great Northern F-3 A Unit Dummy "366A" (See 11724)			
(18105) Great Northern F-3 B Unit Dummy "370B" (See 11724)			
(18106) Great Northern F-3 A Unit Dummy "351C" (See 11724)			
(18107) D&RGW Alco PA-1 ABA set "6001" and "6002", *92*	750	900	___
(18108) Great Northern F-3 B Unit "371B", *93*	120	150	___
(18109) Erie Alco A Unit "725A" (See 11734)			
(18110) Erie Alco B Unit "725B" (See 11734)			
(18111) Erie Alco A Unit Dummy "736A" (See 11734)			
(18112) TCA F-3 A Unit "40" (See 11737)			
(18113) TCA F-3 B Unit (See 11737)			
(18114) TCA F-3 A Unit Dummy "40" (See 11737)			
(18115) Santa Fe F-3 B Unit, *93*	120	165	___
(18116) Erie-Lackawanna Alco PA-1 AA set "858" and "859", *93*	525	650	___
(18117)/ (18118) Santa Fe F-3 AA set "200", *93*	350	400	___
(18119)/ (18120) UP Alco AA set "8119" and "8120", *94*	300	360	___
(18121) Santa Fe F-3 B Unit "200A", *94*	95	125	___
(18122) Santa Fe F-3 B Unit "200B", *95*		CP	___
(18123) ACL F-3 A Unit "342" (See 11903)			
(18124) ACL F-3 B Unit "342B" (See 11903)			
(18125) Atlantic Coast Line F-3 A Unit Dummy "343" (See 11903)			
(18200) Conrail SD-40 "8200", *87*	275	325	___
(18201) Chessie System SD-40 "8201", *88*	275	325	___
(18202) Erie-Lackawanna SD-40 Dummy "8459", *89 u*	150	175	___
(18203) CP Rail SD-40 "8203", *89*	225	300	___

LTI MODERN ERA (1987–1996)

	Exc	New	Cond/$
(18204) Chessie System SD-40 Dummy "8204", *90 u*	150	175	_____
(18205) Union Pacific Dash 8-40C "9100", *89*	300	350	_____
(18206) Santa Fe Dash 8-40B "8206", *90*	250	275	_____
(18207) Norfolk Southern Dash 8-40C "8689", *92*	300	350	_____
(18208) BN SD-40 Dummy "8586", *91 u*	150	175	_____
(18209) CP Rail SD-40 Dummy "8209", *92 u*	175	200	_____
(18210) Illinois Central SD-40 "6006", *93*	275	300	_____
(18211) Susquehanna Dash 8-40B "4002", *93*	275	300	_____
(18212) Santa Fe Dash 8-40B Dummy "8212", *93*	175	200	_____
(18213) Norfolk Southern Dash 8-40C "8688", *94*	325	360	_____
(18214) CSX Dash 8-40C "7500", *94*	325	360	_____
(18215) CSX Dash 8-40C "7643", *94*	325	360	_____
(18216) Conrail SD-60M "5500", *94*	400	450	_____
(18217) Illinois Central SD-40 "6007", *94*	325	360	_____
(18218) Susquehanna Dash 8-40B "4004", *94*	325	360	_____
(18219) C&NW Dash 8-40C "8501", *95*		CP	_____
(18220) C&NW Dash 8-40C "8502", *95*		CP	_____
(18221) D&RGW SD-50 "5512", *95*		CP	_____
(18222) D&RGW SD-50 "5517", *95*		CP	_____
(18223) Milwaukee Road SD-40 "154", *95*		CP	_____
(18224) Milwaukee Road SD-40 "155", *95*		CP	_____
(18300) PRR GG-1 "8300", *87*	425	500	_____
(18301) Southern FM Trainmaster "8301", *88*	300	395	_____
(18302) GN EP-5 "8302" (FF#3), *88*	200	260	_____
(18303) Amtrak GG-1 "8303", *89*	375	425	_____
(18304) Lackawanna MU Car set Powered and Dummy "2401" and "2402", *91*	400	450	_____
(18305) Lackawanna MU Car set, Dummies "2400" and "2403", *92*	300	350	_____
(18306) PRR MU Car set, Powered and Dummy "4574" and "483", *92*	400	475	_____
(18307) PRR FM Trainmaster "8699", *94*	300	350	_____
(18308) PRR GG-1 "4866", *92*	500	600	_____
(18309) Reading FM Trainmaster "863", *93*	300	350	_____
(18310) PRR MU Car set, Dummies "484" and "485", *93*	300	375	_____
(18311) Disney EP-5 "8311", *94*	200	250	_____
(18313) Pennsylvania GG-1 "4907", *96*		CP	_____
(18400) Santa Fe Vulcan Rotary Snowplow			

		Exc	New	Cond/$
	"8400", *87*	150	200	____
(18401)	Workmen Handcar, *87–88*	35	45	____
18402	Lionel Lines Burro Crane, *88*	90	105	____
(18403)	Santa Claus Handcar, *88*	30	35	____
(18404)	San Francisco Trolley "8404", *88*	100	160	____
18405	Santa Fe Burro Crane, *89*	70	80	____
18406	Lionel Track Maintenance Car, *89, 91*	50	65	____
(18407)	Snoopy and Woodstock Handcar, *90–91*	40	60	____
(18408)	Santa Claus Handcar, *89*	30	45	____
18410	PRR Burro Crane, *90*	125	140	____
18411	Canadian Pacific Fire Car, *90*	115	140	____
18412	Union Pacific Fire Car, *91*		NM	
(18413)	Charlie Brown and Lucy Handcar, *91*	30	60	____
(18416)	Bugs Bunny and Daffy Duck Handcar, *92–93*	55	70	____
18417	Lionel Gang Car, *93*	85	105	____
(18419)	Lionelville Electric Trolley "8419", *94*	110	130	____
(18421)	Sylvester and Tweety Handcar, *94*	45	60	____
(18422)	Santa and Snowman Handcar, *94*	40	50	____
(18423)	On-Track Step Van, *95*		CP	____
(18424)	On-Track Pick-up Truck, *95*		CP	____
(18425)	Goofy and Pluto Handcar, *95*		CP	____
(18426)	Santa and Snowman Handcar, *95*		CP	____
(18429)	Workmen Handcar, *96*		CP	____
(18500)	Milwaukee Road GP-9 "8500" (FF#2), *87*	200	225	____
(18500)	(See 18550)			
(18501)	WM NW-2 "8501" (FF#4), *89*	200	230	____
(18502)	Lionel Lines 90th Anniversary GP-9 "1900", *90*	175	200	____
(18503)	Southern Pacific NW-2 "8503", *90*	225	275	____
(18504)	Frisco GP-7 "504" (FF#5), *91*	200	230	____
(18505)	NKP GP-7 Powered and Dummy set "400" and "401" (FF#6), *92*	340	440	____
(18506)	CN Budd RDC Powered and Dummy set "D202" and "D203", *92*	275	300	____
(18507)	CN Budd RDC Baggage "D202" (See 18506)			
(18508)	CN Budd RDC Passenger Dummy "D203" (See 18506)			
(18510)	CN Budd RDC Passenger Dummy "D200" (See 18512)			

	Exc	New	Cond/$
18511) CN Budd RDC Passenger Dummy "D250" (See 18512)			
18512) CN Budd RDC Dummies set "D200" and "D250", *93*	225	275	_____
18513) NYC GP-7 "7420", *94*	200	225	_____
18514) Missouri Pacific GP-7 "4124", *95*		CP	_____
18550) JCPenney MILW GP-9 "8500" w/ display case, *87 u*		NRS	_____
18551) JCPenney Susquehanna RS-3 "8809" w/ display case, *89 u*	200	225	_____
18552) JCPenney DM&IR SD-18 "8813" w/ display case, *90 u*	200	225	_____
18553) Sears UP GP-9 "150" w/ display case, *91 u*	175	200	_____
18554) JCPenney GM&O RS-3 "721" w/ display case, *92–93 u*	175	200	_____
18555) Sears C&IM SD-9 "52", *92 u*	175	200	_____
18556) Sears Chicago & Illinois Midland Caboose and Freight Car set, *92 u*	150	175	_____
18557) Chessie System 4-8-4 "2101" w/ display case for export, *92 u*		NRS	_____
18558) JCPenney MKT GP-9 "91" w/ display case, *94 u*	150	195	_____
18600) ACL 4-4-2 "8600", *87 u*	75	90	_____
18601) Great Northern 4-4-2 "8601", *88*	75	90	_____
18602) PRR 4-4-2 "8602", *87*	100	125	_____
18604) Wabash 4-4-2 "8604", *88–91*	75	90	_____
18605) Mopar Express 4-4-2 "1987", *87–88 u*	80	125	_____
18606) NYC 2-6-4 "8606", *89*	125	150	_____
18607) Union Pacific 2-6-4 "8607", *89*	125	150	_____
18608) D&RGW 2-6-4 "8608", *89 (SSS)*	125	150	_____
18609) Northern Pacific 2-6-4 "8609", *90*	150	175	_____
18610) Rock Island 0-4-0 "8610", *90*	175	210	_____
18611) Lionel Lines 2-6-4 "8611", *90 (SSS)*	130	150	_____
18612) C&NW 4-4-2 "8612", *89*	75	90	_____
18613) NYC 4-4-2 "8613", *89 u*	85	110	_____
18614) Circus Train 4-4-2 "1989", *89 u*	85	110	_____
18615) GTW 4-4-2 "8615", *90*	75	90	_____
18616) Northern Pacific 4-4-2 "8616", *90 u*	85	110	_____
18617) Adolphus III 4-4-2, *89–92 u*	100	125	_____

	Exc	New	Cond/$
(18618) B&O 4-4-2 "8618", *91*		NM	
(18620) Illinois Central 2-6-2 "8620", *91*	175	200	____
(18621) Western Pacific 0-4-0 "8621", *92*		NM	
(18622) Union Pacific 4-4-2 "8622", *90–91 u*	75	95	____
(18623) Texas & Pacific 4-4-2 "8623", *92*	80	110	____
(18625) Illinois Central 4-4-2 "8625", *91 u*	80	110	____
(18626) Delaware & Hudson 2-6-2 "8626", *92*	175	200	____
(18627) C&O 4-4-2 "8627" or "8633", *92, 93 u, 94, 95 u*		CP	____
(18628) MKT 4-4-2 "8628", *92, 93 u*	75	90	____
(18630) C&NW 4-6-2 "2903", *93*	300	360	____
(18632) NYC 4-4-2 "8632", *93–95*		CP	____
(18633) Union Pacific 4-4-2 "8633", *93–95*		CP	____
(18633) (See 18627, 18637)			
(18635) Santa Fe 2-6-4 "8625", *93*	200	225	____
(18636) B&O 4-6-2 "5300", *94*	300	325	____
(18637) United Auto Workers 4-4-2 "8633", *93 u*		NRS	
(18638) Norfolk & Western 2-6-4 "638", *94*	175	225	____
(18639) Reading 4-6-2 "639", *95*		CP	____
(18640) Union Pacific 4-6-2 "8640", *95*		CP	____
(18641) Ford 4-4-2 "8641", *94 u*	75	100	____
(18642) Lionel Lines 4-6-2 "8642", *95*		CP	____
(18689) (See 18207)			
(18700) Rock Island 0-4-0T "8700", *87–88*	40	50	____
(18702) V&TRR 4-4-0 "8702", *88 (SSS)*	125	150	____
(18704) Lionel Lines 2-4-0 "8704", *89 u*	40	50	____
(18705) "Neptune" 0-4-0T "8705", *90–91*	40	50	____
(18706) Santa Fe 2-4-0 "8706", *91*	40	50	____
(18707) Mickey's World Tour 2-4-0 "8707", *91, 92 u*	60	75	____
(18709) Lionel Employee Learning Center "Blue Engine" 0-4-0T, *92 u*	—	200	____
(18710) Southern Pacific 2-4-0 "2000", *93*	35	45	____
(18711) Southern 2-4-0 "2000", *93*	35	45	____
(18712) Jersey Central 2-4-0 "2000", *93*	35	45	____
(18713) Chessie System 2-4-0 "1993", *94–95*		CP	____
(18716) Lionelville Circus 4-4-0 "8716", *90–91*	100	125	____
(18800) Lehigh Valley GP-9 "8800", *87*	95	115	____
(18801) Santa Fe U36B "8801", *87*	100	120	____
(18802) Southern GP-9 "8802", *87 (SSS)*	115	140	____

		Exc	New	Cond/$
(18803)	Santa Fe RS-3 "8803", *88*	100	120	_____
(18804)	Soo Line RS-3 "8804", *88*	100	120	_____
(18805)	Union Pacific RS-3 "8805", *89*	100	120	_____
(18806)	New Haven SD-18 "8806", *89*	100	120	_____
(18807)	Lehigh Valley RS-3 "8807", *90*	100	125	_____
(18808)	ACL SD-18 "8808", *90*	100	125	_____
(18809)	Susquehanna RS-3 "8809", *89 u* (See 18551)			
(18810)	CSX SD-18 "8810", *90*	100	135	_____
(18811)	Alaska SD-9 "8811", *91*	125	175	_____
(18812)	Kansas City Southern GP-38 "4000", *91*	100	135	_____
(18813)	DM&IR SD-18 "8813", *90 u* (See 18552)			
(18814)	D&H RS-3 "8814", *91 (SSS)*	100	125	_____
(18815)	Amtrak RS-3 "1815", *91, 92 u*	100	135	_____
(18816)	C&NW GP-38-2 "4600", *92*	125	150	_____
(18817)	UP GP-9 "150", *91 u* (See 18553)			
(18818)	Lionel Railroader Club GP-38-2 "1992", *92 u*	125	155	_____
(18819)	L&N GP-38-2 "4136", *92*	125	160	_____
(18820)	WP GP-9 "8820", *92 (SSS)*	125	150	_____
(18821)	Clinchfield GP-38-2 "6005", *93*	125	150	_____
(18822)	Gulf, Mobile & Ohio RS-3 "721", *92–93 u* (See 18554)			
(18823)	Chicago & Illinois Midland SD-9 "52", *92 u* (See 18555)			
(18824)	Montana Rail Link SD-9 "600", *93*	125	150	_____
(18825)	Soo Line GP-38-2 "4000", *93 (SSS)*	125	150	_____
(18826)	Conrail GP-7 "5808", *93*	125	150	_____
(18827)	Happy Holidays RS-3 "8827", *93*	150	175	_____
(18830)	Budweiser GP-9 "1947", *93–94 u*	120	140	_____
(18831)	SP GP-20 "4060", *94*	125	145	_____
(18832)	PRR RSD-4 "8446", *95*		CP	_____
(18833)	Milwaukee Road RS-3 "2487", *94*	125	145	_____
(18834)	C&O SD-28 "8834", *94*	110	150	_____
(18835)	NYC RS-3 "8223", *94 (SSS)*	125	145	_____
(18836)	CN/Grand Trunk GP-38-2 "5800", *94*	125	150	_____
(18837)	Happy Holidays RS-3 "8837", *94–95*		CP	_____
(18838)	Seaboard RSC-3 "1538", *95*		CP	_____
(18840)	U.S. Army GP-7 "1821", *95*		CP	_____
(18841)	Western Maryland GP-20 "27", *95 (SSS)*		CP	_____
(18842)	Bessemer & Lake Erie SD-38 "868", *95 u*		CP	_____

LTI MODERN ERA (1987–1996)

	Exc	New	Cond/$
(18843) Great Northern RS-3 "197", *96*		CP	
(18844) NdeM GP-38 "9288", *96*		NM	
(18890) LOTS UP RS-3 "8805", *89 u*	125	150	
(18900) PRR Diesel Switcher "8900", *88 u, 89*	30	40	
(18901)/ (18902) PRR Alco AA set "8901" and "8902", *88*	125	150	
(18903)/ (18904) Amtrak Alco AA set "8903" and "8904", *88–89*	100	150	
(18905) PRR 44-tonner "9312", *92*	125	150	
(18906) Erie-Lackawanna RS-3 "8906", *91 u*	150	175	
(18907) Rock Island 44-tonner "371", *93*	130	160	
(18908)/ (18909) NYC Alco AA set "8908" and "8909", *93*	100	115	
(18910) CSX Diesel Switcher "8910", *93*	30	40	
(18911) UP Diesel Switcher "8911", *93*	30	40	
(18912) Amtrak Diesel Switcher "8912", *93*	30	40	
(18913) Santa Fe Alco A Unit "8913", *93–94*	60	75	
(18915) WM Alco A Unit "8915", *93*	55	70	
(18916) WM Alco A Unit Dummy "8916", *93*	35	40	
18917 Soo Line NW-2, *93*	70	80	
(18918) B&M NW-2 "8918", *93*	70	80	
(18919) Santa Fe Alco A Unit Dummy "8919", *93–94*	30	40	
(18920) Frisco NW-2 "254", *94*	70	80	
(18921) C&NW NW-2 "1017", *94*	70	80	
(18922) New Haven Alco A Unit "8922", *94*	60	75	
(18923) New Haven Alco A Unit Dummy "8923", *94*	30	40	
(18924) Illinois Central Diesel Switcher "8924", *94–95*		CP	
(18925) D&RGW Diesel Switcher "8925", *94–95*		CP	
(18926) Reading Diesel Switcher "8926", *94–95*		CP	
(18927) U.S. Navy NW-2 "65-00637", *94–95*		CP	
(18928) C&NW NW-2 Calf, *95*		CP	
(18929) B&M NW-2 Calf, *95*		CP	
(18930) Crayola Diesel Switcher, *94 u, 95*		CP	
(18931) Chrysler Mopar NW-2 "1818", *94 u*	80	100	
(18932) Jersey Central NW-2 "8932", *96*		CP	
(18933) Jersey Central NW-2 Calf "8933", *96*		CP	
(18934)/ (18935) Reading Alco AA set "300" and "304", *95*		CP	
(18936) Amtrak Alco A Unit "8936", *95*		CP	

		Exc	New	Cond/$
(18937)	Amtrak Alco A Unit Dummy "8937", *95*		CP	____
(18938)	U.S. Navy NW-2 Calf, *95*		CP	____
(18943)	Georgia Power NW-2 "1960", *95 u*		CP	____
19000	Blue Comet Dining Car, *87 u*	65	85	____
19001	Southern Dining Car, *87 u*	65	85	____
19002	Pennsylvania Dining Car, *88 u*	35	55	____
19003	Milwaukee Road Dining Car, *88 u*	35	55	____
19010	B&O Dining Car, *89 u*	35	55	____
(19011)	Lionel Lines Baggage Car "9011", *93*	200	250	____
(19015)	Lionel Lines Passenger Car "9015", *91*	95	115	____
(19016)	Lionel Lines Passenger Car "9016", *91*	95	115	____
(19017)	Lionel Lines Passenger Car "9017", *91*	95	115	____
(19018)	Lionel Lines Observation Car "9018", *91*	95	115	____
(19019)	SP Baggage Car "9019", *93*	125	175	____
(19023)	SP Passenger Car "9023", *92*	110	130	____
(19024)	SP Passenger Car "9024", *92*	110	130	____
(19025)	SP Passenger Car "9025", *92*	110	130	____
(19026)	SP Observation Car "9026", *92*	110	130	____
(19027)	Reading Baggage Car "9027", *92*		NM	
(19031)	Reading Passenger Car "9031", *92*		NM	
(19032)	Reading Passenger Car "9032", *92*		NM	
(19033)	Reading Observation Car "9033", *92*		NM	
(19038)	Adolphus Busch Observation Car, *92–93 u*	—	100	____
(19039)	Pere Marquette Baggage Car, *93*	—	90	____
(19040)	Pere Marquette Passenger Car "1115", *93*	—	90	____
(19041)	Pere Marquette Passenger Car "1116", *93*	—	90	____
(19042)	Pere Marquette Observation Car "36", *93*	—	90	____
(19047)	Baltimore & Ohio Combination Car "9047", *96*		CP	____
(19048)	Baltimore & Ohio Passenger Car "9048", *96*		CP	____
(19049)	Baltimore & Ohio Dining Car "9049", *96*		CP	____
(19050)	Baltimore & Ohio Observation Car "9050", *96*		CP	____
(19100)	Amtrak Baggage Car "9100", *89*	90	110	____
(19101)	Amtrak Combination Car "9101", *89*	90	110	____
(19102)	Amtrak Passenger Car "9102", *89*	90	110	____
(19103)	Amtrak Vista Dome Car "9103", *89*	90	110	____
(19104)	Amtrak Dining Car "9104", *89*	90	110	____
(19105)	Amtrak Full Vista Dome Car "9105", *89 u*	95	115	____
(19106)	Amtrak Observation Car "9106", *89*	90	110	____
(19107)	SP Full Vista Dome Car, *90 u*	85	95	____

LTI MODERN ERA (1987–1996)

	Exc	New	Cond/$
(19108) N&W Full Vista Dome Car "576", *91 u*	100	115	____
(19109) Santa Fe Baggage Car "3400", *91*	110	125	____
(19110) Santa Fe Combination Car "3500", *91*	110	125	____
(19111) Santa Fe Dining Car "601", *91*	110	125	____
(19112) Santa Fe Passenger Car, *91*	110	125	____
(19113) Santa Fe Vista Dome Observation Car, *91*	110	125	____
(19116) Great Northern Baggage Car "1200", *92*	95	110	____
(19117) Great Northern Combination Car "1240", *92*	95	110	____
(19118) Great Northern Passenger Car "1212", *92*	95	110	____
(19119) Great Northern Vista Dome Car "1322", *92*	95	110	____
(19120) Great Northern Observation Car "1192", *92*	95	110	____
(19121) Union Pacific Vista Dome Car "9121", *92 u*	100	125	____
(19122) D&RGW California Zephyr Baggage Car, *93*	100	125	____
(19123) D&RGW California Zephyr "Silver Bronco" Vista Dome Car, *93*	100	125	____
(19124) D&RGW California Zephyr "Silver Colt" Vista Dome Car, *93*	100	125	____
(19125) D&RGW California Zephyr "Silver Mustang" Vista Dome Car, *93*	100	125	____
(19126) D&RGW California Zephyr "Silver Pony" Vista Dome Car, *93*	100	125	____
(19127) D&RGW California Zephyr Vista Dome Observation Car, *93*	100	125	____
(19128) Santa Fe Full Vista Dome Car "507", *92 u*	175	200	____
(19129) Illinois Central Full Vista Dome Car "9129", *93*	100	125	____
(19130) Lackawanna Passenger Cars, set of 4, *94*	400	500	____
(19131) Lackawanna Baggage Car "2000" (See 19130)			
(19132) Lackawanna Dining Car "469" (See 19130)			
(19133) Lackawanna Passenger Car "260" (See 19130)			
(19134) Lackawanna Observation Car "789" (See 19130)			
(19135) Lackawanna Combination Car "425", *94*	100	125	____
(19136) Lackawanna Passenger Car "211", *94*	100	125	____
(19137) New York Central Roomette Car, *95*		CP	____
(19138) Santa Fe Roomette Car, *95*		CP	____
(19139) Norfolk & Western Baggage Car "577", *95*		CP	____
(19140) Norfolk & Western Combination Car "494", *95*		CP	____
(19141) Norfolk & Western Dining Car "495", *95*		CP	____

		Exc	New	Cond/$
19142)	Norfolk & Western Passenger Car "538", *95*		CP	_____
19143)	Norfolk & Western Passenger Car "537", *95*		CP	_____
19144)	Norfolk & Western Observation Car "582", *95*		CP	_____
19145)	Chesapeake & Ohio Combination Car "1403", *96*		CP	_____
19146)	Chesapeake & Ohio Passenger Car "1623", *96*		CP	_____
19147)	Chesapeake & Ohio Passenger Car "1803", *96*		CP	_____
19150)	Chesapeake & Ohio Observation Car "2504", *96*		CP	_____
19153)	Chesapeake & Ohio Passenger Cars, set of 4, *96*		CP	_____
19159)	Norfolk & Western Passenger Cars, set of 4, *95 u*		CP	_____
19200	Tidewater Southern Boxcar, *87*	10	18	_____
19201	Lancaster & Chester Boxcar, *87*	60	75	_____
19202	PRR Boxcar, *87*	35	45	_____
19203	D&TS Boxcar, *87*	10	18	_____
19204	Milwaukee Road Boxcar (FF #2), *87*	25	33	_____
19205	Great Northern DD Boxcar (FF #3), *88*	25	33	_____
19206	Seaboard System Boxcar, *88*	15	18	_____
19207	CP Rail DD Boxcar, *88*	15	18	_____
19208	Southern DD Boxcar, *88*	15	18	_____
19209	Florida East Coast Boxcar, *88*	15	18	_____
19210	Soo Line Boxcar, *89*	15	18	_____
19211	Vermont Railway Boxcar, *89*	15	18	_____
19212	PRR Boxcar, *89*	17	20	_____
19213	SP&S DD Boxcar, *89*	15	18	_____
19214	Western Maryland Boxcar (FF #4), *89*	30	35	_____
19215	Union Pacific DD Boxcar, *90*	15	18	_____
19216	Santa Fe Boxcar, *90*	15	18	_____
19217	Burlington Boxcar, *90*	15	18	_____
19218	New Haven Boxcar, *90*	15	18	_____
19219	Lionel Lines 1900–1906 Boxcar w/ Diesel RailSounds, *90*	140	175	_____
19220	Lionel Lines 1926–1934 Boxcar, *90*	30	35	_____
19221	Lionel Lines 1935–1937 Boxcar, *90*	30	35	_____
19222	Lionel Lines 1948–1950 Boxcar, *90*	30	35	_____
19223	Lionel Lines 1979–1989 Boxcar, *90*	30	35	_____
19228	Cotton Belt Boxcar, *91*	18	20	_____

LTI MODERN ERA (1987–1996)

		Exc	New	Cond/$
19229	Frisco Boxcar w/ Diesel RailSounds (FF #5), *91*	130	150	____
19230	Frisco DD Boxcar (FF #5), *91*	30	35	____
19231	TA&G DD Boxcar, *91*	15	18	____
19232	Rock Island DD Boxcar, *91*	15	18	____
19233	Southern Pacific Boxcar, *91*	15	18	____
19234	NYC Boxcar, *91*	60	75	____
19235	MKT Boxcar, *91*	60	75	____
19236	NKP DD Boxcar (FF #6), *92*	25	35	____
19237	C&IM Boxcar, *92*	15	18	____
19238	Kansas City Southern Boxcar, *92*	15	18	____
19239	Toronto, Hamilton & Buffalo DD Boxcar, *92*	15	18	____
19240	Great Northern DD Boxcar, *92*	15	18	____
19241	Mickey Mouse 60th Anniversary Hi-cube Boxcar, *91 u*	125	150	____
19242	Donald Duck 50th Anniversary Hi-cube Boxcar, *91 u*	125	150	____
(19243)	Clinchfield Boxcar "9790", *91 u*	40	45	____
(19244)	L&N Boxcar "9791", *92*	30	40	____
19245	Mickey's World Tour Hi-cube Boxcar, *92 u*	60	75	____
19246	Disney World 20th Anniversary Hi-cube Boxcar, *92 u*	60	75	____
(19247)	6464 Series Boxcars, 1st Edition, set of 3, *93*	150	175	____
(19248)	Western Pacific Boxcar "6464", *93*	50	60	____
(19249)	Great Northern Boxcar "6464", *93*	50	60	____
(19250)	M&St L Boxcar "6464", *93*	50	60	____
(19251)	Montana Rail Link DD Boxcar "10001", *93*	20	25	____
19254	Erie Boxcar (FF #7), *93*	25	30	____
19255	Erie DD Boxcar (FF #7), *93*	25	30	____
19256	Goofy Hi-cube Boxcar, *93*	40	50	____
(19257)	6464 Series Boxcars, 2nd Edition, set of 3, *94*	125	150	____
(19258)	Rock Island Boxcar "6464", *94*	35	45	____
(19259)	Western Pacific Boxcar "6464100", *94*	45	65	____
(19260)	Western Pacific Boxcar "6464100", *94*	45	65	____
19261	Perils of Mickey Hi-cube Boxcar I, *93*	45	50	____
19262	Perils of Mickey Hi-cube Boxcar II, *93*	45	50	____
19263	NYC DD Boxcar, *94 (SSS)*	35	45	____
19264	Perils of Mickey Hi-cube Boxcar III, *94*	40	45	____
19265	Mickey Mouse 65th Anniversary			

		Exc	New	Cond/$
	Hi-cube Boxcar, *94*	45	50	_____
(19266)	6464 Series Boxcars, 3rd Edition, set of 3, *95*		CP	_____
(19267)	NYC "Pacemaker" Boxcar "6464125", *95*		CP	_____
(19268)	Missouri Pacific Boxcar "6464150", *95*		CP	_____
(19269)	Rock Island Boxcar "6464", *95*		CP	_____
19270	Donald Duck 60th Anniversary Hi-cube Boxcar, *95*		CP	_____
19271	Minnie Mouse Hi-cube Boxcar, *95*		CP	_____
(19272)	6464 Series Boxcars, 4th edition, set of 3, *96*		CP	_____
(19273)	BAR "State of Maine" Boxcar "6464275", *96*		CP	_____
(19274)	Southern Pacific "Overnight" Boxcar "6464225", *96*		CP	_____
(19275)	Pennsylvania Boxcar "6464", *96*		CP	_____
19300	PRR Ore Car, *87*	20	25	_____
19301	Milwaukee Road Ore Car, *87*	20	25	_____
19302	Milwaukee Road Quad Hopper w/ coal load (FF #2), *87*	25	35	_____
19303	Lionel Lines Quad Hopper w/ coal load, *87 u*	25	35	_____
19304	GN Covered Quad Hopper (FF #3), *88*	35	40	_____
19305	Chessie System Ore Car, *88*	15	20	_____
19307	B&LE Ore Car w/ load, *89*	15	20	_____
19308	GN Ore Car w/ load, *89*	15	20	_____
19309	Seaboard Covered Quad Hopper, *89*	15	20	_____
19310	L&C Quad Hopper w/ coal load, *89*	20	30	_____
19311	SP Covered Quad Hopper, *90*	15	20	_____
19312	Reading Quad Hopper w/ coal load, *90*	20	30	_____
19313	B&O Ore Car w/ load, *90–91*	15	20	_____
19315	Amtrak Ore Car w/ load, *91*	20	25	_____
19316	Wabash Covered Quad Hopper, *91*	20	30	_____
19317	Lehigh Valley Quad Hopper w/ coal load, *91*	60	75	_____
19318	NKP Quad Hopper w/ coal load (FF #6), *92*	30	35	_____
19319	Union Pacific Covered Quad Hopper, *92*	20	25	_____
19320	PRR Ore Car w/ load, *92*	20	25	_____
19321	B&LE Ore Car w/ load, *92*	20	25	_____
19322	C&NW Ore Car w/ load, *93*	22	27	_____
19323	Detroit & Mackinac Ore Car w/ load, *93*	22	27	_____
19324	Erie Quad Hopper w/ coal load (FF #7), *93*	30	35	_____
19400	Milwaukee Road Gondola w/ cable reels (FF #2), *87*	25	35	_____

		Exc	New	Cond/$
19400	(See 51701)			
19401	GN Gondola w/ coal load (FF #3), *88*	25	35	___
19402	GN Crane Car (FF #3), *88*	45	65	___
19403	WM Gondola w/ coal load (FF #4), *89*	25	30	___
19404	Trailer Train Flatcar w/ WM trailers (FF #4), *89*	40	45	___
19405	Southern Crane Car, *91*	50	80	___
19406	West Point Mint Car, *91 u*	50	80	___
19408	Frisco Gondola w/ coil covers (FF #5), *91*	30	35	___
19409	Southern Flatcar w/ stakes, *91*	25	35	___
19410	NYC Gondola w/ canisters, *91*	50	60	___
19411	NKP Flatcar w/ Sears trailer (FF #6), *92*	55	65	___
19412	Frisco Crane Car, *92*	50	65	___
19413	Frisco Flatcar w/ stakes, *92*	20	25	___
19414	Union Pacific Flatcar w/ stakes, *92 (SSS)*	20	25	___
(19415)	Erie Flatcar w/ trailer "7200" (FF #7), *93*	30	40	___
(19416)	ICG TTUX Flatcar set w/ trailers "19417" and "19418", *93 (SSS)*	80	100	___
19417/ 19418	ICG TTUX Flatcars w/ trailers (See 19416)			
19419	Charlotte Mint Car, *93*	40	50	___
19420	Lionel Lines Vat Car, *94*	25	30	___
19421	Hirsch Brothers Vat Car, *95*		CP	___
19500	Milwaukee Road Reefer (FF #2), *87*	35	45	___
19502	C&NW Reefer, *87*	35	45	___
19503	Bangor & Aroostook Reefer, *87*	35	40	___
19504	Northern Pacific Reefer, *87*	25	30	___
19505	Great Northern Reefer (FF #3), *88*	40	55	___
19506	Thomas Newcomen Reefer, *88*	20	25	___
19507	Thomas Edison Reefer, *88*	20	25	___
19508	Leonardo da Vinci Reefer, *89*	20	25	___
19509	Alexander Graham Bell Reefer, *89*	20	25	___
19510	PRR Stock Car (FARR #5), *89 u*	35	40	___
19511	WM Reefer (FF #4), *89*	30	35	___
19512	Wright Brothers Reefer, *90*	20	25	___
19513	Ben Franklin Reefer, *90*	20	25	___
19515	Milwaukee Road Stock Car (FF #2), *90 u*	30	35	___
19516	George Washington Reefer, *89 u, 91*	15	20	___
19517	Civil War Reefer, *89 u, 91*	15	20	___
19518	Man on the Moon Reefer, *89 u, 91*	15	20	___

		Exc	New	Cond/$
19519	Frisco Stock Car (FF #5), *91*	35	40	_____
19520	CSX Reefer, *91*	20	25	_____
19522	Guglielmo Marconi Reefer, *91*	20	25	_____
19523	Dr. Robert Goddard Reefer, *91*	20	25	_____
19524	Delaware & Hudson Reefer, *91 (SSS)*	30	35	_____
19525	Speedy Alka Seltzer Reefer, *91 u*	40	50	_____
19526	Jolly Green Giant Reefer, *91 u*	30	45	_____
19527	Nickel Plate Road Reefer (FF #6), *92*	30	40	_____
19528	Joshua L. Cowen Reefer, *92*	30	40	_____
19529	A.C. Gilbert Reefer, *92*	30	40	_____
19530	Rock Island Stock Car, *92 u*	35	40	_____
19531	Rice Krispies Reefer, *92 u*	30	45	_____
(19532)	Hormel Reefer "901", *92 u*	30	45	_____
19535	Erie Reefer (FF #7), *93*	30	35	_____
19536	Soo Line REA Reefer, *93 (SSS)*	25	30	_____
19537	Kellogg's Corn Flakes Reefer, *93*		NM	
(19538)	Hormel Reefer "102", *94*	30	35	_____
19539	Heinz Reefer, *94*	30	35	_____
(19599)	Old Glory Reefers, set of 3, *89 u, 91*	40	45	_____
19600	Milwaukee Road 1-D Tank Car (FF # 2), *87*	40	50	_____
19601	North American 1-D Tank Car (FF #4), *89*	40	50	_____
19602	Johnson 1-D Tank Car (FF #5), *91*	30	40	_____
19603	GATX 1-D Tank Car (FF #6), *92*	35	45	_____
19604	Goodyear 1-D Tank Car, *93 (SSS)*	40	50	_____
19605	Hudson's Bay 1-D Tank Car, *94 (SSS)*	35	40	_____
19651	Santa Fe Tool Car, *87*	25	30	_____
19652	Jersey Central Bunk Car, *88*	20	25	_____
19653	Jersey Central Tool Car, *88*	20	25	_____
19654	Amtrak Bunk Car, *89*	22	27	_____
19655	Amtrak Tool Car, *90–91*	22	27	_____
19656	Milwaukee Road Bunk Car w/ smoke, *90*	45	55	_____
19657	Wabash Bunk Car w/ smoke, *91–92*	50	60	_____
19658	Norfolk & Western Tool Car, *91*	25	30	_____
19700	Chessie System E/V Caboose, *88*	55	65	_____
19701	Milwaukee Road N5C Caboose (FF #2), *87*	40	50	_____
19702	PRR N5C Caboose, *87*	40	50	_____
19703	Great Northern E/V Caboose (FF #3), *88*	50	60	_____
19704	WM E/V Caboose w/ smoke (FF #4), *89*	60	65	_____
19705	CP Rail E/V Caboose w/ smoke, *89*	50	60	_____

LTI MODERN ERA (1987–1996)

		Exc	New	Cond/
(19706)	UP E/V Caboose w/ smoke "9706", *89*	65	75	____
19707	SP Work Caboose w/ searchlight and smoke, *90*	75	100	____
(19708)	Lionel Lines B/W Caboose "1990", *90*	60	65	____
19709	PRR Work Caboose w/ smoke, *89, 91*	65	85	____
19710	Frisco E/V Caboose w/ smoke (FF #5), *91*	60	70	____
19711	Norfolk Southern E/V Caboose w/ smoke, *92*	60	70	____
19712	PRR N5C Caboose, *91*	55	65	____
19714	NYC Work Caboose w/ searchlight and smoke, *92*	75	90	____
(19715)	DM&IR E/V Caboose "C-217", *92 u*	60	70	____
(19716)	Illinois Central E/V Caboose w/ smoke "9405", *93*	55	70	____
(19717)	Susquehanna B/W Caboose "0121", *93*	45	55	____
(19718)	Chicago & Illinois Midland E/V Caboose "74", *92 u*	40	50	____
(19719)	Erie B/W Caboose "C-300" (FF #7), *93*	55	65	____
19720	Soo Line E/V Caboose, *93 (SSS)*	50	60	____
(19721)	GM&O E/V Caboose "2956", *93 u*	60	75	____
19723	Disney E/V Caboose, *94*	40	50	____
(19724)	MKT E/V Caboose "125", *94 u*	60	75	____
19726	NYC B/W Caboose, *95 (SSS)*		CP	____
(19727)	Pennsylvania N5C Caboose "477938", *96*		CP	____
19800	Circle L Ranch Operating Cattle Car, *88*	100	140	____
19801	Poultry Dispatch Chicken Car, *87*	40	60	____
19802	Carnation Milk Car, *87*	85	110	____
19803	Reading Ice Car, *87*	50	60	____
19804	Wabash Operating Hopper, *87*	30	40	____
19805	Santa Fe Operating Boxcar, *87*	30	40	____
19806	PRR Operating Hopper, *88*	35	45	____
19807	PRR E/V Caboose w/ smoke, *88*	55	65	____
19808	NYC Ice Car, *88*	50	60	____
19809	Erie-Lackawanna Operating Boxcar, *88*	30	40	____
19810	Bosco Milk Car, *88*	100	125	____
19811	Monon Brakeman Car, *90*	50	55	____
19813	Northern Pacific Ice Car, *89 u*	45	60	____
19815	Delaware & Hudson Brakeman Car, *92*	50	65	____
(19816)	Madison Hardware Operating Boxcar "190991", *91 u*	125	150	____

TI MODERN ERA (1987–1996)

		Exc	New	Cond/$
19817	Virginian Ice Car, *94*	40	50	_____
19818)	Dairymen's League Milk Car "788", *94*	90	105	_____
19819	Poultry Dispatch Car, *94 (SSS)*	55	65	_____
19820	Diecast Metal Tender w/ RailSounds II, *95–96*		CP	_____
19821)	UP Operating Boxcar "9146", *95*		CP	_____
19822	Pork Dispatch Car, *95*		CP	_____
19823	Burlington Ice Car, *94 u, 95*		CP	_____
19825	EMD Generator Car, *96*		CP	_____
19828	C&NW Operating Cattle Car, *96*		CP	_____
19900	Toy Fair Boxcar, *87 u*	100	125	_____
19901	"I Love Virginia" Boxcar, *87*	25	35	_____
19902	Toy Fair Boxcar, *88 u*	100	125	_____
19903	Christmas Boxcar, *87 u*	40	50	_____
19904	Christmas Boxcar, *88 u*	45	60	_____
19905	"I Love California" Boxcar, *88*	18	22	_____
19906	"I Love Pennsylvania" Boxcar, *89*	18	22	_____
19907	Toy Fair Boxcar, *89 u*	100	125	_____
19908	Christmas Boxcar, *89 u*	35	45	_____
19909	"I Love New Jersey" Boxcar, *90*	20	25	_____
19910	Christmas Boxcar, *90 u*	30	35	_____
19911	Toy Fair Boxcar, *90 u*	100	125	_____
19912	"I Love Ohio" Boxcar, *91*	20	25	_____
19913	Christmas Boxcar, *91 u*	40	50	_____
19913	Christmas Boxcar for Lionel Employees, *91 u*	250	300	_____
19914	Toy Fair Boxcar, *91 u*	100	125	_____
19915	"I Love Texas" Boxcar, *92*	20	25	_____
19916	Christmas Boxcar for Lionel Employees, *92 u*	300	400	_____
19917	Toy Fair Boxcar, *92 u*	125	150	_____
19918	Christmas Boxcar, *92 u*	75	100	_____
19919	"I Love Minnesota" Boxcar, *93*	25	30	_____
(19920)	Lionel Visitor's Center Boxcar, *92 u*	35	45	_____
19921	Christmas Boxcar for Lionel Employees, *93 u*	250	300	_____
19922	Christmas Boxcar, *93*	40	50	_____
19923	Toy Fair Boxcar, *93 u*	100	150	_____
19924	Lionel Railroader Club Boxcar, *93 u*	30	45	_____
19925	Learning Center Boxcar for Lionel Employees, *93 u*	300	350	_____
19926	"I Love Nevada" Boxcar, *94*	20	25	_____
(19927)	Lionel Visitor's Center Boxcar "1993", *93 u*	30	40	_____

		Exc	New	Cond/$
19928	Christmas Boxcar for Lionel Employees, *94 u*	250	300	____
19929	Christmas Boxcar, *94*	30	40	____
19930	Lionel Railroader Club Quad Hopper w/ coal load, *94 u*	30	40	____
19931	Toy Fair Boxcar, *94 u*	100	150	____
19932	Lionel Visitor's Center Boxcar, *94 u*	30	40	____
19933	"I Love Illinois" Boxcar, *95*		CP	____
(19934)	Lionel Visitor's Center Boxcar "1995", *95 u*		CP	____
(19935)	Lionel Railroader Club 1-D Tank Car "1995", *95 u*		CP	____
19937	Toy Fair Boxcar, *95 u*		CP	____
19938	Christmas Boxcar, *95*		CP	____
19939	Christmas Boxcar for Lionel Employees, *95 u*		CP	____
19941	"I Love Colorado" Boxcar, *95*		CP	____
19942	"I Love Florida" Boxcar, *96*		CP	____
(19960)	LOTS Western Pacific Boxcar "1952" (Std. O), *92 u*	75	95	____
19961	Gadsden Pacific Inspiration Consolidated Copper Company Ore Car w/ load, *92 u*	40	50	____
(19962)	Southwest TTOS SP 3-bay ACF Hopper "496035" (Std. O), *92 u*	70	90	____
(19963)	TTOS Union Equity 3-bay ACF Hopper "86892" (Std. O), *92 u*	60	75	____
(19964)	U.S. JCI Senate Boxcar, *92 u*	75	100	____
(21029)	World of Little Choo Choo set, *94 u, 95*		CP	____
21596	(See 17898)			
(23000)	Operating Base Smithsonian NYC Dreyfuss Hudson (2-rail), *92 u*		NRS	____
(23001)	Operating Base NYC Dreyfuss Hudson (3-rail), *93 u*		NRS	____
(23002)	Operating Base NYC Hudson, *92 u, 93–94*	—	120	____
(23003)	Operating Base PRR B-6 Switcher, *92 u, 93–94*	—	120	____
(23004)	Operating Base NP 4-8-4, *92 u, 93–94*	—	120	____
(23005)	Operating Base Reading T-1, *92 u, 93–94*	—	120	____
(23006)	Operating Base Chessie System T-1, *92 u, 93–94*	—	120	____
(23007)	Operating Base SP Daylight, *92 u, 93–94*	—	120	____
(23008)	Operating Base NYC L-3 Mohawk, *92 u, 93–94*	—	120	____
(23009)	Operating Base PRR S-2 Turbine, *92 u, 93–94*	—	120	____
(23010)	Left Remote Switch 31" "3010" (O), *95*		CP	____
(23011)	Right Remote Switch 31" "3011" (O), *95*		CP	____
(23012)	Operating Base F-3 ABA Diesels, *92 u, 93–94*	—	120	____

		Exc	New	Cond/$
24876	(See 17405)			
25766	(See 16561)			
26269	(See 17304)			
DX26925	(See 12810)			
31438	(See 16944)			
31950	(See 16945)			
(33000)	Lionel Lines RailScope GP-9 "3000", *88–90*	175	245	_____
(33002)	RailScope B&W TV, *88–90*	50	75	_____
(33004)	NYC RailScope GP-9 "3004", *90*		NM	
(33005)	Union Pacific RailScope GP-9 "3005", *90*		NM	
33621	(See 12909)			
[38356]	LOTS Dow Chemical 3-D Tank Car, *87*	75	100	_____
45003	(See 17217)			
50224	(See 17124)			
50240	(See 52067)			
51200	(See 17510)			
(51220)	NYC "Imperial Castle" Passenger Car, *93 u*		NRS	_____
(51221)	NYC "Niagara County" Passenger Car, *93 u*		NRS	_____
(51222)	NYC "Cascade Glory" Passenger Car, *93 u*		NRS	_____
(51223)	NYC "City of Detroit" Passenger Car, *93 u*		NRS	_____
(51224)	NYC "Imperial Falls" Passenger Car, *93 u*		NRS	_____
(51225)	NYC "Westchester County" Passenger Car, *93 u*		NRS	_____
(51226)	NYC "Cascade Grotto" Passenger Car, *93 u*		NRS	_____
(51227)	NYC "City of Indianapolis" Passenger Car, *93 u*		NRS	_____
(51228)	NYC "Manhattan Island" Observation Car, *93 u*		NRS	_____
(51229)	NYC Dining Car "680", *93 u*		NRS	_____
(51230)	NYC Baggage Car "5017", *93 u*		NRS	_____
(51231)	NYC "Century Club" Passenger Car, *93 u*		NRS	_____
(51232)	NYC "Thousand Islands" Observation Car, *93 u*		NRS	_____
(51233)	NYC Dining Car "684", *93 u*		NRS	_____
(51234)	NYC Baggage Car "5020", *93 u*		NRS	_____
(51235)	NYC "Century Tavern" Passenger Car, *93 u*		NRS	_____
(51236)	NYC "City of Toledo" Passenger Car, *93 u*		NRS	_____
(51237)	NYC "Imperial Mansion" Passenger Car, *93 u*		NRS	_____
(51238)	NYC "Imperial Palace" Passenger Car, *93 u*		NRS	_____
(51239)	NYC "Cascade Spirit" Passenger Car, *93 u*		NRS	_____
(51240)	NYC Dining Car "681", *93 u*		NRS	_____
(51241)	NYC "City of Chicago" Passenger Car, *93 u*		NRS	_____
(51242)	NYC "Imperial Garden" Passenger Car, *93 u*		NRS	_____

LTI MODERN ERA (1987–1996)

		Exc	New	Cond/$
(51243)	NYC "Imperial Fountain" Passenger Car, 93 u		NRS	___
(51244)	NYC "Cascade Valley" Passenger Car, 93 u		NRS	___
(51245)	NYC Dining Car "685", 93 u		NRS	___
51300	Shell Semi-Scale 1-D Tank Car "8124", 91	—	110	___
(51301)	Lackawanna Semi-Scale Reefer "7000", 92	—	125	___
51401)	PRR Semi-Scale Boxcar "100800", 91	—	110	___
(51402)	C&O Semi-Scale Stock Car "95250", 92	—	135	___
51501	B&O Semi-Scale Hopper "532000", 91	—	110	___
51701	NYC Semi-Scale Caboose "19400", 91	—	140	___
(51702)	PRR N-8 Caboose "478039", 91–92	—	265	___
52000	Detroit-Toledo TCA Flatcar w/ trailer, 92 u	80	100	___
52001	NETCA B&M Quad Hopper w/ coal load, 92 u	50	75	___
[52002]	VTC Passenger Cars (See 7692)			
52003	Ozark TCA "Meet Me in St. Louis" Flatcar w/ trailer, 92 u	—	600	___
[52004]	LCAC Algoma Central Gondola w/ coil covers "9215", 92 u	80	100	___
[52005]	LCAC Canadian National F-3 B Unit "9517", 93 u		NRS	___
[52006]	LCAC CP Boxcar "930016" (Std. O), 93 u		CP	___
[52007]	NLOE Long Island RS-3 "1552", 92 u	130	165	___
(52008)	TCA Bucyrus Erie Crane Car "1993X", 93 u	60	75	___
(52009)	Sacramento Valley TTOS Western Pacific Boxcar "64641993", 93 u	70	90	___
(52010)	TTOS Weyerhaeuser DD Boxcar "838593" (Std. O), 93 u	60	80	___
52011	Gadsden Pacific Tucson, Cornelia & Gila Bend Ore Car w/ load, 93 u	30	40	___
52013	Artrain Norfolk Southern Flatcar w/ trailer (Std. O), 92 u	200	250	___
(52014)	LOTS BN TTUX Flatcar set w/ N&W trailers "637500A" and "637500B", 93 u	125	150	___
52016	NETCA B&M Gondola w/ coil covers, 93 u	50	60	___
52018	Lakes & Pines TCA 3M Boxcar, 93 u	—	600	
[52019]	NLOE Long Island Boxcar "8393", 93 u	35	55	___
[52020]	NLOE Long Island B/W Caboose "8393", 93 u	60	80	___
(52021)	TTOS Weyerhaeuser Tractor and Trailer, 93 u	20	25	___
52022	TTOS Union Pacific Boxcar, 93 u	—	550	___
(52023)	LCCA D&TS 2-bay ACF Hopper "2601" (Std. O), 93 u	60	75	___

		Exc	New	Cond/$
52024	Artrain Conrail Auto Carrier, *93 u*	85	100	_____
52025)	LCCA Madison Hardware Tractor and Trailer, *93 u*	25	30	_____
52026]	NLOE Long Island Flatcar w/ Grumman trailer "8394", *94 u*	80	100	_____
52027	Gadsden Pacific Pinto Valley Mine Ore Car w/ load, *94 u*	35	40	_____
52028)	TTOS Ford Cars, set of 3, *94 u*	60	75	_____
52029)	TTOS Ford 1-D Tank Car "12" (O27), *94 u*		NRS	_____
52030)	TTOS Ford Gondola "4023", *94 u*		NRS	_____
52031)	TTOS Ford Hopper "1458" (O27), *94 u*		NRS	_____
52032)	TTOS Ford 1-D Tank Car "14" w/ Kughn inscription (O27), *94 u*	60	75	_____
52033)	Wolverine TTOS Lionel Lines Tractor and Trailer (See 52040)			
52034)	Wolverine TTOS Grand Trunk Flatcar "52040" (See 52040)			
52035)	TCA Yorkrail GP-9 "1750", shell only, *94 u*	40	50	_____
52036)	TCA 40th Anniversary B/W Caboose, *94 u*	50	60	_____
52037)	TCA Yorkrail GP-9 "1754", *94 u*	125	150	_____
52038)	LCCA Southern Hopper w/ coal load "360794" (Std. O), *94 u*	65	75	_____
52039)	LCCA "Track 29" Bumper, *94 u*	—	20	_____
52040	Wolverine TTOS GTW Flatcar w/ Lionel Lines Tractor and Trailer, *94 u*		CP	_____
52041)	LOTS BN TTUX Flatcar set w/ Conrail trailers "637500D" and "637500E", *94 u*	100	140	_____
52042)	LOTS BN TTUX Flatcar w/ CN trailer "637500C", *94 u*	75	85	_____
52043]	NETCA LL Bean Boxcar "1994", *94 u*	60	75	_____
52044	Eastwood Vat Car, *94 u*	45	60	_____
52045)	TCA Penn Dutch Milk Car "61052", *94 u*	—	135	_____
52046)	TTOS ACL Boxcar "16247", *94 u*	—	125	_____
52047)	Southwest TTOS Cotton Belt Woodside Caboose w/ smoke "1921" (Std. O), *93–94 u*	75	80	_____
52048)	LOTS CN Tractor and Trailer "197993", *94 u*	40	45	_____
52049	Artrain BN Gondola w/ coil covers, *94 u*	75	100	_____
52050]	Schuylkill Haven Borough Day SP-Type Caboose "1994", *94 u*	—	50	_____

LTI MODERN ERA (1987–1996)

		Exc	New	Cond/$
(52051)	TCA Baltimore & Ohio "Sentinel" Boxcar "6464095", *95 u*		CP	___
[52052]	TCA 40th Anniversary Boxcar, *94 u*	—	100	___
52053	TTOS Carail Boxcar, *94 u*	75	90	___
52054	Carail Boxcar, *94 u*		NRS	___
(52055)	LCCA Sovex Tractor and Trailer, *94 u*	20	30	___
(52056)	LCCA Southern Tractor and Trailer "206502", *94 u*	20	30	___
(52057)	TTOS Western Pacific Boxcar "64641995", *95 u*		CP	___
(52058)	Central California TTOS Santa Fe Boxcar "64641895", *95 u*		CP	___
(52059)	Eastern TCA Clinchfield Quad Hopper w/ coal load "16413", *94 u*	150	200	___
[52060]	VTC Tender w/ whistle "7694", *94 u*		CP	___
[52061]	NLOE Long Island Stern's Pickle Products Vat Car "8395", *95 u*		CP	___
(52062)	TCA "Skytop" Observation Car "1995", *95 u*		CP	___
(52063)	TCA New York Central "Pacemaker" Boxcar "6464125", *95 u*		CP	___
(52064)	TCA Missouri Pacific Boxcar "6464150", *95 u*		CP	___
(52066)	Trainmaster Tractor and Trailer, *94 u*	—	225	___
(52067)	LOTS Burlington Ice Car "50240", *95 u*		CP	___
(52068)	Toy Train Parade TTOS Contadina Boxcar "16245", *94 u*	—	50	___
52069	Carail Tractor and Trailer, *94 u*	—	75	___
52070	Knoebel's Boxcar, *95 u*		CP	___
52071	Gadsden Pacific Copper Basin Railway Ore Car w/ load, *95 u*		CP	___
[52072]	NLOE Grumman Tractor, *94 u*		NRS	___
(52073)	Southwest TTOS Pacific Fruit Express Reefer "459402" (Std. O), *95 u*		CP	___
(52074)	LCCA Iowa Beef Packers Reefer "197095" (Std. O), *95 u*		CP	___
52075	United Auto Workers Boxcar, *95 u*		CP	___
[52076]	NLOE Long Island Observation Car "8396", *96 u*		CP	___
(52077)	Pacific Northwest TCA Great Northern Hi-cube Boxcar "9695", *95 u*		CP	___
(52078)	TTOS Southern Pacific SD-9 "5366", *96 u*		CP	___

		Exc	New	Cond/$
(52079)	TTOS SP B/W Caboose "1996", *96 u*		CP	____
[52080]	NETCA Boston & Maine Flatcar w/ trailer "91095", *95 u*		CP	____
(52081)	Chicagoland Lionel Railroad Club C&NW Boxcar "6464555", *96 u*		CP	____
52082	Steamtown Lackawanna Boxcar, *95 u*		CP	____
52083	Eastwood PRR Flatcar w/ Eastwood tanker trailer, *95 u*		CP	____
(52084)	TTOS Union Pacific I-Beam Flatcar w/ load "16380", *95 u*		CP	____
(52085)	TCA Full Vista Dome Car "1996", *96 u*		CP	____
(52086)	Canadian TTOS Pacific Great Eastern Boxcar "64641972", *96 u*		CP	____
(52087)	TTOS New Mexico Central Boxcar "64641996", *96 u*		CP	____
[52088]	Desert TCA 25th Anniversary On-Track Step Van, *96 u*		CP	____
52089	Gadsden Pacific SMARRCO Ore Car w/ load, *96 u*		CP	____
(52090)	LCCA Pere Marquette DD Boxcar (Std. O), *96 u*		CP	____
(52091)	LCCA Lenox Tractor and Trailer, *95 u*		CP	____
(52092)	LCCA Iowa Interstate Tractor and Trailer, *95 u*		CP	____
(52093)	Lone Star TCA Boxcar "6464696", *96 u*		CP	____
52097	Artrain Chessie System Reefer, *95 u*		CP	____
52789	(See 16571)			
59629	(See 17874)			
60029	(See 17118)			
60155	(See 17216)			
61052	(See 52045)			
72867	(See 17121)			
78286	(See 17906)			
79052	(See 16554)			
81487	(See 17871)			
81988	(See 17872)			
82947	(See 16430)			
86892	(See 19963)			
[87010]	LCAC CN Express Reefer, *87 u*		NRS	____
[88011]	LCAC CN Woodside Caboose (Std. O), *88 u*		NRS	____
91095	(See 52080)			
95250	(See 51402)			
100800	(See 51401)			

151161 (See 17890)

173872 (See 17007)

190991 (See 19816)

197095 (See 52074)

197993 (See 52048)

206502 (See 52056)

245998 (See 17404)

295110 (See 17120)

296000 (See 17209)

298011 (See 17882)

360794 (See 52038)

371629 (See 17403)

385405 (See 17406)

459400 (See 17305)

459401 (See 17306)

45940 (See 52073)

477938 (See 19727)

478039 (See 51702)

496035 (See 19962)

532000 (See 51501)

610584 (See 12827)

637500A/B (See 52014)

637500D/E (See 52041)

637500C (See 52042)

640000 (See 16912)

640001 (See 16912)

680441 (See 12910)

800200 (See 17122)

838593 (See 52010)

844304 (See 17123)

[900013] LCAC CN Flatcar w/ trailers, *90 u*   NRS _____

[930016] (See 52006)

3739469 (See 17877)

6106888 (See 16252)

No Number Amtrak Passenger set, *89, 89 u*   800 1000 _____

No Number Baltimore & Ohio set, *94, 96*   CP   _____

No Number C&NW Passenger set, *93*   500   600 _____

No Number Chesapeake & Ohio set, *95–96*   CP   _____

No Number D&RGW "California Zephyr" set, *92, 93* 1400 1600 _____

		Exc	New	Cond/$
No Number	Erie-Lackawanna Passenger set, *93, 94*	1200	1300	_____
No Number	Erie set (FF #7), *93*	500	600	_____
No Number	Frisco set (FF #5), *91*	500	550	_____
No Number	Great Northern "Empire Builder" set, *92, 93*	950	1100	_____
No Number	Great Northern set (FF #3), *88*	450	500	_____
No Number	Illinois Central "City of New Orleans" set, *85, 87, 93*	1300	1500	_____
No Number	Illinois Central set, *91–92, 95*	300	325	_____
No Number	Lionel Lines Madison Car set, *91, 93*	600	700	_____
No Number	The Mint set, *79 u, 80–83, 84 u, 86 u, 87, 91 u, 93*	1200	1400	_____
No Number	Milwaukee Road set (FF #2), *87, 90 u*	450	500	_____
No Number	Missouri Pacific set, *95*		CP	_____
No Number	Norfolk & Western Passenger set, *94*	400	475	_____
No Number	Norfolk & Western "Powhatan Arrow" Passenger set, *95*		CP	_____
No Number	Nickel Plate Road set (FF #6), *92*	500	600	_____
No Number	New Haven set, *94–95*		CP	_____
No Number	Northern Pacific set, *90–92*	250	325	_____
No Number	New York Central set, *89, 91*	300	350	_____
No Number	Pennsylvania set, *87–90, 95*	300	350	_____
No Number	Pere Marquette set, *93*	900	1000	_____
No Number	SP Daylight Steam set, *90, 92, 93*	1000	1200	_____
No Number	Santa Fe "Super Chief" set, *91, 91 u, 92 u, 93, 95*	1800	2200	_____
No Number	Union Pacific set, *94*	550	650	_____
No Number	Wabash set (FF #1), *86, 87*	1000	1200	_____
No Number	Western Maryland set (FF #4), *89*	450	525	_____

O GAUGE CLASSICS

1-263E	Lionel Lines "Blue Comet" 2-4-2 (See 51004)
44E	(See 51100)
350E	Lionel Lines "Hiawatha" 4-4-2 (See 51000)
882	Lionel Lines Combination Car (See 51000)
883	Lionel Lines Passenger Car (See 51000)
884	Lionel Lines Observation Car (See 51000)
892	(See 51202)

		Exc	New	Cond/$
893	(See 51203)			
894	(See 51204)			
895	(See 51205)			
1612	Lionel Lines Passenger Car (See 51004)			
1613	Lionel Lines Passenger Car (See 51004)			
1614	Lionel Lines Baggage Car (See 51004)			
1615	Lionel Lines Observation Car (See 51004)			
8814	(See 51400)			
8816	(See 51500)			
8817	(See 51700)			
8820	(See 51800)			
(51000)	Milwaukee Road "Hiawatha" set, *88 u*	—	825	___
(51001)	Lionel #44 Freight Special set, *89*	—	545	___
(51004)	Blue Comet set, *91*	—	1000	___
(51100)	Lionel Lines Electric "44E", *89* (See 51001)			
(51201)	Rail Chief Passenger Cars, set of 4, *90*	—	550	___
(51202)	Lionel Lines Combination Car "892" (See 51201)			
(51203)	Lionel Lines Passenger Car "893" (See 51201)			
(51204)	Lionel Lines Passenger Car "894" (See 51201)			
(51205)	Lionel Lines Observation Car "895" (See 51201)			
(51400)	Lionel Lines Boxcar "8814", *89* (See 51001)			
(51500)	Lionel Lines Hopper "8816", *89* (See 51001)			
(51700)	Lionel Lines Caboose "8817", *89* (See 51001)			
(51800)	Lionel Lines Searchlight Car "8820", *89* (See 51001)			

STANDARD GAUGE CLASSICS

1-44	(See 13805)
1-214	(See 13605)
1-215	(See 13303)
1-318E	Lionel Lines Electric (See 13001)

			Exc	New	Cond/$
-381E	(See 13102)				
-384E	(See 13101)				
-390E	(See 13100)				
-400E	(See 13103)				
-408E	(See 13107)				
-4390	American Flyer "West Point" Baggage Car (See 13003)				
-4391	American Flyer "Academy" Passenger Car (See 13003)				
-4392	American Flyer "Army/Navy" Observation Car (See 13003)				
-4689	(See 13109)				
2-390E	(See 13106)				
2-400E	(See 13108)				
7E	(See 13104)				
8	(See 13803)				
9	(See 13803)				
426	(See 13801)				
183	(See 13413)				
184	(See 13414)				
185	(See 13415)				
200	(See 13900)				
201	(See 13901)				
323	(See 13400)				
324	(See 13401)				
325	(See 13402)				
326	(See 13416)				
327	(See 13417)				
328	(See 13418)				
437	(See 13804)				
1115	(See 13800)				
1217	(See 13702)				
1412	(See 13404)				
1413	(See 13405)				
1414	(See 13407)				
1416	(See 13406)				
1420	(See 13409)				
1421	(See 13410)				
1422	(See 13411)				

		Exc	New	Cond/
1423	(See 13425)			
1512	(See 13300)			
1513	(See 13600)			
1517	(See 13700)			
1520	(See 13200)			
2412	(See 13421)			
2413	(See 13422)			
2414	(See 13423)			
2416	(See 13424)			
4400C	(See 51900)			
5130	Lionel Lines Flatcar w/ lumber (See 13001)			
5140	Lionel Lines Reefer (See 13001)			
5150	Lionel Lines "Shell" Tank Car (See 13001)			
5160	Lionel Lines Caboose (See 13001)			
(13001)	1-318E Freight Express Train set, *90–91*	—	900	____
(13002)	Fireball Express set, *90 u*	—	1100	____
(13003)	American Flyer "Mayflower" Passenger Car set, *92*	—	1500	____
(13100)	Lionel Lines 2-4-2 "1-390E", *88 u*	—	550	____
(13101)	Lionel Lines 2-4-0 "1-384E", *89 u*	—	590	____
(13102)	Lionel Lines Electric "1-381E", *89 u*	—	800	____
(13103)	Lionel Lines "Blue Comet" 4-4-4 "1-400E", *90*	—	1100	____
(13104)	Lionel Lines "Old #7" 4-4-0 "7E", *90*	—	800	____
(13106)	Lionel Lines "Fireball Express" 2-4-2 "2-390E" (See 13002)			
(13107)	Lionel Lines Electric "1-408E" , *91*	—	800	____
(13108)	Lionel Lines 4-4-4 "2-400E", *91*	—	1030	____
(13109)	American Flyer "Mayflower" Electric "1-4689", *92*	—	1100	____
(13200)	Lionel Lines Searchlight Car "1520", *89 u*	—	145	____
(13300)	Lionel Lines Gondola "1512", *89 u*	—	102	____
(13303)	Lionel Lines Sunoco Tank Car "1-215", *92*	—	200	____
(13400)	Lionel Lines Baggage Car "323", *88 u*	—	200	____
(13401)	Lionel Lines Passenger Car "324", *88 u*	—	200	____
(13402)	Lionel Lines Observation Car "325", *88 u*	—	200	____
(13403)	Lionel Lines State Passenger Car set, *89 u*	—	1500	____
(13404)	Lionel Lines "California" Passenger Car "1412" (See 13403)			

	Exc	New	Cond/$
(13405) Lionel Lines "Colorado" Passenger Car "1413" (See 13403)			
(13406) Lionel Lines "New York" Observation Car "1416" (See 13403)			
(13407) Lionel Lines "Illinois" Passenger Car "1414", *90*	—	575	____
(13408) Lionel Lines "Blue Comet" Passenger Car set, *90*	—	1375	____
(13409) Lionel Lines "Faye" Passenger Car "1420" (See 13408)			
(13410) Lionel Lines "Westphal" Passenger Car "1421" (See 13408)			
(13411) Lionel Lines "Tempel" Observation Car "1422" (See 13408)			
(13412) Lionel Lines "Old #7" Passenger Car set, *90*	—	800	____
(13413) Lionel Lines Combination Car "183" (See 13412)			
(13414) Lionel Lines Passenger Car "184" (See 13412)			
(13415) Lionel Lines Observation Car "185" (See 13412)			
(13416) Lionel Lines "New Jersey" Baggage Car "326" (See 13002)			
(13417) Lionel Lines "Connecticut" Passenger Car "327" (See 13002)			
(13418) Lionel Lines "New York" Observation Car "328" (See 13002)			
(13420) Lionel Lines State Passenger Car set, *91*	—	1800	____
(13421) Lionel Lines "California" Passenger Car "2412" (See 13420)			
(13422) Lionel Lines "Colorado" Passenger Car "2413" (See 13420)			
(13423) Lionel Lines "Illinois" Passenger Car "2414", *92 u*	—	500	____
(13424) Lionel Lines "New York" Observation Car "2416" (See 13420)			
(13425) Lionel Lines "Barnard" Passenger Car "1423", *91 u*	—	600	____
(13600) Lionel Lines Cattle Car "1513", *89 u*	—	120	____

LTI MODERN ERA (1987–1996)

		Exc	New	Cond/$
13601	Season's Greetings Boxcar, *89 u*	—	125	___
13602	Season's Greetings Boxcar, *90 u*	—	125	___
13604	Season's Greetings Boxcar, *91 u*	—	150	___
(13605)	Lionel Lines Boxcar "1-214", *92*	—	200	___
(13700)	Lionel Lines Caboose "1517", *89 u*	—	138	___
(13702)	Lionel Lines Caboose "1217", *91*	—	170	___
(13800)	Lionelville Passenger Station "1115", *88 u*	200	250	___
(13801)	Lionelville Station "126", *89 u*	—	155	___
(13802)	Lionel Runabout Boat, *90*	—	470	___
(13803)	Lionel Racing Automobiles "8" and "9", *91*	—	640	___
(13804)	Lionelville Switch Tower "437", *91*	—	250	___
(13805)	Lionel Racing Boat "1-44", *91*	—	475	___
(13807)	Racing Automobiles Straight Track, *91 u*		NRS	___
(13808)	Racing Automobiles Inner Radius Curve Track, *91 u*		NRS	___
(13809)	Racing Automobiles Outer Radius Curve Track, *91 u*		NRS	___
(13900)	Electric Rapid Transit Trolley "200", *89 u*	—	250	___
(13901)	Electric Rapid Transit Trolley Trailer "201", *89 u*	—	180	___
(51900)	Signal Bridge and Control Panel "4400C", *89 u*	—	280	___

SECTION 5
UNCATALOGED CLUB CARS
AND SPECIAL PRODUCTION

ARTRAIN

____	**9486**	GTW "I Love Michigan" Boxcar, *87*
____	**17885**	Artrain 1-D Tank Car, *90*
____	**17891**	Grand Trunk Boxcar, *91*
____	**52013**	Norfolk Southern Flatcar w/ trailer (Std. O), *92*
____	**52024**	Conrail Auto Carrier, *93*
____	**52049**	Burlington Northern Gondola w/ coil covers, *94*
____	**52097**	Chessie System Reefer, *95*

CHICAGOLAND RAILROAD CLUB

____	**(52081)**	C&NW Boxcar "6464555", *96*

EASTWOOD AUTOMOBILIA

____	**52044**	Eastwood Vat Car, *94*
____	**52083**	Pennsylvania Flatcar w/ Eastwood tanker trailer, *95*

INLAND EMPIRE TRAIN COLLECTORS ASSOC. (IETCA)

____	**[1979]**	IETCA Boxcar, *79*
____	**[1980]**	IETCA SP-Type Caboose, *80*
____	**[1981]**	IETCA Quad Hopper, *81*
____	**[1982]**	IETCA 3-D Tank Car, *82*
____	**[1983]**	IETCA Reefer, *83*
____	**[7518]**	IETCA Carson City Mint Car, *84*
____	**[1986]**	IETCA Bunk Car, *86*

LIONEL CENTRAL OPERATING LINES (LCOL)

____	**[1981]**	LCOL Boxcar, *81*
____	**[9184]**	Erie B/W Caboose, *82*
____	**[6508]**	Canadian Pacific Crane Car, *83*
____	**[5724]**	Pennsylvania Bunk Car, *84*
____	**[9475]**	D&H "I Love NY" Boxcar, *85*
____	**[1986]**	LCOL Work Caboose, shell only, *86*

UNCATALOGED CLUB CARS AND SPECIAL PRODUCTION

LIONEL COLLECTORS ASSOC. OF CANADA (LCAC)

____	[9718]	Canadian National Boxcar, *79*
____	[9413]	Napierville Junction Boxcar, *80*
____	[8103]	Toronto, Hamilton & Buffalo Boxcar, *81*
____	[8204]	Algoma Central Boxcar, *82*
____	[6100]	Ontario Northland Covered Quad Hopper, *82*
____	[830005]	Canadian National Boxcar, *83*
____	[5710]	Canadian Pacific Reefer, *83*
____	[840006]	Canadian Wheat Board Covered Quad Hopper, *84*
____	[8507]/ [8508]	Canadian National F-3 AA, shells only, *85*
____	[5714]	Michigan Central Reefer, *85*
____	[86009]	Canadian National Bunk Car, *86*
____	[87010]	Canadian National Express Reefer, *87*
____	[88011]	Canadian National Woodside Caboose (Std. O), *88*
____	[8912]	Canada Southern Operating Hopper, *89*
____	[900013]	Canadian National Flatcar w/ trailers, *90*
____	[17893]	BAOC 1-D Tank Car "914", *91*
____	[52004]	Algoma Central Gondola w/ coil covers "9215", *92*
____	[52005]	Canadian National F-3 B Unit "9517", *93*
____	[52006]	Canadian Pacific Boxcar "930016" (Std. O), *93*

LIONEL COLLECTORS CLUB OF AMERICA (LCCA)

LCCA National Convention Cars

____	[9701]	Baltimore & Ohio DD Boxcar, *72*
____	9727	TA&G Boxcar, *73*
____	9118	Corning Covered Quad Hopper, *74*
____	9155	Monsanto 1-D Tank Car, *75*
____	9212	Seaboard Coast Line Flatcar w/ trailers, *76*
____	X9259	Southern B/W Caboose, *77*
____	9728	Union Pacific Stock Car, *78*
____	9733	Airco Boxcar w/ tank, *79*
____	9358	Sands of Iowa Covered Quad Hopper, *80*
____	(8068)	Rock Island GP-20 "1980", *80*
____	9435	Central of Georgia Boxcar, *81*
____	9460	D&TS DD Boxcar, *82*
____	6112	Commonwealth Edison Quad Hopper w/ coal load, *83*
____	7403	LNAC Boxcar, *84*
____	(6567)	Illinois Central Gulf Crane Car "100408", *85*
____	6323	Virginia Chemicals 1-D Tank Car, *86*

UNCATALOGED CLUB CARS AND SPECIAL PRODUCTION

___	**17870**	East Camden & Highland Boxcar (Std. O), *87*
___	**17873**	Ashland Oil 3-D Tank Car, *88*
___	**17876**	Columbia, Newberry & Laurens Boxcar (Std. O), *89*
___	**17880**	D&RGW Woodside Caboose (Std. O), *90*
___	**(18090)**	D&RGW 4-6-2 "1990", *90*
___	**17887**	Conrail Flatcar w/ Armstrong Tile trailer (Std. O), *91*
___	**17888**	Conrail Flatcar w/ Ford New Holland trailer (Std. O), *91*
___	**(17899)**	NASA Uni-body Tank Car "190" (Std. O), *92*
___	**(52023)**	D&TS 2-bay ACF Hopper "2601" (Std. O), *93*
___	**(52038)**	Southern Hopper w/ coal load "360794" (Std. O), *94*
___	**(52074)**	Iowa Beef Packers Reefer "197095" (Std. O), *95*
___	**(52090)**	Pere Marquette DD Boxcar (Std. O), *96*

LCCA Meet Specials

___	**[6014-900]**	Frisco Boxcar (O27), *75–76*
___	**[No Number]**	Lionel Lines Tender only, *76–77*
___	**[9142]**	Republic Steel Gondola w/ canisters, *77–78*
___	**[9036]**	Mobilgas 1-D Tank Car (O27), *78–79*
___	**[9016]**	Chessie System Hopper (O27), *79–80*
___	**6483**	Jersey Central SP-Type Caboose, *82*

Other LCCA Production

___	**[9771]**	Norfolk & Western Boxcar, *77*
___	**[9739]**	D&RGW Boxcar, *78*
___	**(17895)**	LCCA Tractor, *91*
___	**(17896)**	Lancaster Lines Tractor, *91*
___	**(52025)**	Madison Hardware Tractor and Trailer, *93*
___	**(52039)**	"Track 29" Bumper, *94*
___	**(52055)**	Sovex Tractor and Trailer, *94*
___	**(52056)**	Southern Tractor and Trailer "206502", *94*
___	**(52091)**	Lenox Tractor and Trailer, *95*
___	**(52092)**	Iowa Interstate Tractor and Trailer, *95*

LIONEL OPERATING TRAIN SOCIETY (LOTS)

LOTS National Convention Cars

___	**[9414]**	Cotton Belt Boxcar, *80*
___	**[3764]**	Kahn Boxcar, *81*
___	**[80948]**	Michigan Central Boxcar, *82*

UNCATALOGED CLUB CARS AND SPECIAL PRODUCTION

____	[6111]	L&N Covered Quad Hopper, *83*
____	[121315]	Pennsylvania Hi-cube Boxcar, *84*
____	[303]	Stauffer Chemical 1-D Tank Car, *85*
____	[6211]	C&O Gondola w/ canisters, *86*
____	[38356]	Dow Chemical 3-D Tank Car, *87*
____	(17874)	Milwaukee Road Log Dump Car "59629", *88*
____	(17875)	PHD Boxcar "1289", *89*
____	(17882)	B&O DD Boxcar w/ ETD "298011", *90*
____	(18890)	Union Pacific RS-3 "8805", *90*
____	(17890)	CSX Auto Carrier "151161", *91*
____	(19960)	Western Pacific Boxcar "1952" (Std. O), *92*
____	(52014)	BN TTUX Flatcar set w/ N&W trailers "637500A/B", *93*
____	(52041)	BN TTUX Flatcar set w/ Conrail trailers "637500D/E", *94*
____	(52067)	Burlington Ice Car "50240", *95*
____		Grand Trunk 2-bay ACF Hopper (Std. O), *96*

Other LOTS Production

____	[1223]	Seattle & North Coast Hi-cube Boxcar, *86*
____	(52042)	BN TTUX Flatcar w/ Canadian National trailer "637500C", *94*
____	(52048)	Canadian National Tractor and Trailer "197993", *94*

LIONEL RAILROADER CLUB (LRRC)

____	0780	LRRC Boxcar, *82*
____	0781	LRRC Flatcar w/ trailers, *83*
____	0784	LRRC Covered Quad Hopper, *84*
____	0782	LRRC 1-D Tank Car, *85*
____	16800	LRRC Ore Car, *86*
____	16801	LRRC Bunk Car, *88*
____	16802	LRRC Tool Car, *89*
____	16803	LRRC Searchlight Car, *90*
____	16804	LRRC B/W Caboose, *91*
____	(18818)	LRRC GP-38-2 "1992", *92*
____	19924	LRRC Boxcar, *93*
____	19930	LRRC Quad Hopper w/ coal load, *94*
____	(12875)	LRRC Tractor and Trailer, *94*
____	(19935)	LRRC 1-D Tank Car "1995", *95*
____	(12921)	LRRC Illuminated Station Platform, *95*

NASSAU LIONEL OPERATING ENGINEERS (NLOE)

____	[8389]	Long Island Boxcar, *89*
____	[8390]	Long Island Covered Quad Hopper, *90*
____	[8391A]	Long Island Bunk Car, *91*
____	[8391B]	Long Island Tool Car, *91*
____	[8392]	Long Island 1-D Tank Car, *92*
____	[52007]	Long Island RS-3 "1552", *93*
____	[52019]	Long Island Boxcar "8393", *93*
____	[52020]	Long Island B/W Caboose "8393", *93*
____	[52026]	Long Island Flatcar w/ Grumman trailer "8394", *94*
____	[52072]	Grumman Tractor, *94*
____	[52061]	Long Island Stern's Pickle Products Vat Car "8395", *95*
____	[52076]	Long Island Observation Car "8396", *96*

TRAIN COLLECTORS ASSOCIATION (TCA)

TCA National Convention Cars

____	6464-1970	TCA Chicago Boxcar, *70*
____	6464-1971	TCA Disneyland Boxcar, *71*
____	6315	TCA Pittsburgh 1-D Tank Car, *72*
____	(9123)	TCA Dearborn Auto Carrier "1973" (3-tier), *73*
____	9864	TCA Seattle Reefer, *74*
____	9774	TCA Orlando Southern Belle Boxcar, *75*
____	(9779)	TCA Philadelphia Boxcar "9700-1976", *76*
____	7812	TCA Houston Stock Car, *77*
____	9611	TCA Boston Hi-cube Boxcar, *78*
____	9319	TCA Silver Jubilee Mint Car, *79*
____	(9544)	TCA Chicago Observation Car "1980", *80*
____	(0511)	TCA St. Louis Baggage Car "1981", *81*
____	(7205)	TCA Denver Combination Car "1982", *82*
____	(7206)	TCA Louisville Passenger Car "1983", *83*
____	(7212)	TCA Pittsburgh Passenger Car "1984", *84*
____	5734	TCA REA Reefer, *85*
____	(8476)	TCA 4-6-4 "5484", *85*
____	6926	TCA New Orleans E/V Caboose, *86*
____	(17879)	TCA Valley Forge Dining Car "1989", *89*
____	(17883)	New Georgia Railroad Passenger Car "1990", *90*
____	(17898)	Wabash Reefer "21596", *92*
____	(52008)	Bucyrus Erie Crane Car "1993X", *93*
____	(11737)	TCA 40th Anniversary F-3 ABA set "40", *93*

UNCATALOGED CLUB CARS AND SPECIAL PRODUCTION

____ **(52035)** Yorkrail GP-9 "1750", shell only, *94*
____ **(52036)** TCA 40th Anniversary B/W Caboose, *94*
____ **(52037)** Yorkrail GP-9 "1754", *94*
____ **(52062)** TCA "Skytop" Observation Car "1995", *95*
____ **(52085)** TCA Full Vista Dome Car "1996", *96*

TCA Museum-Related Cars

____ **[9771]** Norfolk & Western Boxcar, *77*
____ **[1018-1979]** Mortgage Burning Hi-cube Boxcar, *79*
____ **[7780]** TCA Museum Boxcar, *80*
____ **[7781]** Hafner Boxcar, *81*
____ **[7782]** Carlisle & Finch Boxcar, *82*
____ **[7783]** Ives Boxcar, *83*
____ **[7784]** Voltamp Boxcar, *84*
____ **[7785]** Hoge Boxcar, *85*
____ **[5731]** L&N Reefer, *90*
____ **[52045]** Penn Dutch Milk Car "61052", *94*
____ **[52052]** TCA 40th Anniversary Boxcar, *94*
____ **(52051)** Baltimore & Ohio "Sentinel" Boxcar "6464095", *95*
____ **(52063)** NYC "Pacemaker" Boxcar "6464125", *95*
____ **(52064)** Missouri Pacific Boxcar "6464150", *95*

TCA Bicentennial Special Set

____ **1973** TCA Bicentennial Observation Car, *76*
____ **1974** TCA Bicentennial Passenger Car, *76*
____ **1975** TCA Bicentennial Passenger Car, *76*
____ **1976** TCA Bicentennial U36B, *76*

Atlantic Division TCA

____ **[9788]** Lehigh Valley Boxcar, *78*
____ **[9186]** Conrail N5C Caboose, *79*
____ **[1980]** Atlantic Division Flatcar w/ trailers, *80*
____ **[6101]** Burlington Northern Covered Quad Hopper, *82*
____ **[9466]** Wanamaker Boxcar, *83*
____ **[9193]** Budweiser Vat Car, *84*
____ **[No Number]** Pennsylvania Reading Seashore Bunk Car, *85*

UNCATALOGED CLUB CARS AND SPECIAL PRODUCTION

Desert Division TCA

____ **[52088]**   Desert Division 25th Anniversary On-Track Step Van, *96*

Eastern Division TCA

____ **(52059)**   Clinchfield Quad Hopper w/ coal load "16413", *94*

Eastern Division TCA—Washington, Baltimore and Annapolis Chapter

____ **[9740]**   Chessie System Boxcar, *76*
____ **[9783]**   B&O "Time-Saver" Boxcar, *77*
____ **[9771]**   Norfolk & Western Boxcar, *78*
____ **[9412]**   Richmond, Fredericksburg, & Potomac Boxcar, *79*

Ft. Pitt Division TCA

____ **[1984-30X]** Heinz Ketchup Boxcar, *84*
____ **[1984]**   Iron City Beer Reefer, *84*
____ **[1984]**   Iron City Beer Boxcar, *84*
____ **[1984]**   Heinz Pickles Boxcar, *84*

Great Lakes Division TCA

____ **[9740]**   Chessie System Boxcar, *76*
____ **[1983]**   Churchill Downs Boxcar, *83*
____ **[1983]**   Churchill Downs Reefer, *83*

Great Lakes Division TCA—Detroit-Toledo Chapter

____ **[9730]**   CP Rail Boxcar, *76*
____ **[9119]**   Detroit & Mackinac Covered Quad Hopper, *77*
____ **[9401]**   Great Northern Boxcar, *78*
____ **[9272]**   New Haven B/W Caboose, *79*
____ **[8957]**   Burlington Northern GP-20, *80*
____ **[8958]**   Burlington Northern GP-20 Dummy, *80*
____ **52000**   Detroit-Toledo Division Flatcar w/ trailer, *92*

Great Lakes Division TCA—Three Rivers Chapter

____ **[9113]**   Norfolk & Western Quad Hopper, *76*

UNCATALOGED CLUB CARS AND SPECIAL PRODUCTION

Great Lakes Division TCA—Western Michigan Chapter

____ [9730]   CP Rail Boxcar, *74*

Lake & Pines Division TCA

____ 52018   3-M Boxcar, *93*

Lone Star Division TCA

____ [7522]   New Orleans Mint Car w/ coin, *86*
____ (52093)   Lone Star Division Boxcar "6464696", *96*

Lone Star Division TCA—North Texas Chapter

____ [9739]   D&RGW Boxcar, *76*
____ [9184]   Erie B/W Caboose, *77*
____ [9119]   Detroit & Mackinac Covered Quad Hopper, *78*
____ [No Number] Texas Special F-3 A Unit, shell only, *81*
____ [No Number] Texas Special F-3 B Unit, shell only, *82*

METCA

____ [10]   Jersey Central F-3 A Unit, shell only, *71*
____ [9754]   New York Central "Pacemaker" Boxcar, *76*
____ [9272]   New Haven B/W Caboose, *79*

Midwest Division TCA

____ [9725]   Midwest Division Stock Car "00002", *75*
____ [7600]   Frisco "Spirit of '76" N5C Caboose "00003", *76*
____ [4]   C&NW F-3 A Unit, shell only, *77*
____ [00005]   Midwest Division Covered Quad Hopper, *78*
____ [9872]   PFE Reefer "00006", *79*
____ [1287]   C&NW Reefer, *84*
____ [1988]   Illinois Central Boxcar, *88*

Midwest Division TCA Museum Express

____ 9785]   Conrail Boxcar, *77*
____ [9264]   Illinois Central Gulf Covered Quad Hopper, *78*
____ [9786]   Chicago & North Western Boxcar, *79*
____ [9289]   Chicago & North Western N5C Caboose, *80*

UNCATALOGED CLUB CARS AND SPECIAL PRODUCTION

NETCA

____ [1203]   Boston & Maine NW-2, shell only, *72*

____ [9753]   Maine Central Boxcar, *75*

____ [9768]   Boston & Maine Boxcar, *76*

____ [9181]   Boston & Maine N5C Caboose, *77*

____ [9400]   Conrail Boxcar, *78*

____ [9785]   Conrail Boxcar, *78*

____ [9415]   Providence & Worcester Boxcar, *79*

____ [9423]   NYNH&H Boxcar, *80*

____ [9445]   Vermont Northern Boxcar, *81*

____ [5710]   Canadian Pacific Reefer, *82*

____ [5716]   Vermont Central Reefer, *83*

____ [6124]   Delaware & Hudson Covered Quad Hopper, *84*

____ [8051]   Hood's Milk Boxcar, *86*

____ 52001   Boston & Maine Quad Hopper w/ coal load, *92*

____ 52016   Boston & Maine Gondola w/ coil covers, *93*

____ [52043]   LL Bean Boxcar "1994", *94*

____ [52080]   B&M Flatcar w/ trailer "91095", *95*

Ozark Division TCA—Gateway Chapter

____ [9068]   Reading Bobber Caboose, *76*

____ [9601]   Illinois Central Gulf Hi-cube Boxcar, *77*

____ [9767]   Railbox Boxcar, *78*

____ [5700]   Oppenheimer Reefer, *81*

____ 52003   "Meet Me In St. Louis" Flatcar w/ trailer, *92*

Pacific Northwest Division TCA

____ [No Number] Pacific Northwest Division F-3 AA, shells only, *74*

____ (52077)   Great Northern Hi-cube Boxcar "9695", *95*

Rocky Mountain Division TCA

____ 1971-1976 Rocky Mountain Division Reefer, *76*

Sacramento—Sierra Chapter TCA

____ [9723]   Western Pacific Boxcar, *73*

____ [9705]   D&RGW Boxcar, *75*

____ [9301]   US Mail Operating Boxcar, *76*

UNCATALOGED CLUB CARS AND SPECIAL PRODUCTION

____ **[9730]** CP Rail Boxcar, *77*

____ **[9785]** Conrail Boxcar, *78*

____ **[9726]** Erie-Lackawanna Boxcar, *79*

____ **[9414]** Cotton Belt Boxcar, *80*

____ **[9427]** Bay Line Boxcar, *81*

____ **[9444]** Louisiana Midland Boxcar, *82*

____ **[9452]** Western Pacific Boxcar, *83*

____ **[6401]** Virginian B/W Caboose, *84*

____ **[No Number]**Lionel Lines Tender, shell only, *84*

Southern Division TCA

____ **[1976]** Florida East Coast F-3 ABA, shells only, *76*

____ **[9287]** Southern N5C Caboose, *77*

____ **[9403]** Seaboard Coast Line Boxcar, *78*

____ **[9405]** Chattahoochie Boxcar, *79*

____ **[9352]** Trailer Train Flatcar w/ Circus trailers, *80*

____ **[9443]** Florida East Coast Boxcar, *81*

____ **[6111]** L&N Covered Quad Hopper, *83*

____ **[9471]** ACL Boxcar, *84*

____ **[9482]** Norfolk & Southern Boxcar, *85*

____ **[1986]** Southern Division Bunk Car, *86*

____ **[16606]** Southern Searchlight Car, *88*

TOY TRAIN OPERATING SOCIETY (TTOS)

TTOS National Convention Cars

____ **6076** Santa Fe Hopper (O27), *70*

____ **9512** TTOS Summerdale Junction Passenger Car, *74*

____ **9520** TTOS Phoenix Combination Car, *75*

____ **9526** TTOS Snowbird Observation Car, *76*

____ **9535** TTOS Columbus Baggage Car, *77*

____ **9678** TTOS Hollywood Hi-cube Boxcar, *78*

____ **9347** TTOS Niagara Falls 3-D Tank Car, *79*

____ **9868** TTOS Oklahoma City Reefer, *80*

____ **[9326]** Burlington Northern B/W Caboose, *82*

____ **[9355]** Delaware & Hudson B/W Caboose, *82*

____ **[9361]** Chicago & North Western B/W Caboose, *82*

____ **[9382]** Florida East Coast B/W Caboose, *82*

____ **[9883]** TTOS Phoenix Reefer, *83*

____ **[1984]** TTOS Sacramento Northern Boxcar, *84*

UNCATALOGED CLUB CARS AND SPECIAL PRODUCTION

_____ [1985]	TTOS Snowbird Covered Quad Hopper, _85_
_____ 6582	TTOS Portland Flatcar w/ wood load, _86_
_____ (17871)	NYC Flatcar w/ Kodak and Xerox trailers "81487", _87_
_____ (17872)	Anaconda Ore Car "81988", _88_
_____ (17877)	MKT 1-D Tank Car "3739469", _89_
_____ 17884	Columbus & Dayton Terminal Boxcar (Std. O), _90_
_____ (17889)	Southern Pacific Flatcar w/ trailer "15791" (Std. O), _91_
_____ (19963)	Union Equity 3-bay ACF Hopper "86892" (Std. O), _92_
_____ (52010)	Weyerhaeuser DD Boxcar "838593" (Std. O), _93_
_____ (52029)	Ford 1-D Tank Car "12" (O27), _94_
_____ (52030)	Ford Gondola "4023", _94_
_____ (52031)	Ford Hopper "1458" (O27), _94_
_____ (52057)	Western Pacific Boxcar "64641995", _95_
_____ (52087)	New Mexico Central Boxcar "64641996", _96_

TTOS Division Cars

_____ (52009)	Sacramento Valley Division Western Pacfic Boxcar "64641993", _93_
_____ 52040	Wolverine Division GTW Flatcar w/ LL Tractor and Trailer, _94_
_____ (52058)	Central California Division Santa Fe Boxcar "64641895", _95_
_____ (52086)	Canadian Division Pacific Great Eastern Boxcar "64641972", _96_

Southwest Division TTOS—Cal-Stewart

_____ (19962)	Southern Pacific 3-bay ACF Hopper "496035" (Std. O), _92_
_____ (52047)	Cotton Belt Woodside Caboose w/ smoke "1921" (Std. O), _93-94_
_____ (52073)	Pacific Fruit Express Reefer "459402" (Std. O), _95_

Other TTOS Production

_____ [1983]	TTOS Phoenix 3-D Tank Car, _83_
_____ (17894)	Southern Pacific Tractor, _91_
_____ (52021)	Weyerhaeuser Tractor and Trailer, _93_
_____ 52022	Union Pacific Boxcar, _93_
_____ (52032)	Ford 1-D Tank Car "14" w/ Kughn inscription (O27), _94_
_____ (52046)	ACL Boxcar "16247", _94_
_____ 52053	TTOS Carail Boxcar, _94_

UNCATALOGED CLUB CARS AND SPECIAL PRODUCTION

_____	**(52068)**	Toy Train Parade TTOS Contadina Boxcar "16245", *94*
_____	**(52084)**	Union Pacific I-Beam Flatcar w/ load "16380", *95*
_____	**(52078)**	Southern Pacific SD-9 "5366", *96*
_____	**(52079)**	Southern Pacific B/W Caboose "1996", *96*

TTOM Gadsden Pacific Ore Cars

_____	**17878**	Magma Ore Car w/ load, *89*
_____	**17881**	Phelps-Dodge Ore Car w/ load, *90*
_____	**17886**	Cyprus Ore Car w/ load, *91*
_____	**19961**	Inspiration Consolidated Copper Co. Ore Car w/ load, *92*
_____	**52011**	Tucson, Cornelia & Gila Bend Ore Car w/ load, *93*
_____	**52027**	Pinto Valley Mine Ore Car w/ load, *94*
_____	**52071**	Copper Basin Railway Ore Car w/ load, *95*
_____	**52089**	SMARRCO Ore Car w/ load, *96*

VIRGINIA TRAIN COLLECTORS (VTC)

_____	**[7679]**	VTC Boxcar, *79*
_____	**[7681]**	VTC N5C Caboose, *81*
_____	**[7682]**	VTC Covered Quad Hopper, *82*
_____	**[7683]**	Virginia Fruit Express Reefer, *83*
_____	**[7684]**	Vitraco 3-D Tank Car, *84*
_____	**[7685]**	VTC Boxcar, *85*
_____	**[7686]**	VTC GP-7, *86*
_____	**[7692-1]**	VTC Baggage Car (O27), *92*
_____	**[7692-2]**	VTC Combination Car (O27), *92*
_____	**[7692-3]**	VTC Dining Car (O27), *92*
_____	**[7692-4]**	VTC Passenger Car (O27), *92*
_____	**[7692-5]**	VTC Vista Dome Car (O27), *92*
_____	**[7692-6]**	VTC Passenger Car (O27), *92*
_____	**[7692-7]**	VTC Observation Car (O27), *92*
_____	**[52060]**	VTC Tender w/ whistle "7694", *94*

1	(See 85120)
3	(See 85115)
4	(See 85117)
5	(See 85121)
3	(See 85122)
100	(See 85100)
101	(See 85101, 85124)
112	(See 85112)
400	(See 87400)
401	(See 87401)
404	(See 87404)
485	(See 85006)
486	(See 85007)
700	(See 87700)
701	(See 87701, 87724)
709	(See 87709)
712	(See 85008, 87712)
722	(See 85013)
2003	(See 85003)
2004	(See 85005)
5000	(See 55000, 85000)
5001	(See 85001)
5102	(See 85102)
5103	(See 85103)
5104	(See 85104)
5105	(See 85105)
5106	(See 85106)
5107	(See 85107)
5108	(See 85108)
5109	(See 85109)
5110	(See 85110)
5111	(See 85111)
5113	(See 85113)
5114	(See 85114)
6000	(See 86000)
6001	(See 86001)
6002	(See 86002)

		Exc	New	Cond/$
6003	(See 86003)			
6004	(See 86004)			
6005	(See 86005)			
7402	(See 87402)			
7403	(See 87403)			
7405	(See 87405)			
7406	(See 87406)			
7407	(See 87407)			
7500	(See 87500)			
7501	(See 87501)			
7502	(See 87502)			
7503	(See 87503)			
7504	(See 87504)			
7508	(See 87508)			
7702	(See 87702)			
7703	(See 87703)			
7704	(See 87704)			
7705	(See 87705)			
7706	(See 87706)			
7707	(See 87707)			
7708	(See 87708)			
7711	(See 87711)			
7713	(See 87713)			
7716	(See 87716)			
7800	(See 87800)			
7806	(See 87806)			
7808	(See 87808)			
(55000)	Lionel Lines RailScope 0-4-0T "5000", *88–90*	—	225	___
(81000)	Gold Rush Special set, *87–90*	—	190	___
(81001)	Thunder Mountain Express set, *88–89*	—	200	___
(81002)	Frontier Freight set, *88–89*	—	175	___
(81003)	Great Northern set, *90*		NM	___
(81004)	North Pole Railroad set, *89–91*	—	165	___
(81006)	Union Pacific Limited set, *90–91*	—	220	___
(81007)	Disney Magic Express set, *90*	—	250	___
(81008)	Walt Disney World set, *91*		NM	___
(81011)	Thomas the Tank Engine set, *93 u*	110	130	___
(81014)	James & Troublesome Trucks set, *94–95*		CP	___
(81016)	Thomas the Tank Engine Deluxe set, *94–95*		CP	___

	Exc	New	Cond/$
(81017) Ornament Express set, *94–95*		CP	_____
(81050) Gold Rush Special set w/ mailer, *87 u*		NRS	_____
(81051) Spiegel PRR set, *87 u*		NRS	_____
(81054) Gold Rush Special set w/o transformer, *90 u*		NRS	_____
(81057) North Pole Railroad set w/ mailer, *90 u*		NRS	_____
(81059) JCPenney Thomas the Tank Engine set, *94 u*	125	150	_____
(81061) Thomas the Tank Engine set, *95*		CP	_____
(82000) Straight Track, *87–95*		CP	_____
(82001) Curved Track 4.3', *87–95*		CP	_____
(82002) Straight Track, box of 4, *87–95*		CP	_____
(82003) Curved Track 4.3', box of 4, *87–95*		CP	_____
(82004) Curved Track 5.3', *88–95*		CP	_____
(82006) 35" Straight Track, *88–95*		CP	_____
(82007) Right Remote Switch, *89–95*		CP	_____
(82008) Left Remote Switch, *89–95*		CP	_____
(82010) Thomas Track Pack, *94–95*		CP	_____
(82011) Thomas Left Manual Switch, *94–95*		CP	_____
(82012) Thomas Right Manual Switch, *94–95*		CP	_____
(82013) Thomas Curved Track 4.3', box of 4, *94–95*		CP	_____
(82014) Thomas Straight Track, box of 4, *94–95*		CP	_____
(82015) Right Manual Switch, *95*		CP	_____
(82016) Left Manual Switch, *95*		CP	_____
(82101) Lockon w/ wires, *88–95*		CP	_____
(82102) Conversion Rail Joiners (6), *88–95*		CP	_____
(82103) Conversion Knuckle Couplers (2), *88–91*	—	5	_____
(82104) Water Tower kit, *88–89*	—	50	_____
(82105) Engine House kit, *88–89*	—	125	_____
(82106) Watchman Shanty kit, *88–89*	—	65	_____
(82107) Passenger & Freight Station kit, *88–89*	—	100	_____
(82108) Manual Uncoupler, *88–95*		CP	_____
(82109) Brass Pins (12), *88–95*		CP	_____
(82110) Lumber Shed kit, *89*	—	65	_____
(82111) Freight Platform kit, *89*	—	90	_____
(82112) Figure set (6), *89–95*		CP	_____
(82115) RailSounds Control Box, *90–95*		CP	_____
(82115) Wooden Vehicle Assortment, *89*		NM	_____
(82116) DC Converter Box, *91 u, 92–95*		CP	_____
(82116) 1936 Ford Pickup, *89*		NM	_____
(82117) Crossing Gate and Signal, *91*		NM	_____

	Exc	New	Cond/$
(82117) 1928 Ford Model A Coupe, *89*		NM	
(82118) 1936 Ford "Woody" Station Wagon, *89*		NM	
(82120) Thomas Sound System, *94–95*		CP	
(82121) Thomas Play Pack, *94–95*		CP	
(82122) Thomas Building Pack, *94–95*		CP	
(85000) Seaboard System GP-9 "5000", *90–91*	—	350	
(85001) Conrail GP-7 "5001", *90–91*	—	350	
(85003) BN GP-20 "2003", *91 u, 92–94*	—	375	
(85005) BN GP-20 Dummy "2004", *92–94*	—	225	
(85006) Union Pacific GP-20 "485", *93–95*		CP	
(85007) Union Pacific GP-20 Dummy "486", *93–95*		CP	
(85008) Santa Fe GP-9 "712", *95*		NM	
(85013) Santa Fe GP-9 Dummy "722", *95*		NM	
(85100) Pennsylvania 0-6-0T "100", *87*	—	110	
(85101) D&RG 0-6-0T "101", *87–90*	—	100	
(85102) New York Central 4-4-2 "5102", *88*	—	200	
(85103) Santa Fe 4-4-2 "5103", *88*	—	200	
(85104) Santa Fe 0-4-0T "5104", *88–89*	—	90	
(85105) Pennsylvania 0-4-0T "5105", *88–89*	—	90	
(85106) Chessie System 4-4-2 "5106", *89*	—	200	
(85107) Great Northern 4-4-2 "5107", *89*	—	200	
(85108) B&O 0-4-0T "5108", *89*	—	95	
(85109) Canadian Pacific 0-6-0T "5109", *89*	—	100	
(85110) PRR 4-4-2 "5110", *90, 94–95*		CP	
(85111) Great Northern 0-4-0T "5111", *90*		NM	
(85112) RI&P 0-6-0T "112", *90*		NM	
(85113) Union Pacific 0-4-0T "5113", *90–91*	—	100	
(85114) North Pole Railroad 0-4-0T "5114", *89–91*	—	105	
(85115) Disneyland 0-6-0T "3", *90*	—	110	
(85117) Disney World 0-6-0T "4", *91*		NM	
(85120) Thomas the Tank Engine 0-6-0T "1", *93 u, 94–95*		CP	
(85121) James the Red Engine 2-6-0 "5", *94–95*		CP	
(85122) Ornament Express 0-6-0T "8", *94–95*		CP	
(85124) D&RG 0-6-0T "101", *95*		CP	
(86000) PRR Passenger Car "6000", *88–89*	—	65	
(86001) PRR Observation Car "6001", *88–89*	—	65	
(86002) Union Pacific Passenger Car "6002", *90–91*	—	65	
(86003) Union Pacific Observation Car "6003", *90–91*	—	65	
(86004) Disney World Passenger Car "6004", *91*		NM	

		Exc	New	Cond/$
(86005)	Disney World Observation Car "6005", 91		NM	_____
(86006)	"Annie" Passenger Car, 93 u, 94–95		CP	_____
(86007)	"Clarabel" Passenger Car, 93 u, 94–95		CP	_____
87000	New York Central Boxcar, 89	—	45	_____
87001	Pennsylvania Boxcar, 88	—	45	_____
87002	Santa Fe Boxcar, 88	—	45	_____
87003	Great Northern Boxcar, 89	—	45	_____
87004	Southern Boxcar, 90	—	50	_____
87005	Northern Pacific Boxcar, 90	—	50	_____
87006	Christmas Boxcar, 89 u	—	80	_____
87007	Christmas Boxcar, 90 u	—	85	_____
87009	Western Pacific Boxcar, 91	—	50	_____
87013	Christmas Boxcar, 95		CP	_____
87100	Union Pacific PFE Reefer, 88	—	50	_____
87101	Pennsylvania Reefer, 88	—	50	_____
87102	Chesapeake & Ohio Reefer, 89	—	50	_____
87103	Tropicana Reefer, 90	—	60	_____
87104	Gerber Reefer, 90	—	60	_____
87105	Seaboard Reefer, 89	—	50	_____
87107	A&P Reefer, 91	—	65	_____
87108	Pacific Fruit Express Reefer, 95		CP	_____
87109	Santa Fe Reefer, 95		CP	_____
87200	Buford & Roscoe Handcar, 89–90	—	70	_____
87201	Milwaukee Road Ore Car, 89	—	35	_____
87202	Chessie System Ore Car, 89	—	35	_____
87203	Santa & Snowman Handcar, 90	—	90	_____
87204	Northern Pacific Ore Car, 90	—	40	_____
87205	Pennsylvania Ore Car, 90	—	40	_____
87207	Mickey & Donald Handcar, 91, 95		CP	_____
87208	Wile E. Coyote & Roadrunner Handcar, 92	—	100	_____
87210	Santa Fe Ore Car, 95		CP	_____
(87400)	PRR Gondola "400", 87	—	35	_____
(87401)	D&RG Gondola "401", 87–90	—	30	_____
(87402)	Santa Fe Gondola "7402", 88	—	35	_____
(87403)	New York Central Gondola "7403", 88	—	35	_____
(87404)	Disneyland Gondola "404", 90	—	40	_____
(87405)	Chessie System Gondola "7405", 89	—	35	_____
(87406)	Southern Gondola "7406", 89	—	35	_____
(87407)	MKT Gondola "7407", 90	—	40	_____

		Exc	New	Cond/$
(87410)	Ornament Express Gondola w/ ornaments, *94–95*		CP	___
(87411)	"Troublesome Trucks" Gondola, *94–95*		CP	___
(87500)	D&RG Flatcar "7500", *88*	—	35	___
(87501)	Pennsylvania Flatcar "7501", *88*	—	35	___
(87502)	Santa Fe Flatcar "7502", *88–89*	—	30	___
(87503)	ICG Flatcar "7503", *89*	—	30	___
(87504)	Union Pacific Flatcar "7504", *89*	—	30	___
87505	Soo Line Flatcar w/ logs, *90*	—	45	___
87507	Great Northern Flatcar, *90*		NM	
(87508)	Merry Christmas Lines Flatcar "7508", *89–91*	—	35	___
87600	Alaska Tank Car, *89*	—	55	___
87601	Santa Fe Tank Car, *89*	—	50	___
87602	Gulf Tank Car, *90*	—	55	___
87603	Borden Tank Car, *90*	—	55	___
87604	Shell Tank Car, *91*	—	65	___
87612	Santa Fe Tank Car, *95*		CP	___
(87700)	Pennsylvania Caboose "700", *87*	—	50	___
(87701)	D&RG Caboose "701", *87–90*	—	50	___
(87702)	Santa Fe Caboose "7702", *88*	—	45	___
(87703)	New York Central Caboose "7703", *88*	—	45	___
(87704)	Santa Fe Bobber Caboose "7704", *88–89*	—	40	___
(87705)	Great Northern Caboose "7705", *89*	—	50	___
(87706)	Chessie System Caboose "7706", *89*	—	50	___
(87707)	B&O Bobber Caboose "7707", *89*	—	40	___
(87708)	Canadian Pacific Bobber Caboose "7708", *89*	—	45	___
(87709)	Disneyland Caboose "709", *90*	—	50	___
(87711)	Great Northern Bobber Caboose "7711", *90*		NM	
(87712)	RI&P Caboose "712", *90*		NM	
(87713)	Pennsylvania Caboose "7713", *90*	—	50	___
(87716)	North Pole Railroad Bobber Caboose "7716", *89–91*	—	45	___
(87722)	Ornament Express Bobber Caboose, *94–95*		CP	___
(87724)	D&RG Caboose "701", *95*		CP	___
(87800)	NYC Searchlight Car "7800", *89–90*	—	85	___
87802	Conrail Boxcar w/ ETD, *90–91*	—	70	___
87803	Seaboard Boxcar w/ ETD, *90–91*	—	70	___
(87806)	REA Boxcar w/ Steam RailSounds "7806", *91*		NM	
(87808)	Union Pacific Searchlight Car "7808", *95*		CP	
87809	Railbox Boxcar, *95*		CP	___

	Year	Catalog	Size	Pages	Exc	New
___	1945	Consumer Catalog	8½" x 11"	4 pages		NRS
___	1946	Consumer Catalog	8⅜" x 11¼"	20 pages	40	65
___	1947	Consumer Catalog	11¼" x 7⅝"	32 pages	30	45
___	1948	Consumer Catalog	11¼" x 8"	36 pages	30	45
___	1949	Consumer Catalog	11¼" x 8"	40 pages	75	125
___	1950	Consumer Catalog	11¼" x 8"	44 pages	35	60
___	1951	Consumer Catalog	11¼" x 7¾"	36 pages	25	45
___	1952	Consumer Catalog	11¼" x 7¾"	36 pages	20	35
___	1953	Consumer Catalog	11¼" x 7⅝"	40 pages	20	30
___	1954	Consumer Catalog	11¼" x 7⅝"	44 pages	20	28
___	1955	Consumer Catalog	11¼" x 7⅝"	44 pages	20	30
___	1956	Consumer Catalog	11¼" x 7⅝"	40 pages	12	20
___	1957	Consumer Catalog	11¼" x 7½"	52 pages	10	15
___	1958	Consumer Catalog	11¼" x 7⅝"	56 pages	8	12
___	1959	Consumer Catalog	11" x 8½"	56 pages	10	15
___	1960	Consumer Catalog	11" x 8⅜"	56 pages	6	10
___	1961	Consumer Catalog	8½" x 11"	72 pages	6	10
___	1962	Consumer Catalog	8½" x 11"	100 pages	8	12
___	1963	Consumer Catalog	8⅜" x 10⅞"	56 pages	4	6
___	1964	Consumer Catalog	8⅜" x 10⅞"	24 pages	4	6
___	1965	Consumer Catalog	8½" x 10⅞"	40 pages	4	6
___	1966	Consumer Catalog	10⅞" x 8⅜"	40 pages	4	6
	1967	Same Catalog as 1966				
___	1968	Consumer Catalog	8½" x 11"	8 pages	4	6
___	1969	Consumer Catalog	11" x 8½"	8 pages	3	5
___	1970	Consumer Catalog w/ foldout poster	8½" x 11"	8 pages	3	5
___	1971	Consumer Catalog	8½" x 11"	12 pages	3	5
___	1972	Consumer Catalog	8½" x 11"	16 pages	3	5
___	1973	Consumer Catalog	8½" x 11"	16 pages	2	4
___	1974	Consumer Catalog	8½" x 11"	20 pages	2	4
___	1975	Consumer Catalog	8½" x 11"	24 pages	2	4
___	1976	Consumer Catalog	8½" x 11"	24 pages	2	4
___	1977	Consumer Catalog	8½" x 11"	24 pages	2	4
___	1978	Consumer Catalog	8½" x 11"	24 pages	2	4
___	1979	Consumer Catalog	8½" x 11"	24 pages	2	4
___	1980	Consumer Catalog	8½" x 11"	28 pages	2	4
___	1981	Consumer Catalog	5½" x 7"	32 pages	1	2

	Year	Description	Size	Pages	Exc	New
____	1982	Traditional Series Consumer Catalog	8½" x 11"	20 pages	2	4
____	1982	Collector Series Consumer Catalog	8½" x 11"	12 pages	2	4
____	1983	Traditional Series Consumer Catalog	8½" x 11"	20 pages	2	3
____	1983	Collector Series Consumer Catalog	8½" x 11"	16 pages	2	3
____	1984	Traditional Series Consumer Catalog	8½" x 11"	20 pages	2	3
____	1984	Collector Series Consumer Catalog	8½" x 11"	16 pages	2	3
____	1985	Traditional Series Consumer Catalog	8½" x 11"	20 pages	2	3
____	1985	Collector Series Consumer Catalog	8½" x 11"	12 pages	2	3
____	1986	Traditional Series Consumer Catalog	8½" x 11"	16 pages	2	3
____	1986	Collector Series Consumer Catalog	8½" x 11"	16 pages	2	3
____	1986	Stocking Stuffers Brochure	8½" x 11"	4 pages	2	3
____	1987	Consumer Catalog	8½" x 11"	40 pages	3	4
____	1987	Large Scale Brochure	11" x 8½"	6 pages	1	2
____	1987	Stocking Stuffers Brochure	8½" x 11"	4 pages	2	3
____	1988	Consumer Catalog	8½" x 11"	40 pages	2	3
____	1988	Large Scale Catalog	8½" x 11"	16 pages	1	2
____	1988	Classics Brochure	8½" x 11"	4 pages	1	2
____	1988	Hiawatha Brochure	8½" x 11"	4 pages	2	3
____	1988	Stocking Stuffers Flyer	8½" x 11"	1 page	2	3
____	1989	Pre-Toy Fair Consumer Catalog	8½" x 11"	20 pages	2	3
____	1989	Toy Fair Consumer Catalog	8½" x 11"	28 pages	2	3
____	1989	Pre-Toy Fair Classics Brochure	8½" x 11"	4 pages	1	2
____	1989	Toy Fair Classics Brochure	8½" x 11"	4 pages	1	2
____	1989	Large Scale Catalog	8½" x 11"	20 pages	1	2
____	1989	Stocking Stuffers Brochure	8½" x 11"	4 pages	2	3

					Exc	New
____	1990	Book 1				
		Consumer Catalog	8½" x 11"	20 pages	2	4
____	1990	Book 2				
		Consumer Catalog	8½" x 11"	36 pages	2	3
____	1990	Large Scale Catalog	8½" x 11"	16 pages	1	2
____	1990	Stocking Stuffers				
		Brochure	8½" x 11"	6 pages	2	3
____	1991	Book 1				
		Consumer Catalog	8½" x 11"	24 pages	2	4
____	1991	Book 2				
		Consumer Catalog	8½" x 11"	60 pages	2	3
____	1991	Stocking Stuffers				
		Brochure	8½" x 11"	6 pages	2	3
____	1992	Book 1				
		Consumer Catalog	8½" x 11"	32 pages	2	4
____	1992	Book 2				
		Consumer Catalog	8½" x 11"	48 pages	2	3
____	1992	Stocking Stuffers				
		Brochure	8½" x 11"	8 pages	2	3
____	1993	Book 1				
		Consumer Catalog	8½" x 11"	32 pages	2	4
____	1993	Book 2				
		Consumer Catalog	8½" x 11"	52 pages	2	3
____	1993	Stocking Stuffers/1994				
		Spring Releases Catalog	8½" x 11"	28 pages	2	3
____	1994	Consumer Catalog	8½" x 11"	64 pages	2	3
____	1994	Thomas the Tank				
		Engine Catalog	8½" x 11"	8 pages	1	2
____	1994	Trainmaster				
		Transformer Catalog	8½" x 11"	8 pages	1	2
____	1994	Stocking Stuffers/1995				
		Spring Releases Catalog	8½" x 11"	32 pages	2	3
____	1995	Consumer Catalog	8½" x 11"	88 pages		CP
____	1995	Stocking Stuffers/1996				
		Spring Releases Catalog	8½" x 11"	32 pages		CP

ABBREVIATIONS
Pocket Guide Descriptions

A—diesel A unit
AA—two diesel A units
AAR—Association of American Railroads (truck type)
AC—alternating current
acc.—accessory
ACF—hopper type
Alco—diesel type
Alco A—diesel type
Alco FA-2A —diesel type
Alco FA-2B—diesel type
Anniv.—Anniversary
appro.—approaches
auto.—automatic
B—diesel B unit
Bag.—baggage
Bldg.—building
Blvd.—boulevard
Box.—boxcar
b/w—black and white
B/W—bay window
bump.—bumper(s)
Cab.—caboose
cata.—catalog
CC — center cupola
cent.—central
chem.—chemical
con.—connection
cont.—control
Conv.—conversion
CP—current production
C.V.—Commodore Vanderbilt
Dash-8—diesel type
DC—direct current
DD—double-door
dep.—depressed
d.p.d.t.—double-pole, double-throw switches
dir.—direct
dum.—dummy

dz.—dozen
elec.—electric
electr.—electronic
EP-5—electric type locomotive
ETD—end-of-train device
Exp.—express
ext.—extended
E/V—extended vision
F-3—diesel type
F.A.O.S.—F A O Schwarz
FARR—Famous American Railroad Series
FF—Fallen Flag Series
Flat.—flatcar
FM—Fairbanks-Morse
GG-1—electric type locomotive
GE—switcher type
Gen.—General, steam type
Gon.—gondola
GP-7—diesel type
GP-9—diesel type
GP-20—diesel type
GP-35—diesel type
GP-38-2—diesel type
Hi-cube—boxcar type
Hop.—hopper
HS—heat-stamped
illum.—illuminated
ins.—insulated, insulator
lett.—lettering
litho.—lithographed
low-cup.—low-cupola
maint.—maintenance
man.—manual
MB—multi-block door
mech.—mechanical
merch.—merchandise
MU—multiple unit (commuter cars)
N5C—caboose type

ABBREVIATIONS

J8—caboose type
JBA—National Basketball Assoc.
NHL—National Hockey League
NM—not manufactured
NW-2—diesel type
O—Lionel gauge (1¼" between outside rails)
OO—Lionel gauge (¾" between outside rails)
Obs.—observation
oper.—operating
or.—orange
pass.—passenger
pc(s).—piece(s)
port.—porthole
pow.—power, powered
pr.—pair
Pull.—Pullman
Quad—quad hopper
Rad.—radius
R.C.—remote control
RDC—diesel-powered passenger unit
rect.—rectifier
rectifier—electric type locomotive
Reefer—refrigerator car
Refrig.—refrigerator
rem.—remote
rnd.—round
RS—rubber-stamped
RS-3—diesel type
RSC-3—diesel type
RSD-4—diesel type
SB—single-block door
SD-9—diesel type
SD-18—diesel type
SD-24—diesel type
SD-28—diesel type
SD-38—diesel type
SD-40—diesel type
SD-50—diesel type

SD-60M—diesel type
sec.—section
SP—caboose type
spec.—special
SSS—Service Station Special
St.—state
Sta.—station
Std.—Standard gauge (2⅛" between outside rails
Steam—steam engine
str.—straight
Sup.—super
S/W—square window
Switch.—switcher
Tdr.—tender
TOFC—flatcar type
TT—TruTrack
TTUX—flatcar type
Trk.—track
Trans.—transformer
u or uncat.—uncataloged
U36B—diesel type
U36C—diesel type
V. D.—Vista Dome
w/—with
w/o—without
whl.—wheel
1-D—one dome
2-D—two dome
3-D—three dome

Railroad Name Abbreviations

ACL—Atlantic Coast Line

ACY—Akron, Canton and Youngstown

ALASK—Alaska Railroad

AT&SF (ATSF)—Atchison, Topeka, and Santa Fe

B&A—Boston and Albany

BAOC—British American Oil Co.

BAR—Bangor and Aroostook

B&LE—Bessemer and Lake Erie

B&M—Boston and Maine

BN—Burlington Northern

B&O—Baltimore and Ohio

C&A—Chicago and Alton

C&IM—Chicago and Illinois Midland

CB&Q (CBQ)—Chicago, Burlington, and Quincy

CCC&St L—Cleveland, Cincinnati, Chicago and St. Louis

CN—Canadian National

CNJ—Central of New Jersey

C&NW (CNW)—Chicago and North Western

C&O—Chesapeake and Ohio

CP—Canadian Pacific

CRI&P—Chicago, Rock Island, and Peoria

D&H—Delaware and Hudson

DL&W—Delaware, Lackawanna, and Western

DM&IR—Duluth, Missabe, and Iron Range

D&RG—Denver and Rio Grande

D&RGW—Denver and Rio Grande Western

DT&I—Detroit, Toledo, and Ironton

D&TS—Detroit and Toledo Shore Line

EJ&E—Elgin, Joliet, and Eastern

EMD—Electro-Motive Division

Erie-Lack.—Erie-Lackawanna

FEC—Florida East Coast

GM&O—Gulf, Mobile, and Ohio

GN—Great Northern

GTW—Grand Trunk Western

IC—Illinois Central

ICG—Illinois Central Gulf

IETCA—Inland Empire Train Collectors Association

L&C—Lancaster and Chester

Lack—Lackawanna

LCAC—Lionel Collectors Association of Canada

ABBREVIATIONS

LCCA—Lionel Collectors Club of America
LCOL—Lionel Central Operating Lines
LL—Lionel Lines
L&N—Louisville and Nashville
LNAC—Louisville, New Albany, and Corydon
LOTS—Lionel Operating Train Society
LRRC—Lionel Railroader Club
LV—Lehigh Valley
MD&W—Minnesota, Dakota, and Western
METCA—New York Metropolitan Division TCA
MKT—Missouri, Kansas, Texas (KATY)
MNS (MN&S)—Minneapolis, Northfield, and Southern
MP (MoPac)—Missouri Pacific
MPA—Maryland and Pennsylvania (Ma and Pa)
MILW—Milwaukee Road
M&St L—Minneapolis and St. Louis
NC&St L—Nashville, Chattanooga, and St. Louis
NdeM—Nacionales de Mexico Railway
NETCA—New England Division Train Collectors Association
NH—New Haven
NKP—Nickel Plate Road
NLOE—Nassau Lionel Operating Engineers
NP—Northern Pacific
N&W—Norfolk and Western
NYC—New York Central
NYNH&H—New York, New Haven, and Hartford
ON—Ontario Northland
PC—Penn Central
P&E—Peoria and Eastern
PFE—Pacific Fruit Express
PHD—Port Huron and Detroit
P&LE—Pittsburgh and Lake Erie
PRR—Pennsylvania Railroad
REA—Railway Express Agency
RF&P—Richmond, Fredericksburg, and Potomac
RI—Rock Island
RI&P—Rock Island and Peoria
SCL—Seaboard Coast Line
SMARRCO—San Manuel Arizona Railroad Company
SP—Southern Pacific
SP&S—Spokane, Portland, and Seattle
SUNX—Sunoco

ABBREVIATIONS

TA&G—Tennessee, Alabama, and Georgia

TCA—Train Collectors Association

T&P—Texas and Pacific

TP&W—Toledo, Peoria, and Western

TTOS—Toy Train Operating Society

UP—Union Pacific

USMC—United States Marine Corps

VTC—Virginia Train Collectors

V&TRR—Virginia and Truckee Railroad

Wab.—Wabash

W&ARR (W&A)—Western and Atlantic Railroad

WB&A—Washington, Baltimore, and Annapolis Chapter TCA

WM—Western Maryland

WP—Western Pacific

NOTES

NOTES

NOTES

GREENBERG'S®
GREAT TRAIN, DOLLHOUSE & TOY SHOW

Saturday 11 a.m. to 5 p.m. and Sunday 11 a.m. to 4 p.m.;

$5 adults/$2 ages 6-12. Parking included unless noted.

For a current show schedule or directions to a show location, please send SASE to Greenberg Shows, Inc., 7566 Main Street, Sykesville, MD 2178‹ Changes may occur due to circumstances beyond our control, therefore we recommend calling 410-795-7447 for show confirmation.

1995

ATLANTA, GA — *North Atlanta Trade Center*	Oct. 21-2:
KING OF PRUSSIA, PA — *Valley Forge Convention Center*	Oct. 21-2:
UPPER MARLBORO, MD — *The Show Place Arena*	Oct. 28-2:
NOVI, MI — *Novi Expo Center* (\$6 adult admission incl. p)	Oct. 28-2:
EDISON, NJ — *Raritan Center Expo Hall*	Nov. 4-:
ST. CHARLES, MO — *St. Charles Exhibition Hall*	Nov. 4-:
PENNSAUKEN, NJ — *South Jersey Expo Center*	Nov. 11-1:
MONROEVILLE, PA — *Pittsburgh Expo Mart*	Nov. 18-1:
HOUSTON, TX — *George R. Brown Convention Center* (\$3p)	Nov. 18-1:
DALLAS, TX — *Dallas Convention Center* (\$4p)	Nov. 25-2:
WILMINGTON, MA — *Shriner's Auditorium*	Nov. 25-2:
TIMONIUM, MD — *Timonium Fairgrounds*	Dec. 2-:
FORT WASHINGTON, PA — *Expo Center*	Dec. 9-1:
WEST PALM BEACH, FL — *So. Florida Fairgrounds*	Dec. 30-3:

— January through September, 1996 —

VIRGINIA BEACH, VA—*Virginia Beach Convention Center*	Jan. 6-:
JACKSONVILLE, FL—*Greater Jacksonville Fairgrounds* (\$3p)	Jan. 6-:
ATLANTA, GA—*North Atlanta Trade Center*	Jan. 13-1
TAMPA, FL—*Florida State Fairgrounds*	Jan. 20-2:
UPPER MARLBORO, MD—*The Show Place Arena*	Jan. 27-2:
EDISON, NJ—*Raritan Center Expo Hall*	Feb. 3-:
COLUMBUS, OH—*Franklin Co. Veterans Memorial* (\$2.50p)	Feb. 10-1:
MONROEVILLE, PA—*Pittsburgh Expo Mart*	Feb. 24-2:
PENNSAUKEN, NJ—*South Jersey Expo Center*	Mar. 2-:
TIMONIUM, MD—*Timonium Fairgrounds*	Mar. 16-1:
ST. CHARLES, MO—*St. Charles Exhibition Hall*	Mar. 16-1:
HACKENSACK, NJ—*Fairleigh Dickinson University*	Mar. 23-2:
NILES, OH—*Eastwood Expo Center*	Mar. 23-2:
NOVI, MI—*Novi Expo Center* (\$6 adult admission incl. p)	Mar. 30-3:
WILMINGTON, MA—*Shriner's Auditorium*	April 13-1:
KING OF PRUSSIA, PA—*Valley Forge Convention Center*	June 15-1:
FITCHBURG, MA—*Royal Plaza Trade Center*	July 13-1:
MONROEVILLE, PA—*Pittsburgh Expo Mart*	July 20-2:
TIMONIUM, MD—*Timonium Fairgrounds*	July 27-2:
EDISON, NJ—*Raritan Center Expo Hall*	Aug. 3-:
PENNSAUKEN, NJ—*South Jersey Expo Center*	Aug. 17-1:
HEMPSTEAD, NY—*Hofstra University*	Sept. TB:
CLEVELAND, OH—*I-X Center*	Sept. TB: